D0887114

ROBERT LOWELL
IN LOVE

Books by Jeffrey Meyers

BIOGRAPHY

A Fever at the Core: The Idealist in Politics

Married to Genius

Katherine Mansfield

The Enemy: A Biography of Wyndham Lewis

Hemingway

Manic Power: Robert Lowell and His Circle

D. H. Lawrence

Joseph Conrad

Edgar Allan Poe: His Life and Legacy

Scott Fitzgerald

Edmund Wilson

Robert Frost

Bogart: A Life in Hollywood

Gary Cooper: American Hero

Privileged Moments: Encounters with Writers

Wintry Conscience: A Biography of George Orwell

Inherited Risk: Errol and Sean Flynn in Hollywood and Vietnam

Somerset Maugham

Impressionist Quartet: The Intimate Genius of Manet and Morisot, Degas and Cassatt

Modigliani

Samuel Johnson: The Struggle

The Genius and the Goddess: Arthur Miller and Marilyn Monroe

John Huston: Courage and Art

CRITICISM

Fiction and the Colonial Experience

The Wounded Spirit: T. E. Lawrence's Seven Pillars of Wisdom

A Reader's Guide to George Orwell

Painting and the Novel
Homosexuality and Literature
D. H. Lawrence and the Experience of Italy
Disease and the Novel
The Spirit of Biography
Hemingway: Life into Art
Orwell: Life and Art
Thomas Mann's Artist-Heroes

BIBLIOGRAPHY

T. E. Lawrence: A Bibliography
Catalogue of the Library of the Late Siegfried Sassoon
George Orwell: An Annotated Bibliography of Criticism

EDITED COLLECTIONS

George Orwell: The Critical Heritage
Hemingway: The Critical Heritage
Robert Lowell: Interviews and Memoirs
The Sir Arthur Conan Doyle Reader
The W. Somerset Maugham Reader
Remembering Iris Murdoch: Letters and Interviews

EDITED ORIGINAL ESSAYS

Wyndham Lewis: A Revaluation
Wyndham Lewis by Roy Campbell
D. H. Lawrence and Tradition
The Legacy of D. H. Lawrence
The Craft of Literary Biography
The Biographer's Art
T. E. Lawrence: Soldier, Writer, Legend
Graham Greene: A Revaluation

Robert Lowell in Love

Jeffrey Meyers

University of Massachusetts Press
Amherst & Boston

ISBN 978-1-62534-186-0

Set in Adobe Garamond Pro with Quadraat display
Printed and bound by Sheridan Books, Inc.

Library of Congress Cataloging-in-Publication Data
Names: Meyers, Jeffrey.
Title: Robert Lowell in love / Jeffrey Meyers.
Description: Amherst : University of Massachusetts Press, 2015. |
Includes bibliographical references and index.
Identifiers: LCCN 2015028020 | ISBN 9781625341860 (cloth : alk. paper)
Subjects: LCSH: Lowell, Robert, 1917–1977—Relations with women. |
Lowell, Robert, 1917-1977—Family. | Poets, American—20th century—Biography. |
Poets—Psychology.
Classification: LCC PS3523.089 Z7878 2015 |
DDC 811/.52—dc23 LC record available at http://lccn.loc.gov/2015028020

British Library Cataloguing in Publication Data
A catalogue record for this book is available from the British Library.

CONTENTS

PHOTOGRAPHS FOLLOW PAGE 142

ILLUSTRATIONS

1. Anne Dick and Frank Parker, 1941 (Judith Parker)

2. Lowell and Jean Stafford, 1946 (Robert Giroux)

3. Gertrude Buckman and Delmore Schwartz, 1943

4. Carley Dawson, age 16, 1925 (University of Oregon)

5. Lowell and Elizabeth Hardwick, 1977 (Castine Historical Society)

6. Giovanna Madonia, c. 1950 (Pietro Cremonini)

7. Ann Adden, 1960 (Ann Adden)

8. Sandra Hochman, 1974 (Sandra Hochman)

9. Vija Vetra, 1962 (Vija Vetra)

10. Martha Ritter, 1970 (Martha Ritter)

11. Elizabeth Bishop, 1964 (Vassar College Library)

12. Lowell, Caroline Blackwood and her two daughters, c. 1970 (British Library)

ACKNOWLEDGMENTS

This is the first biographical book to use Lowell's fully annotated *Collected Poems* (2003), *Letters* (2005) and correspondence with Elizabeth Bishop (2008), and the family memoirs by Sarah Payne Stuart, *My First Cousin Once Removed* (1998), and Ivana Lowell, *Why Not Say What Happened?* (2010). For my previous books on Lowell and Robert Frost, I interviewed many of Lowell's friends who are now gone: Janice Biala, Caroline Blackwood, Gertrude Buckman, Jack Cutler, Peter Davison, James Dickey, Richard Eberhart, Paul Engle, Robert Fitzgerald, Anthony Hecht, Stanley Kunitz, Robie Macauley, William Meredith, Arthur Miller, Howard Nemerov, J. F. Powers, Adrienne Rich, Beatrice Roethke and Karl Shapiro, and had substantial letters from Elizabeth Hardwick, Mary McCarthy and W. D. Snodgrass.

For this book I've used unpublished material from the British Library (Helen Melody): Ian Hamilton's interviews; the FBI: file on Lowell; Houghton Library, Harvard University (Mary Haegert): Lowell's "Autobiographical Fragment" and letters from Ann Adden, Anne Dick, Elizabeth Hardwick, Mary Keelan and Giovanna Madonia; the Lyndon B. Johnson Presidential Library: White House Festival of the Arts; National Personnel Records Center: Commander Robert T. S. Lowell; St. Mark's School (Nick Noble): prep school archives; United States Naval Academy (Christopher Davis and Jennifer Bryan): Commander Lowell; University of Colorado: Jean Stafford Papers; University of Oregon (Bruce Tabb): Lowell's letters to Carley Dawson; University of Texas: letters from Elizabeth Hardwick and Caroline Blackwood. The library of the University of California, Berkeley, a major source for all my work since the 1960s, has been enormously helpful.

I am grateful for illuminating interviews with Ann Adden, Al and Ann Alvarez, Frank Bidart, Shepherd Bliss, Keith Botsford, Esther Brooks, Robert Gardner, Grey Gowrie, Donald Hall, Fanny Howe, Ivana Lowell,

Catharine Mack Smith, Gail Mazur, Karl Miller, Antonia Kern Mills, May Eliot Paddock (Anne Dick's daughter), Robert Pinsky, Christopher Ricks, Martha Ritter, Gaia Servadio, Richard Tillinghast, Vija Vetra, Richard Wilbur and Alan Williamson.

I also received useful information in letters and phone calls from Steven Axelrod, Xandra Bingley, Perdita Blackwood, Thomas Bonnell, Robert Boyers, Evgenia Citkowitz, Stephen Corey, Pietro Cremonini (Giovanna Madonia's son) and Giovanna Madonia (Giovanna's namesake and niece), Sarah Curtis, Anthony Daniels, Denis Donoghue and W. J. McCormack, Senator Dianne Feinstein, Jonathan Galassi, John Haffenden, Matthew Hamilton, Saskia Hamilton, Henry Hardy, Peggy Hawkins (Carley Dawson's daughter-in-law), Seamus Heaney, Judith Herzberg and Valti Van Leeuwen (via the Dutch Consulate in Los Angeles and De Harmonie Publishers in Amsterdam), Sandra Hochman, Darin Jensen, Jonathan Kozol, Harriet Lowell, Alison Lurie, David Lynn, Anne Newman, Judith Parker, David Reynolds, Peter Robinson, Robert Silvers, Sally Bedell Smith, Ahdaf Soueif, Kathleen Spivack, David Stafford, Paul Theroux, Jean Valentine, Reuel Wilson and Dudley Young; and from All Souls College, Oxford, the alumni records office of Bennington College, Columbia University, Harvard University (David Fahey) and New York University as well as the American Library Association, Burma Star Association (Stephen Fogden) and National Archives, Kew, London, Koren Publishers (Matthew Miller), McLean Hospital, Mid-Hudson Library System (Michael Nyerges), Mount St. Mary's College and National Library of Australia.

Some people failed to respond and have been confined in what Lowell called "Mary McCarthy's spanking machine": Helen Chasin, Mary Gordon, Mary Keelan, Sheridan Lowell, William Merwin, Jonathan Miller and Derek Walcott.

My wife, Valerie Meyers, with sound judgment and critical perception, scrutinized and improved the book, and compiled the index.

For Rachel Meyers

Art was war—a grilling, exhausting struggle that nowadays wore one out before one could grow old. It had been a life of self-conquest, a life against odds, dour, steadfast; he had made it symbolical of the kind of overstrained heroism the time admired, and he was entitled to call it manly, even courageous.

THOMAS MANN, *Death in Venice*

ROBERT LOWELL
IN LOVE

Introduction

The opening chapters of *Robert Lowell in Love* (my third book on the poet) describe his background, character and formative influences: his difficult mother; his early mentors: Ford Madox Ford, Allen Tate and John Crowe Ransom; and his education at Kenyon College. Chapter One describes his family's response to their gifted only child, which accentuated his mental illness, and portrays his first girlfriend Anne Dick. Chapter Two, "Southern Comfort," introduces his first wife, Jean Stafford, in Baton Rouge. It narrates how Lowell, a disturbed and unloved young man, was rescued by distinguished Southern writers who recognized his promise and poetic talent. He acknowledged their influence, and his gratitude for the first warm family life he'd ever known, by adopting a Southern accent and identity and a chivalric code he sometimes found difficult to uphold. This chapter shows how Lowell's unusual education and the development of his mind and character influenced his relations with women and his search for an ideal wife. His attitude toward women cannot be properly understood without a knowledge of the biographical context.

The rest of the book focuses on his three wives: Jean Stafford, Elizabeth Hardwick and Caroline Blackwood; nine of his many lovers: the heart of this work; his close women friends: Mary McCarthy, Elizabeth Bishop and Adrienne Rich; and his most talented pupils: Anne Sexton and Sylvia Plath. His wives and young muses inspired Lowell, and this book traces the volatile course of his emotional life—as son, husband, lover, friend and teacher—through the brilliant trail of his poetry. Lowell did not want to have transient affairs, but regarded each new romance as permanent. He wanted to dominate as well as to nurture his women, and struggled to be an exemplary writer who was both a private man and public citizen.

This book is meant for the general reader who is not familiar with the details of Lowell's life as well as for the specialist on modern poetry. My focus is wide, not narrow, and I interpret his major autobiographical poems when they are relevant. Though numerous books have been published on Lowell, I have made many discoveries. I draw on my interviews with Gertrude Buckman, Caroline Blackwood, Stanley Kunitz and Karl Shapiro in the 1980s; Ian Hamilton's revealing unpublished interviews in the British Library; Hardwick's unpublished letters to Lowell; an interview with the nanny who took care of Harriet Lowell in Brazil; and material about Lowell in the Lyndon Johnson Library, which shows his engagement in politics and the creation of his public image that drew more young admirers into his orbit. I reveal new information about the naval duties of Lowell's father; the character and career of Dr. Merrill Moore and his disastrous impact on the young Lowell; Lowell's year in Holland; Lowell's children and stepdaughters; Plath's influence on Lowell's poetry; and the mysterious death of Caroline's father, Basil Blackwood. I also show the real identity of "Billy Harkness," a friend of Lowell's father in "91 Revere Street," and the circumstances of Lowell's arrival in Rapallo at the time of his mother's death.

Lowell had the most distinguished background of any of his contemporaries. He studied with the most influential teachers, had the greatest talent, earned the most awards and money, had the most powerful personality, attracted the most devoted friends, married the most impressive wives, attracted the most lovers, had the most political power, enjoyed the greatest reputation and prestige, and survived to bury and elegize his leading rivals. As Monroe Spears observed, "Lowell was a remarkable and fascinating person; whatever his faults, nobody ever found him boring. His life obviously had a kind of representative quality: at worst, he was a scapegoat figure representing our defects in their extremity; at best, he was our culture hero, never forgetting in the heights and depths of his madness his responsibilities both to the republic of letters and to the political republic."[1]

Lowell's mania as well as his poetry attracted many women who were frightened and excited by the danger and wanted to help him. He was keenly aware of the western literary tradition that assumed, in John Dryden's words, "Great wits are sure to madness near allied" and was himself its great modern exemplar.[2] In two dialogues Plato described the divine madness that was essential for the creation of the greatest poetry.

In *Ion* he equated poetic power with derangement, a godlike mania: "The composers of lyrical poetry create those admired songs of theirs in a state of divine insanity. . . . For a Poet is indeed a thing ethereally light, winged and sacred, nor can he compose anything worth calling poetry until he becomes inspired, and, as it were, mad, or whilst any reason remains in him."[3] In *Phaedrus* Plato declared that "madness, provided it comes as a gift of heaven, is a channel by which we receive the greatest blessings."[4]

In the nineteenth century the Danish philosopher Søren Kierkegaard described the Romantic view of art, and shifted the focus from the poetry to the poet, doomed to suffer in order to create. Comparing the torments of the artist to the agonizing shrieks of tortured prisoners, he wrote that the poet is "an unhappy man who in his heart harbors a deep anguish. . . . His fate is like that of the unfortunate victims whom the tyrant Phalaris imprisoned in a brazen bull, and slowly tortured over a steady fire; their cries could not reach the tyrant's ears so as to strike terror into his heart; when they reached his ears they sounded like sweet music."[5]

In *Notes from Underground,* Fyodor Dostoyevsky insisted that "too great a lucidity is a disease, a true, full-fledged disease,"[6] that the artist's heightened consciousness forced him to recognize unbearable truths, hidden from ordinary mortals. Lowell expressed the same idea in "Home" when he exclaimed that the thin-skinned poet, who sees too much and feels too deeply, can never be contented. Friedrich Nietzsche—who confessed that Dostoyevsky was "the only psychologist, incidentally, from whom I had something to learn"[7] —also associated the creative spirit with extreme pain and mental anguish, but took this idea one stage further. He argued that artistic greatness could be earned only by suffering, and that the artist must induce the creative spirit: "To make oneself sick, mad, to provoke the symptoms of derangement and ruin—that was becoming stronger, more superhuman, more terrible, wiser."[8] The artist's derangement gave him the power to see and tell the truth, and his suffering was repaid with insight.

Following Nietzsche's belief, Arthur Rimbaud called for an artificially induced, deliberate derangement of all the senses. This would transform the tormented, self-sacrificial, even insane poet into "the great invalid, the great criminal, the great accursed" and plunge him into unknown, "unheard of, unnamable" spiritual visions.[9] Later on, Lowell's contemporary Jean-Paul Sartre voiced the quintessential modern idea that the writer's talent was closely connected to his capacity for self-ruin: "In relation to Gauguin, van Gogh and Rimbaud, I have a distinct inferiority complex because they managed to destroy themselves. . . . I am more and more convinced that, in order to achieve authenticity, something has to snap."[10] In Sartre's view, suicide became the ultimate question. All these writers described the pathology of modern culture and believed that the mad artist is both the product of a sick society and uniquely qualified to provide its cultural expression.

Throughout his life Lowell struggled against insanity, resisted the urge to commit suicide and continued to dedicate himself to poetry. Though his family motto was "*Occasionem cognosce*" (know your opportunity), "*Per aspera ad astra*" (through difficulties to the stars) would have been more appropriate for Lowell himself. It's astonishing that he managed to achieve so much between his manic breakdowns and to become the greatest postwar American poet.

Lowell exemplified the extremes of experience and the sickness of society. His personal revelations seemed universal and he spoke directly to readers about many of the major problems of his time. Assuming the roles of father, mentor and lover, he discussed sex and love, marriage and mistresses, psychological difficulties and recurrent insanity, drug and shock treatments, confinement in prisons and mental asylums, guilt and redemption, struggle and self-conquest, the authority of suffering and courageous creativity.

As compensation for his mania, Lowell needed women and loved the idea of falling in love, and each affair became an intense dramatic episode. His impressive achievements came at great cost to himself as well as to the women who were attracted to his intellect, generosity and charismatic personality. This book tells the stories of the women who inspired his poetry and were at the emotional and aesthetic center of his life.

ONE

Charlotte's Web, 1917–1954

I

Many people don't think about their ancestors—don't even go back far enough to have any. They lack two middle names and have to buy their own furniture. But the poet Robert Traill Spence Lowell IV had a trust fund and inherited bountiful legacies when his parents died. The Lowells had arrived in America in 1639 and belonged to the first families of Boston, but by his father's time, two-and-a-half centuries later, the blood had run thin. Ian Hamilton noted that "the Lowell millions were elsewhere, with the bankers and the lawyers and the cotton magnates: cousins all, but hardly intimates, and in a quite separate financial league."[1] The poet was born on March 1, 1917—the same year as John Kennedy and Andrew Wyeth—one month before America entered the Great War.

The French philosopher Blaise Pascal observed, "What a great advantage nobility confers! It places a man at eighteen in a grand position, where he is as well-known and respected as another would be at fifty, who depended only on his merit. Here is a gain of thirty years that costs no trouble."[2] Lowell's distinguished ancestry has usually been considered a tremendous advantage. He used it to gain a great deal of attention as a conscientious objector in World War II and as an angry protester against the war in Vietnam. Richard Tillinghast expressed the traditional view by saying he had "the luck to have been born with a name and family tradition that lent authority to his utterances."[3] Lowell's close friend Randall Jarrell, who came from a humble background, slyly mocked his impressive pedigree by remarking, "I'm sure the Lowells . . . have all sorts of [ancient]

Egyptian connections, were in the old days Egyptians."[4] Yet Lowell did have a dynastic "IV" after his name and wrote that his grandfather's house on Chestnut Street in Beacon Hill had "two loutish, brownstone pillars copied from the [Egyptian] Temple of the Kings at Memphis."[5] The poet Elizabeth Bishop, awed by his heritage, famously told him, "In some ways you are the luckiest poet I know!" Most poets could write about their ancestors, she continued, "but what would be the significance? Nothing at all. . . . Whereas all you have to do is put down the names! And it seems significant, illustrative, American."[6] David Heymann's *American Aristocracy* (1980), about three generations of poetical Lowells, seems to substantiate Bishop's claim.

But Lowell's ancestry was a curse as well as a blessing. He carried the burden of privilege and was consumed as well as nourished, embalmed as well as exalted by his past. The menacing recollections and anguished expressions of despair in his autobiographical essays—"91 Revere Street," "Antebellum Boston" and "Near the Unbalanced Aquarium"—explored the dark side of his family. He thought it no great feat to surpass his talentless predecessors. He called James Russell Lowell, minister to Great Britain, "a poet pedestalled for oblivion"—statuesque but destined to be dumped on by pigeons.[7] His connection to the huge, eccentric and scandalous Amy Lowell was like having Mae West for a cousin. She'd promoted Imagist poetry with Ezra Pound, who soon mocked what he called "Amy-gism." Lowell quoted with approval a friend's description of Amy as "that cigar-chawing, guffawing, senseless and meterless, multimillionheiress, heavyweight mascot on a floating fortress."[8] These versifying mediocrities were merely deadwood who had to be cleared away to open the path for his own triumphs.

Amy's brother and Lowell's distant cousin, Abbott Lawrence Lowell (his great-grandfather and Robert's great-great-grandfather were stepbrothers), was a member of the Massachusetts Governor's Advisory Committee who ruled that the anarchists, Nicola Sacco and Bartolomeo Vanzetti, had had a fair trial and rejected the plea for a new one. The two men were unjustly convicted and executed on August 15, 1927. Abbott Lawrence Lowell also opposed, for anti-Semitic reasons, the nomination of the distinguished jurist Louis Brandeis to the Supreme Court. As the long-serving president of Harvard from 1909 to 1933, he limited Jewish enrollment, banned African American students from living in Freshmen Halls, and purged homosexual students and faculty. The "illustrious" Abbott Lawrence Lowell was actually a shameful reactionary and bigot.

Lowell's favorite ancestors were military heroes, both of whom died gloriously in the American Civil War. Colonel Robert Gould Shaw, who commanded the first black regiment in the North, was killed while leading a gallant but unsuccessful assault on Fort Wagner, South Carolina, in July 1863. Augustus Saint-Gaudens created a monument on the Boston Common to Shaw, who became the hero of Lowell's major poem "For the Union Dead." Shaw was connected by marriage to Major Charles Russell Lowell, the dashing cavalry officer known as "Beau Sabreur," who was killed in Virginia while leading a charge on horseback in October 1864. James Russell Lowell called him "the pride of the family . . . by far, the best we had."[9]

Lowell's great-grandfather, the first Robert Traill Spence Lowell, had been the founder and first headmaster of St. Mark's prep school, which both Lowell and his father attended. When Lowell walked near Eliot House with T. S. Eliot, whose cousin Charles W. Eliot had been an innovative president of Harvard, the older poet struck a chord with Lowell by exclaiming, "Don't you loathe to be compared with your relatives?"[10] When Eliot said he was delighted to find that two of his relatives had been savaged in a review by Edgar Allan Poe, he was also slyly hinting that his literary ancestors were important enough to be reviewed by a great writer. (Eliot, another New Englander influenced by the South, left Harvard to study at Oxford and never returned to finish his doctorate.)

Lowell portrayed himself as an aristocratic descendant, bearing his personal genealogy like Aeneas carrying old Anchises from the flames of Troy. With great subtlety, he both exploited and repudiated, embodied and rejected his family traditions, rebelling against its ancestral values and spiritual emptiness, its tensions and pretensions. David Heymann defined these traditions as "businesses, banks, mill towns, society balls— the mordant proprieties of Brahmin wealth, the classbound symbols of a universal order . . . the excruciating rites of high WASP gentility, with its aristocratic trappings and special advantages, its incivility, despair, and moral disarray."[11]

Lowell's guilt-ridden rebellion against his New England heritage was closely connected to his feelings about his family. He turned his back on the textile town of Lowell, Massachusetts, and Lowell House at Harvard, for the small and comparatively obscure Kenyon College in rural Ohio in order to study poetry with John Crowe Ransom. In the Midwest, his new teacher offered the descendant of Civil War heroes a completely different, reactionary Southern tradition that Lowell eagerly adopted, along with the honeyed, drawling accent that overlaid his native speech. Lowell's mother and maternal grandparents had been born in North Carolina; and his Southern identity was reinforced by studying with Allen Tate in Tennessee and with Robert Penn Warren in Louisiana, by his father's friend "Billy Harkness" who drank whisky to renew his Bourbon blood and by his second wife, Elizabeth Hardwick. The last three were all born in Kentucky, a state redolent to the Bostonian of bluegrass racehorses, tobacco fields, folk ballads, honeyed hams, sour mash whiskey, mint juleps, decaying plantations, feuding mountain men, honorary colonels, good ole boys and lost causes.

Lowell also rebelled against his WASP background and anti-Semitic parents by emphasizing in his essay "91 Revere Street" Grandmother Lowell's grandfather, Mordecai Myers, a soldier, "a dark man, a German Jew." This autobiographical memoir, featuring an ancestor whose existence embarrassed his father and infuriated his mother, began and ended with a discussion of Major Mordecai and his son Colonel Theodorus. Lowell wrote of their portraits, incongruously displayed by his family: "The artist painted Major Myers in his sanguine War of 1812 uniform with epaulets, white breeches, and a scarlet frogged waistcoat. . . . [He was] a Grand Old Man, who impressed strangers with the poise of his old-time manners." A friend caustically commented that the portrait of Mordecai's son looked like "King Solomon about the receive the Queen of Sheba's shares in the Boston and Albany Railroad."[12]

When Delmore Schwartz visited the family, Lowell senior kept remarking that the New York poet sounded "like a Jew" while young Lowell kept pointing to Mordecai's portrait and insisting that he himself was one-eighth Jewish. Later on, Jean Stafford liked to call A. J. Liebling her "first completely Jewish husband."[13] In the latter half of the twentieth century intellectuals began to prize their Jewish connections. Iris Murdoch (who had several Jewish lovers) believed that "any worthwhile person ought to have at least *some* Jewish blood."[14] Like Lowell, his friend Mary McCarthy, Louis Simpson, the college president John Silber, Madeleine Albright, Tom Stoppard, Joyce Carol Oates, the film director Stephen Frears, Mary Gordon and Christopher Hitchens were all pleased to discover that they were, if not Jews, at least Jew-ish.

The paternal Lowells and maternal Winslows struggled to dominate and control Robert Lowell's character and destiny. It's not clear exactly where the Winslows stood in the hierarchy in Boston, "Where the Lowells talk to the Cabots, / And the Cabots talk only to God." But more historically impressive than the Lowells, they resembled the family of the aristocratic Diana Spencer, whose ancient lineage was superior to the royal Windsors. Heymann wrote that the patrician Winslows, like the Lowells,

> were early New England colonists, dating back to the *Mayflower* journeyman Edward Winslow (1595–1655), the Pilgrim father responsible for the colonists' first treaty with the . . . Indians. Edward Winslow was three times the governor of Plymouth. . . .
>
> Mary Chilton, later married to the early settler John Winslow, was the first female to step foot off the *Mayflower*. Other notable Winslows . . . included Edward II, "a mighty Indian killer" and twice elected governor of Plymouth colony. His son, Edward III, was a high sheriff and a noted silversmith. . . . Also a ferocious Indian-killer was Josiah Winslow, commander-in-chief of the colonial forces in the brutal King Philip's War [against the Indians in 1675–78]. Lowell's mother was related to the New Hampshire frontiersman John Stark, a Revolutionary War brigadier general, who in 1759 founded the New Hampshire township of Starkstown, later named Dunbarton.[15]

The Winslows later paid dearly for their loyalty to the English Tories in the American Revolution.

Lowell's most formidable Winslow relative was his grandfather Arthur (1860–1938). Born in Winston-Salem, North Carolina, the six-foot, self-made millionaire and mountain climber was educated at the University of Stuttgart and at MIT. A gold-and-silver mining engineer and geologist, he founded the Liberty Bell gold mine in Telluride, Colorado, and with Germanic efficiency tore the precious minerals out of the earth. Like Willy Loman's older brother Ben in *Death of a Salesman*, Arthur was, in Lowell's boyhood, "a stolid man, in his sixties, with a mustache and an authoritative air. He is utterly certain of his destiny, and there is an aura of far places about him." Ben boasts, "when I was seventeen I walked into the jungle, and when I was twenty-one I walked out. And by God I was rich."[16] When Bob Lowell was away on sea duty in the Pacific, the powerful Arthur Winslow, the only surviving grandfather, usurped his son-in-law's role in the family. After the death of his son Devereux, Arthur became the surrogate father of the Winslow Boy. When Arthur's farmer, his chauffeur and even his wife mentioned Bobby's father, they always meant his grandfather. In "Grandparents" Lowell openly cried out for the affection his mother failed to provide and parodied the marriage service by pleading, "Grandpa! Have me, hold me, cherish me!" [17]

II

It was usually considered quite shocking, at the beginning of the modern period, to publicly condemn one's parents. George Orwell once startled a friend at Eton by cynically criticizing his parents: "He'd been the first person I had ever heard running down his own father and mother." [18] Ernest Hemingway—"the only man I ever knew who really hated his mother"—shocked John Dos Passos in the same way. [19] But Lowell, who found his parents a source of inspiration, thought it quite natural to make searing revelations about them, and attack their characters and values in his poems and prose.

Bob Lowell's father had died of pneumonia five months before he was born, and the posthumous only child was not a good father to his own son, Bobby. Raised by his mother, Kate Bailey Lowell, and his grandmother in Schenectady, the senior Lowell (1887–1950) came to Boston as a young man. He entered Annapolis when he was sixteen and earned an engineering degree from the Naval Academy in 1906. Since the navy needed junior officers, he graduated in three years (instead of four), a weak 62nd in a class of 87. The archivist of the Naval Academy wrote, "At that time, midshipmen had to perform two years of sea duty after the four-year course at the Academy. At the completion of the six years, they were then commissioned as ensigns." [20]

The matey familiarity, adolescent humor and satirical tone of *The Lucky Bag,* the Academy yearbook, portrayed Bob as a rather anxious and trifling nerd:

An out-of-hours grub fiend with a Terhunesque way of talking and an irrepressible giggle. Recites in an eager, apologetic manner. Tortures his neighbors with a noisy sea-going clock that has a constant error on U.S.N.A. Mean Time. Holds the record for frenching paps [kissing nipples], but is a statement adept and immune to the Santee, except the quarter deck. Electrician, First Class, and McKeehan's partner in the construction of various heathenish contrivances. A constant fusser who sends flowers before and after taking out girls.

Albert Payson Terhune was the author of popular books about collies. Santee was the station ship used to punish disobedient midshipmen; the quarter deck housed the commanding officer.

Bob's entry begins with a couplet from Alexander Pope's "Epistle to Dr. Arbuthnot"—"Eternal smiles his emptiness betray, / As shallow streams run dimpling all the way"—and ends with a description of him as "Greaser and fusser with a smily smile and a 'way.'"[21] Bob's caustic entry suggests that his giggles and ingratiating grins failed to cover his nervous superficiality. In "Antebellum Boston" Lowell, emphasizing this trait, recalled that his father "smiled and smiled in his photographs, just as he smiled and smiled in life,"[22] and in "Commander Lowell" portrayed Bob "Smiling on all," like the doomed wife in Robert Browning's "My Last Duchess."[23]

The high point of his life was the never-to-be-equaled adventure that took place after graduation in 1906. In "91 Revere Street" Lowell wrote that Bob and a classmate called "Billy Harkness" would frequently "talk about their ensigns' cruise around the world, escaping the 'reeport,' gunboating on the upper Yangtze during the Chinese Civil War, keeping sane and sanitary [from venereal disease] at Guantánamo, patrolling the Golfo de Papa[ga]yo during the two-bit Nicaraguan Revolution" in 1912. In "Commander Lowell," the satiric elegy on his father, Lowell wrote: "And once / nineteen, the youngest ensign in his class, / he was the 'old man' of a gunboat on the Yangtze."[24] In the days of aggressive American gunboat diplomacy, Bob sailed the Yangtze, which flows near Shanghai and into the Yellow Sea, after the Boxer Revolution (1899–1901) and before the Chinese Civil War (1908–1913). After graduate school in radio telegraphy at Columbia (M.S., 1914), Harvard (master's in electrical engineering, 1915) and MIT while in the navy, Bob became an expert in mathematics, and in radio design and installation in ships and shore stations. A brainy man but not an impressive scholar or natural leader, he never engaged in naval combat and when not at sea was later stationed at navy shipyards in Washington, Philadelphia and Boston.

Despite their grand dynastic alliance, Lowell's parents were eminently unsuited to each other. His mother Charlotte (1894–1954) was born in Raleigh, North Carolina, her mother's home town. The one-time high school prom queen—with her tiny waist, dark eyes, rosy cheeks, strong

chin, swanlike neck and pyramid of hair—looked like one of the handsome eighteenth-century aristocrats painted by Sir Joshua Reynolds. But
her expression was lifeless, her voice falsely dramatic. Lowell wrote that
"She had the lower jaw of a waterbuffalo / the weak intelligence, the iron
will."[25] She never read anything and he thought she was rather stupid.
Her father's great wealth gave the spoiled darling—like Maggie Verver in
Henry James' *The Golden Bowl*—the best of everything: a small army of
servants, art-filled mansions, expansive summer "cottages," luxurious cars,
fashionable clothes and leisurely journeys to Europe. Lowell wrote that
his narcissistic mother, who lacked self-assurance, needed to feel liked,
admired, surrounded by the approved and familiar. Her haughtiness and
chilliness derived from some deep apprehension.[26]

In her unpublished autobiography Charlotte, prone to self-analysis,
criticized her own youthful character. She also shrewdly explained her
strangely mixed motives for accepting the patently mediocre Bob Lowell,
the tensions in her marriage and the mounting hostility to her husband:
"As a child Miss B was self-conscious, introverted, aggressive and rather
deceitful. . . . Miss B married because she thought it was time to. She
was not at all in love with the man, nor did she really admire him. But he
seemed the best that was offered. . . . After this marriage, having to live in
constant companionship with this comparative stranger, whom she found
neither agreeable, interesting nor admirable, was a terrible nervous strain.
She became increasingly critical and unappreciative. . . . Her husband
could not understand at all, was always kind, though irresponsible; and
thought her half crazy."[27] Bob's aunt, in a caustic condemnation, agreed
that he was indeed a hollow man: "Bob hasn't a mean bone, an original
bone, a funny bone in his body! That's why I can't get a word he says. If
he were mine, I'd lobotomize him and stuff his brain with green peppers."
Emphasizing Charlotte's strong attachment to her powerful father, who
could not be supplanted by her weak husband, as well as the emotional
emptiness of her marriage, Lowell wrote in "During Fever":

> Terrible that old life of decency
> without unseemly intimacy
> or quarrels, when the unemancipated woman
> still had her Freudian papá and maids![28]

A martinet in the household, she inspected the furniture with white gloves
to make sure the maids had not overlooked any dust.

There were, of course, endless bitter quarrels beneath the respectable Boston Brahmin façade and most of them focused on Bob's career. Lowell recalled that "Mother hated the Navy, hated naval society, naval pay, and the trip-hammer rote of settling and unsettling a house every other year when Father was transferred to a new station or ship." Her status in the navy was based on her husband's relatively low rank. Bob's colleagues failed to recognize her own exalted social position and his superiors disapproved of her critical attitude and defiant behavior. Marshaling her arguments, "she would start talking like a *grande dame* and then stand back rigid and faltering, as if she feared being crushed by her own massively intimidating offensive." She particularly hated Bob's colorful friend "Billy Harkness," who opposed her plots and glorified the navy.

Lowell observed that even as a young officer Billy "breathed the power that would make him a vice-admiral and hero in World War II. I can hear him boasting in lofty language of how he had stood up for democracy in the days of Lenin and Béla Kun [the Hungarian Communist leader in 1919]; of how he 'practiced the sport of kings' (i.e., commanded a destroyer) and combed the Mediterranean, Adriatic and Black Seas like gypsies." "Why in God's name," Billy asked Charlotte, "should a man with Bob's brilliant cerebellum go and mess up his record by actually *begging* for that impotent field nigger's job of second in command at the defunct Boston Yard!"[29] The answer was that Bob pulled strings in Washington so he could remain in Boston—building ships, then supplying, refitting, maintaining and repairing them—in order to please Charlotte.

Bob also had to pay other penalties. After he'd flouted naval tradition and bought a house at 91 Revere Street in Beacon Hill, his outraged commandant, Admiral De Stahl, ordered him to spend every night in an official house in the Charlestown Navy Yard. This dispute continued until the end of Bob's career. On July 22, 1925, another admiral told Bob: "It is believed by the Commandant that the Engineer Officer should live in the Yard in his assigned quarters, and that he cannot properly carry out his duties if he lives out in town, due to lack of supervision."[30]

Though Charlotte surrendered her husband, she won a small victory (no doubt at Bob's expense) by remaining in Revere Street. Charlotte also defeated Bob by insisting, after he'd changed from his dinner jacket (they always dressed formally in the evening), that he take the nightly trolley instead of his beloved car to the Yard. Alluding to Edward Gibbon's "I sighed as a lover; I obeyed as a son," when Gibbon's father insisted he break off his engagement to a Swiss girl, Lowell noted, "Father sighed and obeyed."[31] Sunk in his berth on the base, Bob surrendered his son to his father-in-law and wife, and Charlotte's overwhelming presence filled the vacuum left by her husband. In his "Autobiographical Fragment," Lowell wrote that Bob gave him no paternal affection and disowned him by handing him over to the Winslows: "Always, he seemed to treat me as though I were some relation of Mother's who was visiting. He could remember my Christian name and even my nicknames, but somehow or other my surname had escaped. He would rather have had his fingernails pulled one by one than have said anything to me that was impolite, called for, or fatherly."[32]

Bob was also deprived of marital bliss, which provoked Billy's sly remark, "I know why Young Bob is an only child." Charlotte, putting a burden on her young son and drawing him into her emotional whirlpool, exclaimed, "Oh Bobby, it's such a comfort to have a man in the house." Rejecting his role as surrogate husband, he replied, "I am not a man . . . I am a boy." Charlotte first torpedoed, then terminated Bob's career and drove him from dry dock to shipwreck. His last real job was liaison between the Charlestown Navy Yard and MIT. In 1927 she delivered the fatal blow by persuading him to leave the navy. Noting Bob's public degradation, Billy bitterly observed, "Bob Lowell, our bright boy, our class baby, is now on a par with 'Rattle-Ass Rats' Richardson," who'd left the navy to become a press agent for a circus.[33]

Amazingly enough, the heroic, realistic and vividly portrayed "Billy Harkness," who dominates the last third of "91 Revere Street," did not actually exist. Lowell either changed his name or invented him as a feisty adversary to Charlotte and as a model for the kind of dashing career Bob might have had if he'd resisted her onslaughts and remained loyal to the navy. The registrar of the Naval Academy wrote that he was "unable to find anything in the Alumni books or registers of a person with the last name of 'Harkness' (or similar) who would have graduated in (or around) 1907."[34]

Cut adrift from the discipline and duties, the security and prestige of naval life, Bob felt like a deserter who'd jumped ship and was anxious about his future prospects. If Arthur Winslow resembled Willy Loman's dynamic brother Ben, Bob Lowell, like Willy himself, soon got fired from his promising job as soap salesman. Then, stripped of his powers, he made a prolonged and desperate effort to fill up the empty hours of his life. Bob was completely dispossessed: the admiral took his home, Charlotte's lover took his wife, his wife took his career and his father-in-law took his son.

Lowell portrayed his fatherless father, an obsessive-compulsive personality, as a ludicrous and pathetic failure, and recorded his slow deterioration and trivial death. He wrote that after Bob had been emasculated by Charlotte and stripped of his fatherhood, sexual life, profession and even identity, the apathetic, cuckolded man "treated even himself with the caution and uncertainty of one who had forgotten a name, in this case his own. . . . The strain brought about by his effort to make himself heroically nonexistent was extreme."[35] None of the Winslows liked Bob, and Charlotte undermined Bobby by teaching him to despise his father. Bob failed in his role as commander; Bobby rejected his role in Boston society.

Bob spent his time on menial and often pointless tasks: watering the grass, polishing the furnace and arranging the placement of the furniture. Without realizing the absurdity of his behavior, he proudly stenciled—like letters on a prisoner's back—his three new garbage cans with "R. T. S. Lowell—U.S.N." During the Depression and after trading martial values for material gain, Bob set himself up as a financial advisor. On innumerable graphs, Lowell remarked, "Father had plotted out catastrophic systems for his private investments in those years before the war when he had been an investment counsel and his own chief customer."[36] Fortunately, no others were gullible enough to trust the novice with their funds, and he lost sixty thousand dollars—an enormous chunk of his trust fund—in only three years. Drifting from job to job, failing in many fields and living on the fantasies of past glory, Bob also resembled James Joyce's portrayal of his father as Simon Dedalus: "a small investor, a drinker, a good fellow, a storyteller, somebody's secretary, something in a distillery . . . and a praiser of his own past."[37] Finally, after a serious heart attack when he was fifty-four, Bob became unemployable. Two years later, in February 1943, Bob tried to join the naval reserve, but was rejected on medical grounds. His report read: "Cerebration appears slightly retarded, speech indistinct; questionable cerebral arteriosclerosis; and defective vision."[38]

Lowell's fury with his parents fueled his poems. The heroine of "The Mills of the Kavanaughs," partly based on Charlotte and speaking ironically, criticizes her husband's fateful decision: "My husband was a fool / To run out from the navy when disgrace / Still wanted zeal to look him in the face."[39] *Life Studies* moves from Lowell's poems about his family to poems about his mental illness to show the clear connection between them. The title of his elegy "Commander Lowell" is also ironic: Charlotte was the real commander and Bob couldn't even command himself. The condescending

portrait of paternal weakness and decline contrasts the promise of Bob's
past with the hopelessness of his future. Bob sang "Anchors Aweigh" in the
bathtub when Lever Brothers offered to double his navy salary:

> I nagged for his dress sword with gold braid,
> and cringed because Mother, new
> caps on all her teeth, was born anew
> at forty. With seamanlike celerity,
> Father left the Navy,
> and deeded Mother his property. [40]

Charlotte was revived as Bob, substituting bathtub for boat, surrendered
his authority. By blackmailing him and threatening to leave with Bobby,
Charlotte dominated the contentious house on Revere Street.

Bobby's first major quarrel with his parents occurred in 1936 when the
nineteen-year-old Harvard freshman suddenly became engaged to Anne
Dick (1911–1981). The oldest of four sisters, Anne grew up on Pinckney Street in Beacon Hill and on the family estate, Appleton Farms, in
Ipswich, Massachusetts. Six years older than Bobby and a cousin of his
close school friend Frank Parker, she was pretty, hedonistic and rather
empty-headed, with a blond pageboy haircut, small neat features and a
girlish look. Her oval face, slightly protruding eyes and seductive manner
reminded Bobby of Bette Davis. Jean Stafford, Lowell's first wife, used
to exclaim, "If you say that Anne Dick looks like Bette Davis one more
time, I'll do you violence!"

But the former debutante in Boston, New York and Philadelphia had
been seeing a psychiatrist (a plus for Bobby) and was considered unmar-
riageable. She described herself as horribly driven and ultra-neurotic,
couldn't bear to sleep alone in a room and when she felt the psychological
pressure was unbearable would exclaim, "I must call my analyst!" Frank
Parker said, "an aura of glamour surrounded her because she had been
psychoanalyzed for her depressions. Her parents were afraid of her—her
beaus were afraid of her—she and her sisters fought like cats and dogs. She
could get very edgy." [41] In Richard Eberhart's verse play about Lowell, *The
Mad Magician*, the character based on Charlotte concedes that Anne "was
at least an aristocrat, / At least a girl of the social whirl, although a creature / Of frail edge, who had twice been in an institution." [42] Anne both
accepted and (like Bobby) rebelled against her privileged background,

which she called "that Social Register grossity"—the incivility, despair and moral disarray that he was also trying to escape.

Anne, Bobby's first girlfriend, eagerly welcomed his awkward and pedantic overtures. She later recalled, "The first time we met I said the only thing I knew how to say, 'Do you like dances?' And he said, 'I've never been to one.' Well, I'd been to maybe a thousand. I'd never spoken to anyone who hadn't been to one. It was different." But when he tried to impress her by reading one of his poems, she found it "the most pathetic, wretched thing." After Anne explained why she wasn't married, Bobby asked, with studied formality, "May I be one of your suitors?" It was a *coup de foudre* and they fell instantly in love. This was the first of Lowell's many gauche and ultimately unhappy courtships.

Bobby would turn up in the evening with Frank Parker and their friend Blair Clark and casually announce, "We're all staying for dinner," as if they were conferring the greatest honor on their hosts. Anne said, "My father hated their guts because they didn't even say 'Good evening, Mr. Dick.' They sat at his table and acted as if he didn't exist." But Anne greatly enjoyed their high-flying dinner conversation about the kings of England, which gave the boys the chance to show off their schoolboy knowledge: "It was completely spontaneous and humorful and yet learned in the right way." She succumbed to Bobby's dominating personality, and was willing to tolerate his rude behavior, strict educational regime and crude sexual advances. Deprived of intellectual stimulation and a congenial family, Anne said, "I felt the happiest I think I've ever felt in my entire life." During their year-long engagement they never went to the theater or a movie. Anne, who later saw the absurdity of his courtship and could describe it in an amusing way, recalled, "I always had to drive so he could think. There was never any question of me wanting to think, though I sure had something to think about."[43]

Bobby's engagement to Anne cemented his bond with her cousin Frank Parker, to whom he expressed some serious doubts: "I love her and know her as deeply and as much as anyone could in a few weeks, but must admit that she has not yet the same reality to me as you have. . . . Can she or should she burn thru her neuroses?" His letter to Anne was much more formal and restrained. He believed that reading books was more important than physical attraction, sympathetic understanding and mutual love. In a didactic rather than seductive letter, Bobby told his fiancée: "Your point is . . . how can you work with me toward marriage, how you can profitably develop in the interim. See that your talk is on that basis. . . . Read Ezra [Pound], keep up my organization, *and prepare for our marriage.* I miss you terribly but refuse to say anything [more]. . . . love Cal." [44]

Bobby impulsively planned to drop out of Harvard, elope to Europe and marry her. Like Flaubert's romantic Emma Bovary, who exclaimed, "I have a lover! a lover!," [45] Anne kept thinking, " 'I'm engaged, I'm *engaged.'* It seemed very unreal"—and it was. [46] Bobby was too young, inexperienced and unstable to get married. His plan was clearly unwise and all reasonable parents would have strongly disapproved. Charlotte, knowing Bobby couldn't support himself, resorted to a traditional ploy and threatened to cut off his funds if he disobeyed her.

Defiant as ever, Bobby continued his clumsy courtship. After he'd told Anne to read Shakespeare's *Troilus and Cressida* and send him her comments on the play, she was gratified by his abusive reaction: "I loved being mocked so wittily. I adored it. The more he criticized me, the more I adored it." She also wittily expressed her disappointment with his amorous approach: "He told me he didn't like kissing. I guess he'd never kissed anyone before. But that was very disturbing because kissing was all I was interested in, with anybody. It was my main thing. But it's true, there was very little kissing after that. . . . I was a virgin, but [with] a lot of necking. But I was engaged. I somehow felt I wanted it to be a complete rounded experience." At a crucial moment, he entered his fiancée's bedroom, she declared herself a virgin, and he roughly pulled her down from her pedestal. Instead of gently talking about love and expressing his feelings about Anne, he announced: "I've been to a whorehouse, twice. And I can tell you what the whores do. I can tell you and you can try and do it." [47] Anne, who was sexually adventurous, gave it her best shot, but it didn't work out and things went downhill from then on.

Bobby's older relative, observing Anne's affectionate behavior, recalled, "It was a very hot and heavy romance, and everyone just assumed they were sleeping together. It was a great release for Bobby. She was very much in love with him, sincerely so." [48] Terrified that Bobby would impregnate Anne and be forced to marry her, and determined to thwart their engagement, Bob Lowell sent an insulting letter (possibly dictated by Charlotte) to Anne's father: "I wish to ask that you and Mrs. Dick do not allow Anne to go to Bobby's rooms at college without proper chaperonage. . . . Such behavior is contrary to all college rules, and most improper for a girl of good repute." Anne's parents were too polite—and perhaps too eager to marry off their daughter—to be offended by Bob's suggestion that the immoral woman was attempting to seduce his son. But Anne got hold of the incendiary letter and gave it to Bobby, with predictably disastrous results. Taking up the prostitute theme, Bobby thought his father had described Anne as "no better than a whore" and felt obliged to defend the honor of his beloved.[49]

Bob Lowell, repeatedly defeated by Charlotte, was a soft target. Bobby, a bully at school, was much taller and stronger than Bob. He displaced his anger toward his mother onto his father and described their violent confrontation in "Rebellion":

> There was rebellion, father, when the mock
> French windows slammed and you hove backward, rammed
> Into your heirlooms, screens, a glass-cased clock,
> The highboy quaking to its toes. You damned
> My arms that cast your house upon your head
> And broke the chimney flintlock on your skull.[50]

In revolt against his heritage as well as his father—and using naval diction—Lowell destroyed his ancestral possessions, quaking like his father and crashing to the ground. He earned Bob's curse for hitting him on the head with a weapon from the Revolutionary era.

Knocking down his father violated both primitive taboo and the Mosaic law in Exodus 21:15: "He that smiteth his father, or his mother, shall be surely put to death." In *Troilus and Cressida,* Ulysses warns that society will break down and descend into chaos when "Strength should be the lord of imbecility, / And the rude son should strike the father dead" (1.3.114–115). Charlotte, who witnessed the domestic attack from the top of the stairs, told Frank Parker, with a brutal comparison: "If you had a German shepherd, taking care of it and getting the best food and care and so on, and then it bit you, wouldn't you shoot it?"[51] Her idea of taking care of Bobby, whom she described as a rabid dog, was to kill him. Though punching his father was the physical equivalent of Charlotte's verbal abuse, she wanted her psychiatrist Merrill Moore to commit her son to an insane asylum. The crisis was diffused when Bobby agreed to apologize, and told Bob: "One can not get away with striking his father or for that matter using violence to anyone. I am sorry and wish to be forgiven."

In the summer of 1937 Frank Parker organized a car trip to Tennessee with Blair Clark and Anne. But Bobby, who could suddenly turn off his feelings, had lost interest in Anne, rudely ignored her, and left her bewildered and hurt. Parker took up the slack and the trip ended rather sadly. In the fall of 1937, after Lowell had left Harvard for Kenyon College, he suddenly broke off their engagement and sent Anne the bad news in a series of contorted sentences that revealed his embarrassment: "Without putting my head into a well I want to say I am sorry and that although it would be doing a favor to neither of us I'd like to see you again. . . . I hardly as ever yet want to let go, and want you to let me do something for—but preferably with you."[52] After interviewing her, Ian Hamilton wrote, "Anne was quietly acquiescent; after all, she barely knew what she had lost: 'I guess Cal cared for me—loved me, as he would say—for about 10 days, the first 10 days of our engagement.'"[53]

Three years later, in 1940, Anne got married and had a daughter, May, in 1942. Patricia Bosworth wrote that "Anne was thirty when she met Alex Eliot; he was nineteen. She was terrified of becoming a spinster. 'Getting married was essential to Anne,' [Frank] Parker said. 'Having a man to depend on—to live through—was of prime importance. And Alex was intelligent and charming and sexy—and he came from a distinguished family.'" Alex would later "tell people he'd been totally unaware of Anne's violent mood swings—one day she would be euphoric, the next so despondent she became physically ill and took to her bed." After their divorce in 1949, Anne became permanently frail and ill: "her drinking and depressions had increased and she was spending more and more time in mental hospitals."[54] Parker revealed that Anne's life ended tragically. She hanged herself in a mental institution near Framingham, Massachusetts, with curtain ropes she found in the theater.[55]

Lowell wrote two poems about his relations with Anne Dick in 1936. The first one sets the scene and recalls the violent conflict with his father, which he would remember, write about and regret throughout his life: Bob's incendiary letter, which made her father florid and Anne outraged, Bobby cooling his nerves at the Harvard Fieldhouse by reciting Milton's *Lycidas,* their furious drive from Cambridge to Boston, Anne waiting for him outside the house in a station wagon and Lowell knocking down his father. The second, more objective poem places his relations with Anne in several contexts. He refers to the classical: the Emperor Nero, who had his mother murdered; aesthetic: the seventeenth-century French landscapes by Claude Lorrain; historical: Hitler's annexation of Austria in 1938 and the millions dead in World War II; and urban: the view of MIT across the Charles River from Boston. Apart from the banal phrase, "I wanted to marry you," Anne—never quite real to him as he played at being her lover—disappears in the poem. Anne Dick set the pattern for Lowell's troubled relations with Jean Stafford and Carley Dawson. With all three women he was pedantic and sexually maladroit, domineering and insensitive to their feelings. He broke with them abruptly and caused severe emotional damage.

In the Lowells' home, where Bobby returned on college vacations, Charlotte continued to torment Bob with sarcasm and disdain. After his first heart attack, she banished the convalescent to the country club, explaining that it was "an impossible situation, so *inconvenient* having Bob at home."[56] In 1949, after Bob's near-fatal coronary, Lowell was horrified to hear Charlotte's grating voice continuing to assail the shuffling invalid. Bob's last words were "I feel awful." Lowell said the death of his father in 1950 seemed "almost meaningless, as is perhaps always the case when the life has long resigned itself to a terrible, dim diffused pathos."[57] In "Sailing Home from Rapallo" he wrote that his father was literally placed under and metaphorically smothered by generations of Winslows, who'd been interred for centuries in their Dunbarton cemetery and seemed to resent the presence of his corpse: "The only 'unhistoric' soul to come here / was Father, now buried beneath his recent / unweathered pink-veined slice of marble."[58] Lowell himself was destined to be buried there.

The Lowells resembled the desperately unhappy family in D. H. Lawrence's story "The Rocking-Horse Winner," published in 1926 when Bobby was nine years old. They had the same social pretensions and financial anxiety, the insignificant absent husband, the parents' remoteness from each other, the wife's sexual dissatisfaction, the impossible demands she makes on her young son and the desire to have her son replace his father in her emotional life.

III

Many modern American writers—from Fitzgerald and Hemingway to Berryman and Jarrell—had strong, domineering mothers and weak, often absent, fathers. Lowell fit this pattern perfectly. There was universal agreement among Bobby's friends that Charlotte was a monster mom, the prototype of the cruel tyrants from Nero to Stalin who fascinated him throughout his life. Bobby was caught in Charlotte's web and his relations with her were sometimes quite funny in a ghoulish sort of way. When Bob was stationed at Guantánamo and Charlotte was staying with his mother on Staten Island, she grieved over her pregnancy and rejected Bobby even before he was born. In his last book, *Day by Day* (1977), published a month before his death, the unwanted son of a mother trapped in an unwanted marriage finally exposed the festering wound that had tormented him for a lifetime. Lowell probed his psychological pain in his high-octane poem "Unwanted," in which Charlotte, heavy with child, laments, "I wish I were dead, I wish I were dead"—and by doing so also wished that he were dead.[59] Lowell thought it was unforgivable for a mother to tell her child that she didn't want him to be born and give him the perpetual dread of not being wanted. Lowell's cousin Christina Brazelton recalled that his father also rejected Bobby. When Charlotte brought him the baby when he was an infant, Bob said, "Bring him back when he's three."[60]

Lowell tried to ease the pain with the extraordinary claim that "anyone is unwanted in a medical sense—lust [is] our only father." This strange idea had also appeared in a letter from the illegitimate T. E. Lawrence, another man who knew he was unwanted. On March 27, 1923, he wrote to his friend Robert Graves: "I believe it's we who led our parents on to bear us, and it's our unborn children who make our flesh itch."[61] Graves took up the idea that unborn infants inspire lust in their own parents and are, in a sense, their own begetters in "Children of Darkness" (1923):

> We spurred our parents to the kiss,
> Though doubtfully they shrank from this—
> Day had no courage to pursue
> What lusty dark alone might do:
> Then we were joined from their caress
> In heat of midnight, one from two.[62]

To Graves this was a clever conceit; to Lawrence and Lowell it was a source of deep-rooted guilt and misery. Lowell said that Charlotte devoured him with her love, but lacked a truly affectionate nature. Unwilling to crease her dress, she never allowed him to sit in her lap. So he always wanted what he never had: a "mother to lift me in her arms."[63]

Characteristically, Charlotte remained hysterical even in her calm. "She was not," Lowell wrote, "one whose hand was stayed from destruction by sentiment,"[64] and was merciless with both her husband and son. But Bobby's earliest memory offered a unique example of Charlotte's ability to exhibit sharp wit while observing the social proprieties. Fascinated by a cracked ivory elephant, no bigger than a molar, which a visitor wore on her necklace, he begged to have it. When his wish was granted, he promptly swallowed it. Comically exaggerating his Rabelaisian appetite, "Mother kept saying with Gargantuan suavity, 'Bobby has swallowed an elephant.'" After it was unmentionably ascertained that the elephant had passed through and been discharged from his body, Charlotte, sanitizing the offensive process, "managed to mention the chamber-pot, my movement and the marvelous elephant all in one pure, smirking breath."[65]

Bobby felt drenched in his parents' passions. Ashamed of his father's humiliation yet mocking his weakness, he was determined to resist his mother's domination and as a small boy felt the first stirrings of revolt against her. Blair Clark recalled her incessant nagging: "He was so clumsy, so sloppy, so ill-mannered. She would say things to him like 'See what nice manners Blair has.' And I played that role because it was helpful to him. I really think there was a psychological fixation on dominating Cal by that woman. And what does an only child do—with an obsessed mother and a weak father who goes along with that obsession?"[66] Bobby had two possibilities: he could rebel or escape, and he did both.

Lowell inherited his four dynastic names from his father, and was called the childish "Bobby" to distinguish him from the elder "Bob." But he changed his name to "Cal" in prep school and reveled in its negative associations, which also suggested calculating, callow and callous. Caligula was a Roman emperor and insane tyrant, known for his extravagance, sexual perversity and cruelty. Caliban, the son of a witch, was the brutal and evil monster in Shakespeare's *The Tempest*. "Cal" also hinted at the fanatical religious reformer John Calvin and, ironically, to the stodgy and boring Calvin Coolidge, American president when Cal was a boy in the 1920s. His first letter to his parents, in August 1936, was addressed to "Mother" (formal) and "Daddy" (familiar), and signed "Cal."

As a young man he quarreled with them about his plans to leave Harvard and ambition to become a poet (which Charlotte thought was a worthless pursuit), about his lack of employment and engagement to Anne Dick. He was angry about their interfering in his life and roundly condemned their "false Back Bay morality and true sophistry." Always trying to mold him in their image, they had disloyally written to his friends and secretly sent his letters to Dr. Merrill Moore, Charlotte's psychiatrist. Four years later, as these quarrels persisted, he again warned Charlotte to stop meddling in his affairs and seized the moral high ground by telling her: "I am not flattered by the remark that you do not know where I am heading or that my ways are not your ways. . . . One can hardly be ostracized for taking the intellect and aristocracy and family tradition seriously."[67] Charlotte wanted him to be an obedient and conformist son, but he became defiant and rebellious. Bobby's parents never expected to have a gifted son and didn't know what to do with him.

In the last years of their marriage Bob was ashamed of being oppressed by his wife and Charlotte dreaded the empty years that loomed ahead. She despised him for being less manly than her forceful father and for allowing himself to be enslaved. She expressed her lifelong dissatisfaction by taunting her hapless husband. She often called Bob a weakling whose only interests were steamships, radio and his former comrades. When visitors provided an appreciative audience, she would say, "Don't you think Bob looks peaceful? They call him the undertaker at Lever Brothers. I think he is in love with his soap vat" or "Bob is the only man in America who really believes it is criminal to buy Ivory Soap instead of Lux."[68] Ironically alluding to Ivory Soap's advertising slogan, Lowell slyly wrote that his father's (single) bedroom "was ninety-nine one-hundredths [percent] white."[69] Heymann defined the sterile atmosphere of the household: "although grievously unsuited for one another, both Lowells were traumatically formal and remote, Charlotte dreading any kind of lapse from the protocol of class, the Commander shirking all parental and social responsibility."[70] Though weak, Bob deflected and absorbed some of Charlotte's antagonism to Bobby. She treated her son as a backward boy and felt obliged to remind him to put on his socks before his shoes.

Charlotte both denigrated Bobby and, after transferring her ambitions from her husband to her son, counted on him to restore the declining family fortunes. He had to resist her assaults or become emasculated like his father. In "Commander Lowell" he stressed his father's ineptitude by noting that sailor Bob was no good at sailing and took four shots to sink a putt. Elizabeth Hardwick, Lowell's second wife, recalled that in a similar fashion Grandfather Winslow expressed intense disappointment at Bobby's ineptitude, and humiliated the boy by telling him: "One year thin and handsome and the next year bulky and brooding. Cannot shoot a gun, cannot ride a horse. What prizes have you won, except for collecting snakes and mismatched socks? On a sailboat, a menace."[71] Lowell complained that Charlotte drilled home her father's disdain and thought his only practical accomplishment was fishing. It's scarcely surprising, as one critic noted, that the fierce, sinister and destructive "women in Lowell's poetry seem monster, [husband-murdering] Clytemnestra-projections" of his mother,[72] and that he felt his generous cousin Harriet Winslow, who left his family her grand house in Castine, Maine, "was more to me than my mother."[73]

The red-haired Dr. Merrill Moore (1903–1957) was Charlotte's ally in her psychological assault on Bobby. Born (like Ransom and Tate) in Tennessee, Moore earned his medical degree at Vanderbilt and was married with four children. The poet Louis Untermeyer described him as "an enthusiast and yea-sayer, an athlete, walker and gardener." An expert in the treatment of alcoholism and syphilis, known for his personal "euphoria, or chronic state of well-being," he would serve in the Pacific in World War II and became the personal physician of Chiang Kai-shek. He also treated Robert Frost and the poet's emotionally disturbed children. Frost's generous obituary of Moore in the *Harvard Alumni Bulletin* of 1957 alluded to his self-importance and called him "a serious physician and serious artist who had no notion of being taken lightly; still there was something of the rogue there that was part of his great charm."[74]

Moore was a member of the Fugitive group of Southern poets. In the course of his undistinguished literary career, he cranked out thousands of sonnets, averaging one a day for seventeen years, in his self-styled "Sonnetorium"—more than all the sonnets, he proudly claimed, that had been written in the entire history of English literature. All the Fugitives advised Moore to control his obsession, be more self-critical and take time to revise his verse. But undeterred by harsh and unforgiving reviews from the beginning to the end of his career, he continued to pour it out. The exact opposite of Ransom, the refined perfectionist, Moore was an example of how to write bad poetry.[75] Lowell quoted Allen Tate exclaiming that his "tenant with ten children had more art / than Merrill Moore."[76]

Yvor Winters, in *Poetry* (May 1930), was merciless: "The meters are a kind of rhymed and butchered prose, and the diction is for the most part very, very approximate, to speak as charitably as possible. The fact that Mr. Moore has written badly with a deliberate intention and consistent effect does not alter the fact that he has written badly."[77] A decade later Dudley Fitts, in the *Sewanee Review* (April 1939), harpooned his habits and agreed with Winters: "There is a Merrill Moore legend—the ten sonnets daily, the fifty-thousand yet unpublished sonnets in the bound files, the prescription blank, the laundry-check, the telephone-pad jottings for poems, the sonnets scribbled at crossings between changes of traffic lights—and while, like most literary legends, this is amusing, it is also unfortunate. . . . I do not know any contemporary poetry that yields so many points of adverse criticism. It invites attacks of every kind."[78] It's ironic that Moore, one of the worst contemporary poets, pronounced judgment on the psychological condition of one of the greatest poets of his time.

In his poem "Unwanted," Lowell agonized over his relations with both Charlotte and Moore. When he was in college and still unaware of Charlotte's prenatal hostility, Moore deliberately undermined his precarious balance by informing him that he was an unwanted child. Moore even suggested that he and Charlotte collaborate on a case study of Bobby— just the thing to cheer him up. Her amateur diagnosis of Bobby's mental state was both cruel and wounding. Charlotte told Bobby that the authoritative Carl Jung (who'd unsuccessfully treated Zelda Fitzgerald and Joyce's daughter Lucia), had said, "If your son is as you have described him, / he is an incurable schizophrenic."[79] Though nine years younger than Charlotte, Moore also became her lover. Lowell's friends described Moore as a charlatan and villain who oozed onto the scene.

Moore's behavior was unprofessional, unethical and perhaps even criminal. If the medical authorities had known about it, they would have revoked his license. He used Bobby to recruit wealthy patients; he slept with his own patient Charlotte; he let her, with no qualifications, take on some of his cases and the "doctor" (as Lowell called her) gave ill-informed advice to disturbed people. Moore simultaneously treated Charlotte's teenaged son and wanted to treat Anne Dick; he betrayed confidentiality by discussing Bobby's case with his mother (who then told Bobby what Moore had revealed about him); and he told Bobby that his mother had not wanted him to be born. The vulnerable Bobby, their prime target and victim, was caught in their emotional crossfire. The kindly John Crowe Ransom thought Moore's "insensibility to Cal's sensibilities was so gross that I had to sit down and write him a very sharp letter."[80]

Lowell was not the only one to criticize his mother. None of his close friends or wives had a kind word to say about her. Blair Clark saw her claws beneath the smooth façade: "Charlotte Lowell's white gloves sheathed steely hands determined to wrest victory from her strange, rebellious only child."[81] Clark added, "I think of her as a monstrous woman, clinically monstrous. I said to Cal in the last summer of his life, 'I think you spared your family.' And he said, 'I probably did—they were awful, quite awful.'"[82] John Thompson, a Kenyon friend, characterized her as the evil figure who lived in a land of permafrost in Hans Christian Andersen's fairy tale: "Charlotte was a Snow Queen who flirted coldly and shamelessly with her son [and his friends]. His father once ordered a half-bottle of wine for five at dinner."[83] Allen Tate, even more caustic about Charlotte's rude behavior, declared that she had no peer "for stupidity, insensitivity, and ill-breeding."[84]

Jean Stafford named her "Charlotte Hideous" and called her a neurotic with very little brain. Elizabeth Hardwick came from a poor family and had made a lucky escape from her background, but was not impressed by his parents. After Charlotte had complacently said that she usually managed to make herself pretty comfortable, Hardwick satirized the parents' self-indulgent but empty way of life: "They were a knotty pair. They were in marvelous shape, very careful and prudent. And yet very sensual about fine bed linens, silk underwear, soft cushions, and the proper purring of household motors. The father's fine eyesight, healthy teeth, good tennis game did not keep him from an early death."[85] Lowell's father was bald and had perfect vision; his son was hairy and myopic.

In 1951, when Lowell and Hardwick were living in Europe, he made the mistake of touring with the recently widowed and impossibly demanding Charlotte, who brought out the worst in him and reinforced his infantile connection with her. He described her character, their mutual misunderstanding and their inexorably deteriorating relations in an amusing letter to Elizabeth Bishop: "She is a very competent, stubborn, uncurious, unBohemian woman with a genius for squeezing luxury out of rocks. That is, she has a long memory for pre-war and pre-first-world-war service; and thinks nothing of calling the American ambassador if there's no toilet-paper on the train etc. Well, under the best conditions, of course, I can't begin to make sense out of or to her. Each year since I was eighteen, it's gotten worse." Emphasizing her oppressive personality, he told Allen Tate, "we sat like stones on each other's heads—inhibiting and inhibited."[86]

In February 1954 Charlotte suddenly suffered a cerebral hemorrhage in Rapallo, on the Italian Riviera. Teaching in Cincinnati at the time, Lowell flew there on a circuitous route to Boston, New York, London and Paris, where he stopped to see his old friend Blair Clark and spent the night drinking with him. He then flew on to Milan, couldn't find a taxi in the heavy rain, caught a tram to the Central Station, and finally took a train southwest to Genoa and another one twenty miles south to Rapallo.

Just after his arrival he wrote Hardwick that he blubbed for half an hour with the gray, bespectacled nurse, sharing their common language of hot tears. "Mother died very suddenly from a second attack just an hour before I arrived," he wrote. "She was quite wandering in her memory all the time and I don't think there was ever much chance. She didn't suffer and didn't altogether know where she was. They thought best not to announce my coming to her, and I don't think she suspected the need. Pretty rough—I spent the morning with her nurse who only speaks Italian, both of us weeping & weeping. I mean I spent it in the room with her body!"[87] The doctors told him that Charlotte had had high blood pressure and arteriosclerosis, and couldn't have lived much longer even if she'd remained at home.

Lowell's claim that he arrived after a very long trip only an hour after her death exaggerated the truth for dramatic effect. In a prose draft of "Sailing Home from Rapallo," Charlotte was still alive when he got there: "Mother lay looking through the blacks and tans and flashings from her window. Her face was too formed and fresh to seem asleep. There was a bruise the size of an earlobe over her right eye."[88] In fact, Charlotte died when Lowell was drinking with Blair Clark. He naturally felt guilty about dallying in Paris instead of hurrying on to Rapallo in time to see Charlotte and be with her when she died. But he was afraid to see her menacingly alive and felt it was better to reach the hospital after she was safely dead. Relieved but devastated, Lowell produced a flood of tears.

Rapallo had strong literary associations. Max Beerbohm lived there, except for the war years, from 1910 until his death in 1956. W. B. Yeats spent two winters there in the late 1920s. Ezra Pound lived there from 1924 until his arrest for treason in 1945, and Lowell discussed Pound's *Jefferson and/or Mussolini* with Charlotte's doctor. The deaths of his parents released Lowell's deepest emotions and left him free to condemn them in his poems. When he asked Robert Frost's advice about whether he could savage his father in "91 Revere Street," the older poet recognized the psychological necessity and replied, "I wish you wouldn't publish the piece against your father unless you find you must to relieve pressure."[89] This memoir, a nostalgic account of his disorder and early sorrow, provided the essential personal context for the poems in *Life Studies*.

Lowell's elegy on his mother, "Sailing Home from Rapallo," more emotionally charged than its satirical companion "Commander Lowell," reveals the contrast between the grief that Lowell was supposed to feel and the relief that he actually felt when he could no longer be tormented by her. It also has strong historical and mythical connotations. Lowell identified with oppressive Roman emperors and, like Nero, had created a kind of "death barge for his mother."[90] By sailing home with his mother's corpse, he seemed like Charon ferrying the dead across the Styx to Hades. In "Near the Unbalanced Aquarium," his prose version of Charlotte's traumatic death, he said the Italians took advantage of his grief to overcharge him for her ugly casket, which had a huge brass crucifix attached to it. Though inappropriately Catholic, the coffin matched her queenly presence and extravagant taste. Since nothing was too good for his luxury-loving mother, she managed to make herself pretty comfortable, as if she were still alive, and traveled "first-class in the hold" while Lowell drank his way across the ocean.

In a letter to Blair Clark, Lowell said his mother's name on the casket had been misspelled *Charlotte Winslon.* His poem states, more convincingly,

> In the grandiloquent lettering on Mother's coffin,
> *Lowell* had been misspelled LOVEL.
> The corpse
> was wrapped like *panetone* in Italian tinfoil.[91]

In any case, there's no letter W in Italian, which may account for the errors in Winslow or Lowell. He also confuses *panettone* with the flat, spicy fruitcake *panforte* which, like Charlotte, is wrapped in tinfoil to preserve it.

Writing to a friend, Hardwick asked if her apparently indestructible mother-in-law was " '*really* dead?' Not out of any sentimentality but from a genuine wonder that such a strange force could suddenly vanish. In my heart I do four times a day pay Mrs. Lowell the compliment of profound disbelief in this latest event."[92] Charlotte had a formidable array of negative qualities. She was self-indulgent, perpetually dissatisfied and a dreadful traveling companion. She constantly mocked her weak husband, and provoked late night arguments that kept her young son anxious and awake. She victimized Bobby and devoured him with love. Unhappily married and with a complaisant husband, she flirted with her son's friends and took lovers. While working for a doctor, she pretended to have medical knowledge and advised his patients. She also alienated everyone who was close to her.[93]

Though Charlotte's death doubled Lowell's income and gave him $50,000 in cash, her real legacy was catastrophic. When it seemed that his dead mother—silently sealed in her coffin, safely frozen and tinfoiled in the hold of the ship—could no longer torment him, she precipitated his next mental breakdown. Immediately after her death, he broke with Hardwick and became involved with an Italian woman he'd met while teaching at the Salzburg Seminar. "When Mother died," he wrote, quoting the *Book of Common Prayer,* "I began to feel tireless, madly sanguine, menaced, and menacing, I entered the Payne-Whitney Clinic [in New York] for 'all those afflicted in mind.'"[94] The mental illness that plagued him throughout his life did not come from his bland and boring father, but from his volatile and unstable mother. Lowell suffered terribly. But as Robert Frost observed, "No tears in the writer, no tears in the reader."[95] Poetry was his means of expressing and conquering his emotional turmoil.

TWO

Southern Comfort, 1930–1941

I

In his first novel, *This Side of Paradise* (1920), Scott Fitzgerald, impressed by the old wealth and hallowed traditions of St. Mark's, wrote that the school recruited boys from "Boston and the Knickerbocker families of New York."[1] The poet and publisher Harry Crosby and the journalist Benjamin Bradlee were prominent alumni, and W. H. Auden taught there in 1939. Lowell's ancestor and namesake, Robert Traill Spence Lowell, the founder and first headmaster of the school, portrayed heroic values in his Indian Mutiny poem "The Relief of Lucknow" (1860).

In 1930 the thirteen-year-old Lowell entered St. Mark's—an all-boys boarding school in Southborough, Massachusetts, twenty-five miles west of Boston—and spent the next four years there. He later called it fearful and cruel, a "curious clubby monosexual, but seething with tentacles world[2] . . . big boys beating small boys, with old men watching fondly from the wings."[3] Lowell, with his brooding, saturnine nature, was miserable at school and, Frank Parker said, "there was a darkness wherever he went."[4] In three poems, written later on, he recalled his old wounds and emphasized the mockery and pervasive sadism. The boys had "high-school nicknames on their tongues, / as if they wished to relive / the rawness that let us meet as animals." Teasing at the school soon turned into public humiliation as his classmates zeroed in on Lowell's unpleasant habits:

> Mid-meal, they began
> To pull me apart.
> "Why is he always grubbing in his nose?"

"Because his nose is always snotty."
"He likes to wipe his thumb in it."
"Cal's a creep of the first water."[5]

He wrote that Bobby Delano, cousin of President Roosevelt, "dug my ass with a compass,/forced me to say 'My Mother is a whore.'" But Lowell soon scared off his predators, and became one of the bullies and tormentors: "my callous unconscious drives me/to torture my closest friend."[6]

Three photos of Lowell appear among his thirty-five classmates in the senior yearbook: one with the rowing crew, two when he was forced to wear a jacket and tie. The surprisingly active Lowell was on the board of the literary magazine; the tall but uncoordinated boy also played on the soccer and football teams. As gym boy he handed out towels and uniforms in the equipment room. In July 1934, as counselor at Brantwood Camp—a summer program for underprivileged inner-city youths— "Lowell lived with ten boys in a cabin, leading them in activities: hiking, camp craft and civics tests, daily inspection, and coaching them in baseball and swimming."[7]

In May 1936 Lowell wrote Ezra Pound that at St. Mark's he was always a resentful outsider, rather out of touch with ordinary life: "I never mixed well or really lived in the usual realities. . . . I was proud, somewhat sullen and violent."[8] His lifelong pal Blair Clark—who became John Kennedy's friend at Harvard, vice-president of CBS News, editor of the *Nation* and Eugene McCarthy's campaign manager in 1968—recalled that Lowell was "dark, menacing, belligerent; always bigger, stronger, shaggier than his contemporaries. . . . He was the strongest boy in the class; people left him alone—they thought he was crazy—because he was so strong. And now and then he proved he ought to be left alone."[9] The loyal and efficient Blair would later rescue Lowell from many crises and disasters.

Lowell's best teacher was Richard Eberhart, born in Minnesota in 1904, who'd graduated from Dartmouth, studied at Cambridge University with I. A. Richards and William Empson, and begun to publish poetry. He'd worked on a tramp steamer and would become a naval gunnery officer in World War II. Lowell liked to refer to him as Ghormley, his weird middle name. He said that Eberhart "smoked honey-scented tobacco, and read Baudelaire and Shakespeare and Hopkins—it made the thing living. . . . He was very encouraging and enthusiastic."[10]

Eberhart described how the teenaged Lowell started coming to see him in the winter of 1934, and recalled his unusual energy and impressive talent:

He entered my study and placed on my desk a typewritten manuscript in a rough brown folder. It contained sixty poems, the first
fruits and trial of his art as a youth yet in school, produced after
some months of talk about poetry and art. . . . The raw power was
there. The forms were scarcely more complicated than the sonnet,
which he yet employs, with variable rhyme schemes. And there was a
heavy driving force and [surge] of prose which would bind the lyric
flow in strict forms. . . .

Between then and the end of School Lowell had written about
one hundred and fifty poems. I thought this a rather remarkable
phenomenon and the man behind the pen promising: I admired
his seriousness (and was appalled at the fabulous beliefs the young
can have about the infallible and gigantic nature of their own powers) and his incipient ability. . . . I felt that his strength of mind, his
determination, and the apparent seriousness of his intentions were
salutary and to be encouraged.[11]

Later on, when Lowell had come under the influence of more forceful
poets, he wrote a rather severe review that offered faint praise of Eberhart's poetry—"He writes a rough iambic line with subtle shifts in speed
and tone. His best poems are entirely his own and masterful"—but also
pointed out his weaknesses: "Elsewhere his lines drag in a rhetorical dog-
gerel. . . . Sometimes his idealistic reflections on himself and the universe
are remarkably foolish."[12] Lowell made it clear that he had now outgrown
his old teacher.

In his student years Lowell, the future disciple of great writers, forced
his friends and girlfriends to become his own disciples. One would expect
him to spend the summer of 1935, liberated from St. Mark's and about
to enter Harvard, going to the beach, drinking beer and chasing girls.
Instead, on Nantucket island, he persuaded Blair Clark and Frank Parker
to read a long list of seventy-five difficult and often boring Elizabethan
plays—more than a graduate student writing a dissertation on Renais-
sance drama would have to swallow. Parker recalled that, like a torturer
keeping prisoners awake until they signed a confession, Lowell did not
"allow them to go to sleep until they agreed."[13]

While pursuing this strict regimen they sustained themselves with peni-
tential rations. They ate tasteless health-food cereal and repulsive cooked
eels, and drank watered cocoa laced with rum. Lowell believed that
involvement with girls would vitiate their lofty ideals and felt his ascetic

tyranny was justified by the acquisition of knowledge. Like the King of Navarre and his lords in Shakespeare's *Love's Labour's Lost,* Lowell swore to keep away from women and live by fasting and studying.

II

Lowell spent his first year and a half of college at Harvard, which seemed to reinforce the conformity and constrictions of his New England prep school. Harvard had an old-fashioned curriculum, no important poet on the faculty and scant interest in contemporary literature. During his second year Lowell took almost all his courses in English literature, and had his poems rejected by the literary magazine, the *Harvard Advocate.* Lowell, whose cousin was president of Harvard, already had all the academic prestige he needed, and it was even more prestigious to reject Harvard than to go there. Abandoning the Ivy League, he went to obscure colleges in remote places to study with distinguished poets who recognized his talent, took him seriously and taught him well.

Well aware of his intellectual powers and poetic potential, the young Lowell felt entitled to consort with many of the leading writers of his time. Like Hemingway—who'd talked about writing with Sherwood Anderson, Gertrude Stein, Pound and Fitzgerald—Lowell studied with the best teachers. While still in his teens he corresponded with Pound, and showed Eberhart and Robert Frost his early poems; in his early twenties he discussed his work with Ford Madox Ford, Allen Tate, John Crowe Ransom and Robert Penn Warren. From these older writers, he not only learned about the craft of poetry, but also how to live as a poet and use a poet's charisma to attract women.

In Boston in the spring of 1937, during his fierce quarrels with his parents about Anne Dick, Lowell met the English novelist Ford Madox Ford at Anne's house. Ford, who'd met Tate in England and was about to visit him in Tennessee, urged young Lowell to follow him there. This salutary advice gave Lowell the chance to escape from his parents, from Harvard and eventually from Anne, and to create a new life in the South.

Lowell knew the ill and aging Ford at the fag end of his life and did not seem to recognize his real distinction. Born into an artistic family in 1873, the grandson of the Pre-Raphaelite painter Ford Madox Brown, he was well known for his literary friendships, fictional achievements and editorial skill. He was the generous friend of several major American writers—Henry James, Stephen Crane, Pound and Hemingway—and a confidant

and collaborator of Joseph Conrad, and had written two innovative mas-
terpieces, *The Good Soldier* and the *Parade's End* tetralogy. Though over
forty when the Great War broke out, he'd volunteered for active service.
In the disastrous 1916 battle of the Somme he'd been shell-shocked and
gassed, which caused his labored breathing and wheezing speech.

"When I knew Ford in America," Lowell wrote, "he was out of cash,
out of fashion, and half out of inspiration, a half-German, half-English
exile in love with the French, and able to sell his books only in the United
States. . . . His conversation, at least as finished as his written reminiscences, came out in ordered, subtly circuitous paragraphs."[14] Lowell later
told Eberhart, with some exaggeration, "I am not on speaking terms with
Mr. Ford, the explanation given, that he is afraid I will write memoirs
30 or 60 years from now, in which I will describe him as an ever stout,
gouty old gentleman, deluded by the [old-fashioned] poetry of Christina
Rossetti."[15] Though Ford may have been trying to avoid Lowell, he also
used him as an assistant and dictated his volume of criticism, *The March of
Literature* (1938), to the importunate poet. When Lowell couldn't read his
own childishly crabbed handwriting, he cavalierly added a few of his own
sentences to Ford's dictation.

Elizabeth Hardwick once quoted the remark of Robert Frost, a veteran
of the lecture circuit, that "hell is a half-filled auditorium."[16] At the University of Colorado Writers' Conference in the summer of 1937, Lowell
witnessed Ford's humiliation when "an audience of hundreds walked out
on him, as he exquisitely, ludicrously, and inaudibly imitated the elaborate
periphrastic style of Henry James."[17] Lowell's later elegy of Ford and his
preface to Ford's poems *Buckshee* were appreciative and did not justify
Ford's prediction that Lowell would denigrate him. In Lowell's poem Ford,
who died in 1939, became a poignant example of a great writer who ended
up impoverished and obscure. Lowell concluded his elegy with, "you were
a kind man and you died in want."[18]

Now that Tate's and Ransom's reputations have declined and the New
Criticism they advocated has been overtaken by more fashionable abstract
theories, it is difficult to recall the great prestige these poets enjoyed when
Lowell knew them in their prime. Tate (eighteen years older than Lowell)
had roomed with Robert Penn Warren at Vanderbilt University in Nashville, where Ransom had been their professor. Tate was thin, pale, blond
and blue-eyed, with a bulging, Poe-like, almost hydrocephalic forehead
that Lowell called an "enormous brow, a snowman's knob."

A heavy drinker and energetic seducer, Tate led a defiantly bohemian life. He'd married the Southern novelist Caroline Gordon in 1925 and their daughter Nancy was born soon after. He divorced Gordon in 1946, remarried her that year and divorced her again in 1959. He converted to Catholicism in 1950 and remained in the Church despite his divorces. In 1959 he became the fourth husband of the New England poet Isabella Gardner and divorced her in 1966. That year he trumped all his rivals by marrying his much younger student, an ex-nun, Helen Heinz. In 1967— as Tate approached seventy—the couple had twin sons, and a third son the following year.

In 1937, when Lowell first turned up, Tate and his entourage were living in an antebellum mansion, Benfolly, bought for him by his wealthy brother Ben. It was attached to an eighty-five acre estate and farm, with a fine view of a fast-flowing river, three miles from Clarksville in north-central Tennessee. In his amusing essay "Visiting the Tates," Lowell (a dangerous driver) described his dramatic arrival: "My only anchor was a suitcase, heavy with bad poetry. I was brought to earth by my bumper mashing the Tates' frail agrarian mailbox post. Getting out to disguise the damage, I turned my back on their peeling, pillared house. I had crashed [in both senses] the civilization of the South." In fact, he didn't stop to inspect the mailbox but to piss on it. Recalling the recent conflicts with his parents about marrying Anne Dick and leaving Harvard, Lowell added, "Like a torn cat, I was taken in when I needed help, and in a sense I have never left." As Tate and the Southern Agrarians captured and began to tame their rare prize, Lowell "realized that the old dead weight of poor James Russell Lowell was now an asset."[19] He both rebelled against his background and benefited from its prestige.

Trying at first to get rid of the brash intruder, Tate told him there was no room in the rambling house and that Lowell would have to camp out on the lawn. Ignoring or oblivious to this polite discouragement, the pioneer took Tate literally, bought a tent in the nearest Sears, Roebuck and incrementally but firmly established himself in the house. His tent on Tate's demesne was an extension of his experience in Brantwood camp. As he proudly told Eberhart, alluding to the plant in Homer's *Odyssey* that made travelers lose their desire to return to their native land, "For the past 3 weeks I have been camping on the Tates' lawn in a translucent green umbrella tent obliquely under a lotus tree. Barnyard stock meander all around me, occasionally scratching the tent sides or pawing the mosquito netting. The Tates live in a shabby plantation house which is not ancestral, high on top of a slope overlooking the brown Cumberland River." [20]

The Tates prided themselves on genteel manners and tried hard to domesticate the unkempt Lowell. Nancy said, "There was a great effort to get him to tie his shoe laces, tuck in his shirt tails and take baths." [21] Lowell, now on his best behavior and acting quite differently than he did with his parents, tried to earn his keep and became a model guest. The motherly Gordon, enchanted by Lowell's pedigree and presence, thought that he looked like "a choirboy or a matinee idol," that he was "such a nice boy—the handiest she ever knew. He would drive her [around on errands], haul the buttermilk, even 'flit' the dining room." [22]

Tate was more sceptical. Aware of Lowell's checkered history and impulsive character, he worried about possible problems: "The Lowell boy turned up twice, and we like him but feel that he is a potential nuisance. His family decided that anybody who wanted to be a writer was insane; so they tried to have him judged crazy and committed to an asylum. Merrill [Moore] evidently put on his bedside manner and got their consent for him to come to Tennessee, which doubtless in the Lowell mind is not unlike a madhouse. Ford says they are the most dreadful people he's ever seen." [23] Despite the initial difficulties, Lowell had found his first in a series of ideal poetic parents. He began with Tate and Gordon, John Crowe and Robb Ransom, and ended with Ezra and Dorothy Pound, William Carlos and Florence Williams.

A generous but acerbic figure, Tate fulfilled Lowell's dream of having an important American poet read his work. After looking at his youthful effusions, Tate wrote Eberhart, "I have great hopes for your pupil Robert Lowell. This past summer he made handsome progress, and I am convinced that he will be a real poet. Besides that he is a fine boy." [24] News of young Lowell's extraordinary arrival soon spread through the Midwest to the East Coast. The Chicago critic Morten Dauwen Zabel, emphasizing Lowell's slovenly appearance and resolute character, wrote Edmund Wilson about "a young Harvard sprout called Robert Lowell (yes: the right Lowells), who'd thrown up that University after two restless years and gone down to Tennessee to learn poetry from Tate and Ransom—a pleasant fellow got up in the best Harvard manner of soiled shoes, unpressed pants, dirty shirt, tousled hair, face slightly broken out, soft voice, and moral earnestness writ large upon his features." [25]

Lowell remained a close friend of Tate till the end of his life. Though they occasionally quarreled about literature, religion and sex, Tate continued to influence his work and advance his career. First Lowell became a serious rival, then surpassed his old mentor in achievement and reputation. Following T. S. Eliot's pronouncements, Tate taught Lowell that the poet should be learned and rooted in history, cultivate classical forms, work within the European tradition, act in a patrician and dignified manner, write in an impersonal and symbolic style, and embrace conservative social and political ideas.

Tate wrote an incisive introduction to Lowell's first book, *Land of Unlikeness* (1944), hand printed by the Cummington Press in Massachusetts in a limited edition of only 250 copies. (It sold for $3 and is now worth as much as $10,000.) Lowell's title suggested that the real world was but a poor reflection of the ideal. Like William Blake, he wanted to build a new Jerusalem—in America's green and pleasant land. Tate, who saw these poems come into being, perceived in Lowell's first book the personal elements that would later dominate *Life Studies:* "The style is bold and powerful, and the symbolic language often has the effect of being *willed;* for it is an intellectual style compounded of brilliant puns and shifts of tone. . . . Shorter poems like 'A Suicidal Nightmare' and 'Death from Cancer' are richer in immediate experience than the explicitly religious poems; they are more dramatic, the references being personal and historical and the symbolism less willed and explicit."[26] This heady mixture of Lowell's original talent and Tate's forceful advocacy sparked an auspicious debut. *Land of Unlikeness* was enthusiastically reviewed by major critics: John Frederick Nims, Arthur Mizener, Richard Blackmur and Lowell's close college friend Randall Jarrell.

In 1949 Tate successfully recommended Lowell for a residency at Yaddo, the writers' colony in Saratoga Springs, New York (where Elizabeth Hardwick, who became his second wife, was also in residence), characterizing him as a serious artist and charming young man. Tate praised Lowell's freely translated version of Baudelaire's major poem "Au Lecteur" ("To the Reader"), calling it "masterly, possibly it is better than the original; it is certainly more powerful." He was also flattered and well pleased by Lowell's affectionate personal essay, "Visiting the Tates": "It's a very fine piece of prose, every word packed and precise, and every word, unless I am wholly bemused, very tender. If I am not bemused, I am at least dazzled. I could not have known that you thought so well of me, or that so many others did, that I can put out of mind for the time being those who don't."[27]

Lowell's first literary conflict with Tate and first break with the Master took place in 1959 when he was about to publish the intensely personal revelations in *Life Studies*. Tate strictly adhered to Eliot's and the New Critics' emphasis on irony and impersonality, distance and decorum—though Eliot, if his readers but knew it, had revealed a great deal about himself in *The Waste Land* and several other poems. Tate, who behaved as priapically as possible in private life while maintaining a respectable façade, did not want Lowell to reveal himself. He disliked Lowell's unhealthy self-obsession and insisted, "*all* the poems about your family, including the one about you and Elizabeth ["Man and Wife"], are definitely *bad*. I do not think you ought to publish them."[28] Lowell ignored Tate's well-intentioned but misguided advice and his warning that the book would damage his standing as a poet. Instead of hurting Lowell, the forceful and innovative *Life Studies* created his charismatic public persona and established his reputation as the leading American poet of his time.

Lowell, whose own sexual affairs were tempestuous and chaotic, made the fatal mistake of getting involved in Tate's love life. Elizabeth Bishop (not interested in men) found Tate creepy and could never understand his sex appeal. But Tate, always on the prowl and impervious to rebuffs, succeeded with Southern gallantry, courtly manners and bold attacks. He was obsessed for a time with Natasha, the wife of the bisexual English poet Stephen Spender, and finally managed to seduce her. But when the guilt-free Tate described himself as a Southern puritan, Hardwick cuttingly replied that he was as puritanical as an ape. Tate was also put down by the Lowells' five-year-old daughter, Harriet. Lowell recalled that when Tate solemnly promised the child, " 'You are very dear to me because your parents are very dear to me. You will be dear to me when you are older.' (One had a feeling she would be more dear to him then.) At that point Harriet stared at him in wonder, and slowly said, 'If you are still alive.' "[29] The complete list of Tate's lovers is still unknown. His biographer, overcome by fears of libel, gave up after his first volume, which stopped in 1939. Lowell entertained friends with amusing imitations, exactly in Tate's tone of voice, of the hot-blooded Southern gentleman challenging his rivals to a duel.

Tate could not resist boasting of his sexual conquests and unwisely entrusted this information to Lowell. Jean Stafford, Lowell's first wife and confidante, then got into the act. When Gordon, separated from Tate, was staying with her in Maine, Stafford told her guest about one of Tate's recent affairs. The hysterical Gordon responded by throwing a glass at the ill-fated messenger and by breaking everything she could get her hands on in the house. During one of his manic states, Lowell even provided Gordon with an expanded list of Tate's lovers and then—in a state of grace— begged him to confess and repent his sins. In one of his most notorious episodes, Lowell suspended the terrified Tate from a second-floor window while he recited his host's "Ode to the Confederate Dead" in his gruff, idiosyncratic "bear's voice." Once Tate was safely inside, it took four cops to subdue and handcuff Lowell and cart him away.

After Tate's second divorce from Gordon, he married Lowell's cousin Isabella (Belle) Gardner, and the friends became relatives. But Lowell made Tate furious by interfering in the acrimonious divorce negotiations and questioning the intelligence of his future wife: "All this has been complicated by a new maniacal outburst of Cal Lowell's. He has had another violent breakdown, at the pitch of which he telephoned Caroline several times and urged her to save me from a Boston divorcée [Isabella Gardner]. . . . The lady is a cousin of Cal's and an old friend whom he trusted. I am the object of his hostility. The Lowell vulgarity reached its height when he told Caroline that the lady wasn't very rich—that I could look around and do better."[30]

Lowell, who'd observed the Tate-Gordon marriage at close quarters, at first remained loyal to Gordon, his ideal mother. Then, after trying to protect Tate from Gardner, suddenly changed his mind and decided that Gordon was destroying Tate and that he had to get rid of her. Lowell told his confessor, Elizabeth Bishop, "I made an awful blunder last spring when I was getting high. I called up Caroline and told her she mustn't let Allen get a divorce, that Allen really loved her and that Belle was extremely stupid. Actually, the marriage is a good thing—Allen is much more settled down after all his gadding. . . . I really feel Belle saved Allen's life from the long inspired nightmare of Caroline. She's slow, imperious, though not to Allen, and sane."[31] Tate's example taught Lowell what was considered to be the poet's prerogative: moving from wife to wife while maintaining a string of mistresses.

III

Following Tate's advice, Lowell had planned to continue his education with Ransom at Vanderbilt, but before he could get there his teacher was lured away by a more attractive offer. In a letter of May 1937 to the chancellor of the university, Tate used the prestige of Lowell's family (even in the South) as an argument for preventing a disastrous loss and keeping Ransom at Vanderbilt: "The Lowell family of Boston and Harvard University has just sent one of its sons to Nashville to study poetry with Mr. Ransom. . . . I can only ask you to imagine Harvard University, at the height of the New England revival, letting Charles Eliot Norton go to a small college in the Middle West."[32] But Ransom left Vanderbilt for Kenyon College in Ohio. Lowell, making the right choice, left Harvard and followed him. Provincial, all-male Kenyon, where Ford and Ransom urged Lowell to expand his interests by studying classics and philosophy, proved to be more intellectual and more literary than Harvard.

John Crowe Ransom, the other important influence on Lowell's early career, was a striking contrast to Tate in character and behavior. Tate, a publisher and novelist as well as a poet, was a Catholic convert, heavy drinker and active fornicator. He taught at Princeton and glided through several other universities before landing a permanent position at the University of Minnesota. Ransom, the son of a Methodist minister, was born in Tennessee in 1888, graduated from Vanderbilt, was a Rhodes Scholar at Christ Church, Oxford, and an officer in World War I. Courtly and dignified, conventional and restrained, a solid family man, Ransom taught at Vanderbilt and then at Kenyon College until he retired. The fiction writer Peter Taylor, Ransom's pupil and Lowell's friend at Kenyon, said, "Mr. Ransom was reserved. His dress and manner reminded you of a preacher. He was like a father to all of us; we wanted his respect. And Lowell was his favorite son."[33] Unlike Tate, Ransom was more of an intellectual mentor than a formal influence on Lowell's poetry.

Though still as scruffy as ever, Caliban, slightly tamed by Gordon and Ransom, had at least learned to put on his socks before his shoes and to greet his host, as he'd failed to do during dinners with Anne Dick's father. "I was nineteen or twenty then," he wrote, "loud-humored, dirty, and frayed—I almost needed to be persuaded to comb my hair, tie my shoes, and say goodbye when leaving a home."[34] Peter Taylor confirmed that Lowell, assuming a defiantly bohemian role, couldn't be bothered about his slovenly appearance: "At Kenyon, he didn't drink, he didn't go out with girls. He was just a big school-boy. . . . He was awful looking. He never cut his hair, he never took a bath. His shoes often had the soles divided, and they were just flapping. He looked terrible."[35] "Cal was dirty and unkempt, intellectual, intense, and overbearing, a big, loutish figure allowed to play tackle on the football team because of his sheer brute force."[36] Another friend recalled Lowell's energetic but ineffectual game of tennis: "Lowell looked formidable on the courts—tall, leonine, he'd sway back and forth ominously, hair tousled in the breeze, awaiting service, as though about to sizzle a return. But his game was all preparation—he was a most indifferent player."[37]

During his first year at Kenyon Lowell actually lived in Ransom's house till Robb Ransom, disturbed by his dirty habits, urged him to move out. The mild-mannered professor became very fond of his talented protégé and recalled, "His animal spirits were high, his personality was spontaneous, so that he was a little overpowering."[38] But Ransom was impressed by Lowell's fierce energy, intellectual commitment and strength of character. Lowell had also made tremendous improvements in his behavior after his release from the conventions of Boston and the torments of his parents. Ransom, who felt he was more like a son than a student, wrote Tate: "Cal is sawing wood and getting out to all his college engagements in a businesslike if surly manner; taking Latin and Greek and philosophy and, of course, English; wants to be really educated; personally is about as gentle and considerate a boy as I've ever dealt with. . . . and applying himself prodigiously. . . . He is a fine boy, very definitely with great literary possibilities. I don't know whether he's better as critic or as poet, but he's making fast progress in both lines."[39] For his part, Lowell was grateful for Ransom's excellent tuition and personal care, and reassured Charlotte that he "looks out for me better than you could wish, getting me to take exercise and even making my bed for me one night."[40]

The eccentric, highly intellectual Lowell did not fit into the social mold at St. Mark's or at Kenyon. Instead, he formed his own inner circle of devoted friends, especially the replacements for Frank Parker and Blair Clark: Peter Taylor and Randall Jarrell. Three years older than Lowell and teaching freshman composition at Kenyon, Jarrell had grown up in Nashville and Los Angeles, and graduated from Vanderbilt. The poet Stanley Kunitz called him "magisterial, cool, aloof, defensive, guarded and protective."[41] He was known for his brilliant mind, and feared for his sharp tongue and caustic criticism. Peter Taylor noted Jarrell's "conceit, his intransigence, his primness: 'Randall never in his life used a four-letter word. He couldn't stand a joke about sex. He wouldn't have it.'"[42] Lowell deferred to Jarrell's superior intellect, but noted his weaknesses and weirdness: "When I first met Randall, he was twenty-three or -four, and unsettlingly brilliant, precocious, knowing, naïve, and vexing.[43] . . . Randall has a better mind than I have, more contemporary interests, is more articulate and talented. I too find him emotionally immature, puritanical, monstrous, odd; but his peculiarity is part of his excellence.[44] . . . Randall doesn't like people and doesn't know much of anything about them."[45] John Thompson, a Kenyon classmate, recalled that Jarrell's friendship for Lowell was limited: "Randall was terrified. He wouldn't have anything to do with Cal when he was sick—he'd go home and read Freud. He must have just recognized that it was not something for him to mess with. He must have realized that he was a little edgy himself."[46]

Jarrell's poems, which could not compete with Lowell's, were fanciful and fey, dreamy and whimsical, and his melancholy tone frequently merged with self-pity. Psychologically precarious and frightened of Lowell's mania, Jarrell disliked Hardwick and became unwillingly entangled with two of Lowell's lovers. But he also became Lowell's poetic conscience, as Pound had been Eliot's. Later on, after Jarrell's suicide, which Lowell found threatening, Elizabeth Bishop replaced him in that role.

Ransom and Kenyon brought out the best in Lowell. He graduated summa cum laude and Phi Beta Kappa, with honors in classics, was first in his class and valedictorian. His parents, still disapproving and perhaps oblivious, did not attend the triumphant graduation of their only child. Lowell fancifully thought he might go to New York, become a Marxist and join the Communist Party, or maybe live in London and learn how to wear stylish clothes. But he never did either. Still attracted to superior teachers, he and his first wife Jean Stafford went on to Louisiana State University, which lacked prestige and was located in a smelly oil town.

In June 1940 Lowell wrote his parents that Baton Rouge is "inland, windless, waterless, suburban. . . . [There] are immense twentieth-century-Mexican dormitories, iron pipes blazing with crude oil, palm-beachy trees and [Governor] Huey Long's two million dollar sky-scraper capitol."[47] In his satiric poem "Louisiana State University in 1940," he suddenly shifted from the emphasis on high intellectual hopes to the horrors of gigantic rats and ironically "cleansing" sewage: "O Baton Rouge, your measureless student prospects, / rats as long as my forearm regrouping toward / the sewage cleansing on the open canals."[48]

The great attractions, amidst the rats and sewage, were the courtly Southern gentlemen, Robert Penn Warren and Cleanth Brooks, who'd both studied with Ransom at Vanderbilt and become Rhodes Scholars.

They'd recently published the influential college textbook *Understanding Poetry* (1938), which, following the principles of New Criticism, gave close readings of complex poems, with special attention to irony, ambiguity and learned allusions. Just as Tate had passed Lowell on to Ransom, Ransom now passed Lowell on to Brooks; and the blessings and promising prophecies continued. Ransom said, "He's a strong man, the last of the line of Lowells bearing the name, due to give a good account of himself before he is done. He is a bit slow and thorough, but he has enormous critical sense. He wants above all things to work into the sort of critic who compares effects in different languages."

To achieve this goal Warren, in an Oxfordian tutorial, spent several hours a week reading Dante in Italian with Lowell. Though Warren didn't know Lowell as well as Tate and Ransom did, he perceived some unusual aspects of his character and wrote: "He was always a naïf of one kind or another. And a calculated naïf, too. But he had a charm and he had great intelligence and he read widely, and he could be wonderfully good company." Warren then retrospectively added, "You talk about a man who was really mad . . . he was on his way." [49]

IV

The South had nurtured Lowell, formed his mature character and trained his mind. When he left LSU at the age of twenty-four he was six feet tall and weighed 160 pounds—black-haired, blue-eyed, square-jawed, broad-shouldered and ruggedly handsome. His massive, Beethoven-like head suggested extraordinary intellectual power. His friends provided a composite picture of his striking appearance and complex personality. One called him "tall, gentle, big-boned, humorous, teasing, sly; . . . myopic, hulking, formidable, wry, companionable, sombre . . . moved to glee over phrases and fantasies." [50] Another added, "awkward, disheveled, somewhat diffident, and gazing around him in what appeared to be a vague and absent way . . . riveting, fascinating, funny, odd, and completely, interestingly original and serious." [51] Lowell was an odd mixture of stiffness and disorder, lethargy and passion. His slow drawl and apparent self-effacement hid a wicked tongue as well as a mind learned, sophisticated and urbane.

Many writers who saw Lowell at his best praised his humor, his human warmth and his capacity for friendship. Grey Gowrie said he was easy to like, funny and warm, clever, sweet and lovable. He broke the upper-class, boarding-school prohibitions with affectionate hugs and open displays of emotion.[52] Derek Walcott remembered his "heartbreaking smile, his wit, his solicitude, his shyness."[53] William Meredith recalled the intense feelings he provoked and the intellectual fireworks he displayed, the "disturbance of heart, dazzle of mind that one experienced in Lowell's company."[54] Daniel Hoffman wrote that Lowell was brainy and intense, friendly yet imperious, but "how enjoyable was his company, what fun he was to be with: witty, quick, courteous, unaffected."[55] Edmund Wilson, a shrewd judge of character and with high intellectual standards, noted, "I always enjoy his wide range of reading and reference, and his feeling for the important things in literature. What he says is probing and witty, sometimes perverse, with a desire to startle."[56]

There was also a dark side to Lowell both when he was manic and when he was sane. He lacked in life and sometimes in his work (in the hundreds of endlessly revised fourteen-line poems he called "sonnets") the restraint and control, the discipline of the conscientious superego, that governs most people's behavior. One of his favorite roles, which greatly amused him and frightened his friends, was his alter ego who—in a whining, sing-song voice—scolded, seized, arrested and chastised people. Flannery O'Connor explained that "Cal Lowell has an imaginary friend named Arms, a policeman, kind of half man and half bear. Arms of the Law he calls him, and Arms says all the outrageous things that Cal is too polite to say."[57] Lowell was not only a severe bear, but also a creative dancing bear who listened to the lively lines in his head while treading dangerously on tongues of fire. His dark side did not express (as he wrote in "Epilogue") Jan Vermeer's ideal "grace of accuracy," but the anguished and intense suffering portrayed in the paintings of Van Gogh, Edvard Munch and Francis Bacon.

Lowell Agonistes, a combative pacifist and brute force adversary, had violent confrontations with many of his friends. (Samuel Johnson and Hemingway, though not manic, were also violent.) He bullied boys in grade school and on the Boston Common, beat up Blair Clark and knocked out Frank Parker at St. Mark's. He punched his father's face and knocked him down. When Lowell wanted to go to sleep at Kenyon and his roommate Peter Taylor refused to turn off the lights, he tore the electric wires out of the lamp and shot sparks into the darkness. He once had a fistfight with Taylor on the train from New York back to Kenyon and a similar punch-up with the poet Delmore Schwartz in Cambridge. He hung Tate out of the window and forcefully resisted a squad of police who tried to subdue him. This violence would also erupt against women. A combustible cocktail of the brooding Hamlet and fierce Tamburlaine, he was (as one friend noted) "Heathcliff played by Boris Karloff."[58]

Tate, Ransom, Jarrell and Warren acclimatized Lowell to the South. In the South he found paternal guidance and expert tuition, a dedication to the rhyme and meter of formalist poetry, and commitment to the tenets of New Criticism. He not only adopted the drawling accent he oddly mixed with his Boston twang, but also gained a different perspective on the heroic defeat in the Civil War and made many stimulating friends. Caroline Blackwood thought that Charlotte Lowell never recognized her son's outstanding qualities and hated everything he represented. In his mother's view, a successful son earned a Harvard degree, had a law career and membership in the best clubs, was a great tennis player and graceful dancer with debutantes.[59] To counter her ideal image, Lowell rejected everything she wanted and even walked (sometimes talked) like a grumpy bear.

Lowell had dutifully toed the line by going to St. Mark's and Harvard, but after that everything he did defied his family and their traditions: his slovenly dress, bad manners, physical violence, devotion to poetry, engagement to Anne Dick, departure from Harvard and enrollment in Kenyon and LSU. He would continue his rebellious trajectory by marrying the unacceptable Jean Stafford, converting to Catholicism, becoming a conscientious objector, having love affairs and then divorcing Stafford.

Despite parental discouragement and damage, the young Lowell had a sense of direction, a conviction of his own talent and an awareness of the kind of education he needed. Eager to learn but socially awkward, he also found substitute parents who remained lifelong friends. During his years with Tate and Ransom, Lowell created himself as an intellectual and poet in a deliberate, self-conscious way. After living in an all-male society in prep school and college, he emerged from the comfort of the South prepared to confront all the women in his adult life.

THREE

Jean Stafford, 1937–1948

I

T. S. Eliot divorced his mentally ill wife; Ezra Pound had a mistress and an illegitimate daughter; William Carlos Williams had many lovers, including some of his patients; and Tate had three wives. The next generation of poets—Lowell, Berryman and Jarrell—also had volatile and broken marriages that influenced their work. All three of Lowell's wives—Jean Stafford, Elizabeth Hardwick and Caroline Blackwood—married him despite clear warnings of impending disaster, and all his marriages were marked by chaos and violence. He was possessed by religious mania in his years with Stafford; he suffered frequent bouts of insanity while married to Hardwick; and, despite improved medication, he had more breakdowns with Blackwood. Egoistic and pursuing his own goals, Lowell seemed unaware of the intense unhappiness of his friends and wives, and forced them to submit to his will: not only Parker and Clark in Nantucket and Anne Dick in Tennessee, but also Stafford in Baton Rouge and Maine, Hardwick in Amsterdam, Blackwood in Boston. His first and third wives were alcoholics and suffered mental breakdowns.

Lowell had the self-absorbed ability to unleash extreme emotions, detach himself from the heartbreak and then leave the ruins as if nothing had happened. He always abandoned the women; they never left him. No matter how badly he treated them, they always admired his virtues and forgave his faults, continued to love him and wanted to remain with him. Despite his destructive behavior, Lowell was irresistible to women. Good-looking, seductively charming and impressively intelligent, he had a distinguished name, poetic genius and great influence in the literary world. He fell passionately in love with his women and gave them, at least at first, his fierce attention. Fascinated by his madness, they wanted to take care of him, believed they could save him, hoped that he'd recover his health and that they could lead a normal life together.

In the summer of 1937 Ford brought Lowell to the Colorado Writers Conference in Boulder and introduced him to Jean Stafford. She was two years older than Lowell, who was still an undergraduate at Kenyon. Her father, an unsuccessful but persistent writer of western stories, published titles like "The Transmogrified Calf" under the pseudonyms of Jack Wonder and Ben Delight, and was still adding to his mountain of rejection slips in his tenth decade. He had inherited and then lost $300,000 in the stock market in 1921, was a religious fanatic, chewed and spat tobacco, seldom shaved and was as dirty as a bum. When Stafford saw him later in life, she was amazed that all his children hadn't committed suicide in their cradles. Her mother supported the family by keeping a boarding house in Boulder. Her sisters' cruel teasing, her father's selfish failures and his loss of the great fortune gave Stafford a lifelong dislike of her family, a sense of social inferiority and a permanent fear of poverty.

In 1936 Stafford won a fellowship from the German government for graduate study in philology at Heidelberg University. During that turbulent year the Spanish Civil War broke out, the fanatical Nazi rallies continued in Nuremberg, the Germans reoccupied the Rhineland and the Olympic games took place in Berlin. But as John Thompson caustically commented, Stafford was unaware of the impending catastrophe: "she didn't know Germany from China—the fact that it was Nazi didn't mean a thing to her."[1] She'd mainly socialized with Americans and did not learn to read, speak or understand German. She came home after only five months among the beer-swilling, goose-stepping, anti-Semitic Nazis, with a dirndl and blond braids. Infected by her German lover, she also had a case of gonorrhea that persisted for years and made her sterile.

Pretty, sharp-tongued and amusing, Stafford had high cheekbones and a pert snub nose. Berryman's first wife, Eileen Simpson, said Stafford's voice "was low and came from deep in her throat. As a storyteller she was as masterly at pacing and timing as a professional comedian."[2] The poet Howard Moss observed that (like Caroline Blackwood) she had a morbid interest in "symptoms, diagnoses, horror stories, freak accidents, diseases."[3] During one of the weirdest literary courtships, Lowell hotly pursued her while she was living in Cambridge with James Robert Hightower (later a professor of Far Eastern languages at Harvard). Ford told Stafford horrible things about Lowell and warned her that he was "really pathological and capable of murder." She prophetically told Hightower that "she was physically afraid of Lowell and afraid of what he'd do to [her]." [4]

In November 1938 Stafford wrote a friend: "Lowell kept saying if I didn't marry him he wd. just run the car off the road, etc., so I said he cd. go to hell . . . and he got savage and I got scared, so I said well I will see you once more but only in the company of other people. . . . [He said he] wanted me more than anything else in his life and that I wd. never be free of him, that he will continue to track me down as long as I live, a very unpleasant thought. It makes me perfectly sick because he is an uncouth, neurotic, psychopathic, murderer-poet." [5] Nevertheless, succumbing to his emotional blackmail and dire threats, she continued to see him. She liked his fine manners and what she called his "raving beauty." He affected a formal mode of address and called her "Miss Stafford" throughout the entire first year of their courtship.

Lowell was handsome, though not with the film-star appearance of the poets William Merwin and Mark Strand. Dark-eyed and soulful looking, he had a soft dangerous voice and was (according to the poet Gail Mazur) physically beautiful and extremely charismatic, gentle, witty and strangely brilliant, lovable, endearing and great company. Fanny Howe added that he was "curious about people, really saw you and gave you his full attention. He was also wounded, a ruin, a mess and fully human." [6] Norman Mailer explained what drew Stafford and all the other women to Lowell: "His personal attractiveness was immense, since his features were at once virile and patrician. . . . Lowell had the most disconcerting mixture of strength and weakness . . . [and was] sensationally attractive." [7]

A traumatic turning point in Stafford's life occurred at Christmas 1938 when Lowell—home from Kenyon, drunk and driving fast, with Stafford in the front seat—crashed his father's precious Packard into the wall of a Cambridge cul-de-sac. Stafford suffered massive head injuries, including a fractured skull and jaw and a crushed nose. She had five operations in the spring and summer of 1939, and bitterly described her disfigurement: "My teeth can't be fixed, and oh god I look so hideous and if I want my old nose back I have to have a complete plastic with two bones completely removed and others grafted in and everyone says oh don't be silly that nose is good enough which is true but it isn't *my* nose." [8]

Friends described the dramatic change in Stafford's appearance. Eileen Simpson said that her eyes "seemed to be bathed in an excess of fluid, so that they looked permanently welled-up, giving the impression that she had been crying or might do so at any moment."[9] Another friend recalled, "before the accident she had been quite a beautiful woman with a classic profile. But the accident broke her face. Afterwards she looked crooked and distorted."[10] Blair Clark, emphasizing the importance of her beauty, thought "there was about a 25 percent reduction in the aesthetic value of her face."[11] Stafford's story "The Interior Castle" (1947), a description of her nose operation performed when she was fully conscious, shows extraordinary objectivity about her own excruciating pain. She wrote, with a series of cruel verbs, "the knives ground and carved and curried and scoured the wounds they made; the scissors clipped hard gristle and the scalpels chipped off bones. It was as if a tangle of tiny nerves were being cut."[12] Lowell's parents were more concerned about the damage to their reputation and their car (which Bob had not been allowed to drive to the Navy Yard at night) than to Stafford's nose and face.

Frank Parker noted that Lowell was strangely detached from the tragic consequences of the crash: "It was just an accident, and he didn't feel responsible particularly. He looked up, there was a dead end. It was not his fault."[13] But every time he looked at Stafford's face he was forced to remember what he'd done to her. His repressed guilt was one reason he married a woman who had contracted a venereal disease and been disfigured by him. If Lowell seemed indifferent, Stafford—still in love with him—was forgiving. Like Jane Eyre, she could say of her "psychopathic, murderer-poet": "Reader, I married him." On April 2, 1940, with Blair Clark and the Tates in attendance, they got joylessly joined in St. Mary's of the Bowery church in New York. It was election day, all the bars were closed and they couldn't even get a much-needed drink to cheer or console themselves.

Stafford came from Colorado, where Lowell's grandfather Winslow had made his mining fortune, and both she and Winslow had studied in German universities. But nothing could staunch Charlotte's cataract of condemnation. It was all right to get rich in the West, but not to marry a woman who came from those parts. Charlotte was appalled by a daughter-in-law who was a writer, whose father wrote trashy westerns and whose mother ran a low-class boarding house. Dramatizing Charlotte's hysterical antagonism, Eberhart imagined the scene in a satiric poem:

Give up that wretched girl. You must!
She is beneath you, not even in the [social] register.
From the West, and her family is unthinkable. . . .
You must give her up, we are not of that kind. . . .
      It is an awful girl again.
It is the same thing as it was last year [with Anne Dick],
Only worse, for this one is an intellectual.[14]

Furious that Bobby had rejected the inbred marriages of Boston, Charlotte subjected Stafford to snobbish criticism: "Your family is just a myth to me, Jean. In our little community here, we all marry our third cousins and know everyone."[15] On awkward visits to her in-laws, Stafford was greeted with frosty politeness and offered unwelcome advice. When she mentioned their financial problems Charlotte, who seemed to be down to her last hundred thousand dollars, refused to help. Even her successful first novel, *Boston Adventure* (1944), was subject to censure. Stafford explained: "There are the same lectures and moral generalizations and refusals to countenance the way we live and the dredging up of all the mistakes of the past. I am more thoroughly, more icily, more deeply disliked than ever . . . even though it is generally admitted that it's a damned good thing Bobby married someone who makes money writing."[16]

II

While Lowell and Stafford were living in Baton Rouge, which had a strong French Catholic ambience and which Stafford hated, Lowell converted to Catholicism. It was 1,500 years older than Protestantism and went almost as far back (as Jarrell said of the Lowells) as the ancient Egyptians. Stafford had also converted a few years earlier but had soon lapsed, so his new religion failed to bring them together. Lowell did everything in extremes, and his religion, like his mental illness, went in cycles and inspired his poetry. His conversion, a case history of religious mania and struggle with guilt and fear, did not bring consolation and tranquillity.

Adopting the fanaticism of a convert, Lowell rejected the hedonistic aspects of the faith and became an anguished ascetic. Not for him the pleasures of a prelate or comforts of a cardinal. The Catholic poet Robert Fitzgerald recalled that when Lowell's mania kicked in with his Catholicism, "he filled the bathtub with cold water and went in first on his hands and knees, then arching on his back, prayed thus to Thérèse of Lisieux in gasps."[17] Alluding to Lowell's nickname and to the puritan element that clashed with his new religion, Stafford sharply remarked, "I fell in love with Caligula and am living with Calvin. He's become a fanatic. During Lent he starved himself. If he could get his hands on one, he'd be wearing a hair shirt."[18] But even a hair shirt was not sufficient to satisfy his spiritual severity; he also required flagellation and a bed of nails. After Lowell insisted on remarriage in a Catholic church, his relations with Stafford began to deteriorate. She started to drink heavily and suffered a series of mysterious, possibly psychosomatic, illnesses. She was appalled by the contrast between Lowell's pious talk and fire-breathing self-righteousness and his complete lack of the Christian virtues of pity and kindness—especially toward herself. Tired of listening to Stafford's laments, he spent a week of silence in a Trappist monastery.

In a brutal replay of his car crash, Lowell continued his assaults on Stafford. In 1941 he punched her in the face during a drunken argument and broke her agonizingly repaired nose for the second time. Aware of what he did, yet not quite knowing his own strength or how it had happened, he felt the nose collapse under his fist. Stafford then had to have it painfully reconstructed all over again. As with the car crash, Lowell felt guilty but portrayed himself as a passive participant, and found it hard to admit that he had been responsible for the violence. When Stafford complained of having trouble breathing through her nose, he told her that she breathed too much. But Stafford, like all Lowell's women, remained loyally in love with him and said (as Sylvia Plath would say of Ted Hughes) that she needed a strong man to dominate her rebellious character and provide a disciplined life for her writing.

The priest who'd converted Lowell got him and Stafford low-level jobs at the New York Catholic publishers Sheed and Ward, who thought (like the Southern poets) that the prominent convert was quite a catch. Lowell read manuscripts (judging the quality, as Ford had advised, by the first sentence), edited texts and wrote copy for the dust wrappers, though he found it hard to be both flattering and truthful. He decorated their apartment with crucifixes, both wooden and iron.

Influenced by T. S. Eliot, Lowell packed his early poetry with religious allusions and symbols that provided a rare feast for the New Critics. Al Alvarez observed, "In much of his earlier poetry the strain was almost unbearable. Only a prodigious effort of poetic will seemed to prevent it from splintering into incoherence."[19] Robert Fitzgerald, citing an extreme example from "A Prayer for My Grandfather to Our Lady," said that when Lowell "besought the Mother of God with her 'scorched, blue thunder-breasts of love' to pour 'buckets of blessings' on his 'burning head,' one apprehended a verse builder working with intensities close to madness."[20] In fact, Lowell was working in the Catholic Baroque tradition exemplified by Richard Crashaw's "The Flaming Heart" (1652). That poem emphasized the cruel and ferocious elements of religion, the desire for mysticism and martyrdom, for sacrifice, salvation and divine annihilation:

> O sweet incendiary! show here thy art,
> Upon this carcass of a hard, cold, heart. . . .
> By all thy brim-fill'd Bowls of fierce desire,
> By the last Morning's draught of liquid fire;
> By the full kingdom of that final kiss,
> That seiz'd thy parting Soul, and seal'd thee his.[21]

Lowell's first political protest—his declaration that he was a conscientious objector to World War II—took place while he was still a fanatical Catholic and Catholic poet, and married to Stafford. She could not restrain Lowell (no one could) and found his attitude difficult to comprehend, but loyally supported his idealistic but quixotic stance. In 1935, while still at St. Mark's, Lowell had published "War: A Justification" in *Vindex,* the school magazine. In June 1940 he dutifully told his parents, "If war comes and they want me, I'll gladly go."[22] When America entered the war he tried to enlist in the army and navy, but was rejected because of defective vision. Though he would not have been drafted even if he'd wanted to serve, he eventually revised his ideas about the war and used his prestigious name to publicize his protest.

Instead of appearing before his draft board and explaining his beliefs, he refused to report and forced the authorities to prosecute him. Assuming a high moral tone, expressing principled arguments and speaking man to man, on September 7, 1943, Lowell sent a cheeky letter to President Franklin Roosevelt. He refused to take part in the horrors of merciless conquest, whose goal, he believed, was the total destruction of Germany and Japan. In September 1943 the FBI file on Lowell reported that he had refused service in World War II because "he no longer felt that the war was justified and because America was attempting to form another

totalitarian kind of civil authority to substitute for the Dictator regimes in
Germany and Italy." [23]

Lowell's attitude was remarkably like Siegfried Sassoon's public protest
to the military authorities in World War I. In June 1917 Sassoon, then a
serving officer who risked execution for treason, wrote: "I believe that the
War is being deliberately prolonged by those who have the power to end
it. . . . I believe that this War, upon which I entered as a war of defence
and liberation, has now become a war of aggression and conquest. . . . I
am protesting against. . . the political errors and insincerities for which the
fighting men are being sacrificed." [24] In order to save human lives, Lowell also advocated a negotiated peace with Germany. In fact Hitler, who
remained in power until the last days of the war, refused to surrender even
after the Russians had entered Berlin. The Allies believed they could end
the war by flattening German cities from the air and destroying enemy
morale. This strategy worked and the mass bombing actually shortened
instead of prolonging the war.

Lowell was justly proud of his military ancestors who'd fought the Indians, the American revolutionaries, the British in 1812, the Confederate reb-
els, and even the Chinese warlords and opium traders. Though somewhat
ashamed of refusing to carry on this patriotic tradition and become a man
of action, he declined to serve in the war. Lowell's protest, condemned by
many as anti-American cowardice, had a private as well as a public motive.
It was the most deadly blow, by far, against his father.

Lowell's defiant gesture earned a light sentence of one year in prison,
first in the West Street Jail in New York City, then in the federal penitentiary in Danbury, sixty miles north in Connecticut. Paradoxically, the jail
contained hardened criminals, including murderers, while the penitentiary—which Lowell called a country club and model prison—contained
C.O.s and first offenders, bootleggers and black marketers. Ring Lardner,
Jr., who later served time in Danbury for refusing to name names during
the anti-Communist witch hunts in Hollywood, wrote:

> The place served as a kind of halfway house for a handful of serious
> street criminals who were nearing release after serving long peniten-
> tiary terms; otherwise, almost all of us had been convicted of white-
> collar crimes, which included mail theft, crossing a state line with
> a stolen automobile, defrauding the military on wartime contracts,
> draft evasion (or, in some cases, conscientious objection on the part

of young men lacking the proper religious credentials), bribery of
Internal Revenue Service agents, and spying for the enemy during
World War II. . . .

Most of the housing at Danbury was in large dormitory rooms
with individual cubicles containing a cot and a table with a couple
of drawers. . . . Most of the food served at our meals came from the
inmate-tended farm. [25]

Lowell almost nostalgically recalled, "I belonged to a gang that walked
outside the prison gates each morning, and worked on building a barn.
The work was mild: the workers were slow and absent-minded. There were
long pauses." [26] "Jail was monotonous and weak on incident. I queued
for hours for cigarettes and chocolate bars, and did slow make-work like
wheeling wheelbarrows of cinders." [27] Jim Peck, a fellow inmate, noted
that Lowell "chose to do manual labor in the mason shop to get experience
in building a Catholic community, which he hoped to do upon release
. . . [and wore] the standard shabby, ill-fitting overalls." [28] Lowell later told
John McCormick that "he rather enjoyed his companions at Danbury,
mostly well-heeled gentlemen from the New York black markets, fallen,
momentarily, from grace." [29]

Paroled after four months in Danbury, Lowell was sent to clean the
nurses' quarters at St. Vincent's Hospital, twenty miles away in Bridgeport.
Finally, he was classified as 4-F, unfit for military service. If he hadn't pro-
tested, his draft rejection would have prevented his jail sentence. Stafford
seems to have suffered more than Lowell during his self-inflicted imprisonment. She remained alone in their New York apartment, struggling to
survive on $100 a month from his trust fund, and visited him in Danbury
for an hour every Saturday. She endured condemnation from Charlotte,
who blamed her for Lowell's behavior, and began to drink heavily. When
he was paroled, they moved to a grim little flat in the Bridgeport suburb
of Black Rock on Long Island Sound. With classic wit, Stafford told Peter
Taylor, "I am frightened, feel that it will be three years before Cal has
recovered from the pleasurable monasticism of the penitentiary." [30] Lowell
enjoyed his punishment, and his imprisonment as a C.O. enhanced his
reputation during the 1960's protests against the war in Vietnam.

Lowell's incarceration inspired one of his best poems, "Memories of
West Street and Lepke." Though no street in Boston could be accurately
described as passionate, he begins the poem by quoting Henry James on

"hardly passionate Marlborough Street," which he contrasts to the violent inmates of West Street.[31] The jail contained an incongruous mixture of pacifist C.O.s and Jehovah's Witnesses as well as gangsters who beat up mild-mannered vegetarians and a professional killer who'd bumped off scores of victims. Two inmates were the Chicago racketeers, George Browne and William Bioff, who wore double-breasted chocolate-colored suits in jail. In 1935 they had seized control of the skilled workers' union in Hollywood, and over the next six years extorted millions of dollars from studio executives by threatening to call strikes and then agreeing to limit their demands. In 1941 they were convicted of extortion and sent to jail. In 1955 Bioff was blown up in Phoenix, Arizona, by a bomb that was planted in his car.

Louis "Lepke" (Yiddish for Louis) Buckalter (1897–1944) looked like the *Partisan Review* art critic Clement Greenberg. He was head of the "Kosher Nostra," the Mafia hit squad called Murder, Inc. that carried out mob contracts with corporate efficiency. Sentenced to death by a New York court in December 1941, he was held in the West Street Jail for two years. Lowell was there with Lepke for ten days in October 1943 while the murderer was awaiting execution. Lepke used his still considerable influence with the authorities to have privileges denied to the distinguished poet: a single cell with radio, dresser and four American flags. Lepke was finally sent to Sing Sing in January 1944 and electrocuted there in March. Lowell has been credited with a famous exchange (not quoted in his "West Street" poem) that never actually took place. When Lepke said, "I'm in for killing. What are you in for?," Lowell supposedly replied, "Oh, I'm in for refusing to kill."[32] But another C.O., Lowell Naeve, was the man who actually said, " 'I was in jail because I refused to kill people.' The Murder, Inc. boss, who was headed for the electric chair, said: 'It don't seem to me to make much sense that they put a man in jail for that.' The law covered both ends—one in for killing, the other for refusing to kill."[33]

III

In August 1945 Stafford, who'd grown up in the family boarding house occupied by strangers, realized her lifelong dream by buying her own home with the royalties from her bestselling novel, *Boston Adventure*. The house was in Damariscotta Mills, Maine, which had sawmills to cut trees from the surrounding dark forest of hemlock and spruce, and was seventeen miles from the ocean. Set on a hill overlooking the town, the house had a tidal river on one side and a lake filled with bass and salmon on the other. Fishing, described in Lowell's poem "The Drunken Fisherman," became his only avocation.

In September 1945 Lowell wrote Peter Taylor, "Not even you could imagine the state of sustained ecstasy Jean is in. . . . I don't think we've ever been so happy. In the 17th century this region was Catholic and had the oldest Catholic Church in New England." But the temperature in this isolated rural retreat and fisherman's paradise dropped to twenty degrees below zero in the winter, and eleven months later Lowell lamented, "Everything is chaos with us. Jean is driving like a cyclone, and we both have had about all we can stand and more. . . . We have got to *leave each other alone,* and the future to time."[34]

Their new home, like their religion, did not bring them closer; and marriage, instead of providing sexual pleasure, brought repression and frustration. Stafford had been frightened in childhood by intrusive boarders and was so shy with Lowell that she always undressed in the closet. Her venereal disease, which made her fearful of infecting her lovers, had permanently warped her attitude toward sex. She wrote James Hightower that she was frigid and sadly confessed that "no aphrodisiac has yet been devised to make me desire; to make me submit, yes, but not to desire."[35]

She told Blair Clark, with some exaggeration, that though she was willing to have sex, she and Lowell had not been intimate for the last four or five years of their marriage. For his part Lowell, still a fanatical Catholic, had smelled the hellfires and thought sex smacked of sin. Stafford also told Frank Parker about Lowell's jealousy of her old loves and his violent substitute for sex: "one night, while she was dreaming of a former lover, Cal had once awakened her to make love and, still half asleep, she'd repeated her lover's name. In a perfect frenzy, Cal tried to strangle her" and tightened his hands on her throat. In a manuscript version of "The Mills of the Kavanaughs," Lowell wrote as if another man had "reached at midnight / for your wind-pipe."[36]

Recalling his parents' experience as well as his own, Lowell thought "marriage was always a rat fight."[37] Whenever things went wrong in his marriage to Stafford—and they often did—she reminded him of Charlotte's worst qualities: her caustic criticism, grating will and oppressive domination. Stafford explained their destructive role-playing: "The trouble all along was that Lowell, with his 'powerful alchemy,' had turned her into a version of his mother and that subconsciously she had assented

to this role 'until she terrifyingly resembled her.'"[38] She added, with
psychoanalytic insight, that "I had become your mother just as you had
become my [slovenly and fanatical] father and both of us by now were so
far gone that we were blindly and savagely attacking those people, not one
another."[39] They were emotionally trapped by and accused each other of
having the worst qualities of their own parents.

Stafford found that liquor brought instant relief from her life with
Lowell, and became an anodyne for both the strain of writing and the
greater torments of imaginative sterility. She got the "wim-wams" in a
bone-dry house and had to take a taxi to the nearest state liquor store in
Bath. She confessed, "I *hated* to drink, it made me unspeakably miserable
but I could not help it because I did not know why I was compelled to
destroy myself."[40] Noting her dependence on alcohol, Lowell seized the
moral high ground and, imitating Charlotte's tone of voice, remarked,
"You don't drink well, dear. Not well at all."[41]

The dramatic appearance of Gertrude Buckman—in the sane period
between Lowell's religious mania and his first breakdown—finally
destroyed their marriage. Born into a Jewish family in 1913, Buckman had
grown up in New York, graduated from New York University and hoped
to become a classical musician. Short, dark, sensual and attractive, she
had green eyes, full breasts and the look of a young Russian peasant. The
poet Delmore Schwartz wrote that "her face was round, her cheeks were
always rosy and her eyes gay, and she looked like the true image of health,
amiability and vivacity."[42] Her father was an unsuccessful manufacturer of
women's clothing and her parents were unhappily married, "so Gertrude
was familiar with scenes of domestic strife." She was an only child and her
parents paid a lot of attention to her, but she felt "it was always the wrong
sort"—nagging rather than guiding her. She married Schwartz in 1938,
left him in 1943 and divorced him the following year. He told Buckman
that during their years together they "made no life for each other, nor any
happiness."[43] After divorcing Schwartz she worked for Pantheon publishers, the Bollingen Foundation and *Collier's* magazine. Between 1942 and
1948 she wrote eight book reviews for the *Partisan Review,* covering fiction
by Nelson Algren and William Maxwell, Caroline Gordon and Katherine
Anne Porter.

Stafford's "An Influx of Poets," a satiric portrait of Buckman and Lowell, described the sudden arrival in 1946 of the femme fatale who dropped
from the sky—like Mrs. Rattery landing at Tony Last's country house

in Evelyn Waugh's *A Handful of Dust:* "She came to us, quixotically and at the expense of her last host, in a Piper Cub, landing on an island in Hawthorne Lake, behind us, flown there by a Seebee so stricken with her that he loitered in the village several days afterwards." She added that the small, dark, *zaftig* girl "was not the kind of woman [Lowell] liked; she was flirtatious, competitive, argumentatively political."[44] She was also an intense and interested listener. Stafford later "accused Buckman of deliberately 'fouling my nest,' of cold-bloodedly setting out to steal her husband: she 'horribly flattered Cal, caused him to fall in love with her and caused herself to fall in love with him.'"[45]

Though Lowell had refused to sleep with Stafford, he was eager to have sex with a new woman. Buckman's description of the affair—which lasted, longer than any other, from 1946 to 1948—was vague, puzzled, fearful, sceptical and joyous. It was also more intensely passionate than her love for her handsome ex-husband:

I don't know what his feelings were. He was so beautiful then. . . . But I did think he was a very odd character. Unlike anyone else I've ever known. . . . It was happening imperceptibly and rather frighteningly, because I had never felt that feeling toward anyone. At the same time, it was very evident that he was feeling the same thing. Whether it was two floundering souls seeking each other's sympathy, I don't know, because it was a very difficult situation, with thunderclouds always hanging over one. I was very happy and feeling romantic about him, but I don't think either of us was sexually needful of each other. He said he loved me, but he was so childlike.[46]

After Lowell had left Stafford in Maine, he resumed his affair with Buckman in New York. There, she recalled, he continued his hair-shirt existence: "He would spend days in my flat working, and I would feed him. He was living in this ghastly rooming house on Third Avenue. I mean, he would get lice and crabs and everything, and he had no money. I really think he preferred that kind of thing. It was a haunt of pimps and prostitutes and God knows what." Early in 1947 Stafford "allowed" (though she could hardly prevent) Lowell to see Buckman and even arranged for the three of them to go to the Bronx Zoo. But the excursion was not a success. They called her possessive and left her as soon as they could, like a married couple at dinner with a boring relative.

Stafford retaliated by calling Buckman a selfish egoist and warning

Lowell not to marry her: "She is a child and if she wishes to eat the last piece of candy in the box, she will consult only her own desire. . . . If you marry her you will not be marrying a woman."[47] But it was not enough to supplant Stafford, Buckman also had to humiliate her: "Gertrude, the clever quicksilver, the heartless fey, the no-woman, the bedeviller. She laughed at me over the telephone and I shall never forget: a melodious laugh of triumph, of double triumph: she had got you, she had laid my life in ruins. I remember the laugh here nights on end."[48] When Stafford divorced Lowell and made reasonable but what he considered outrageous demands for alimony, Buckman loyally supported Lowell and declared that she wanted to marry him: "I have never thought to come up against such determined wickedness, such abandon of scruples, such calculated and unabashed gold-digging; and cashing in on the Lowell name. . . . I don't think it's patience, as much as faith, that will save us for a good and meaningful life together, which I want more than anything in the world."[49]

By 1948, as Lowell's passion cooled and the perils of matrimony loomed larger, the prospective bridegroom began to withdraw. He was grateful to Buckman for rescuing him from Stafford and giving him a joyous eighteen months, but dreaded the bondage of another marriage and told her:

> You know better than anyone how all things changed for me—as though I were re-born, as though I were suffering a second adolescence, with all the first to guide or mislead or what you will. And all this is due to you. . . .
>
> I want to drift a while before I marry. As my friend you can understand this, but in another way you can't, and it will all seem heartless and irresponsible. I suppose, it is so. And yet there is nothing I even believe I can do about it. This is a lousy return to you who have saved my life and always been perfect and kind to me. I think we've never quarreled or been unhappy together. I must be frightened to death of marriage and being tied down.[50]

By May Lowell had fallen in love with another woman, Carley Dawson, and awkwardly announced the end of the affair. But tormented by his puritan conscience, he was overwhelmed by remorse and guilt. He wrote Buckman: "It was a joy to see you, especially the second time. But I have been eating bitter bread. It's been as though I were pounding my soul with two stones to wash it. . . . Why? Because there's some one else, and because the past keeps coming back, and because. . . . But I and what I'm going through are useless to you at the moment—to anyone but myself. You were good to see me; but I know that seeing you now is selfish, irresponsible and self-indulgent. It's hard not to be with one's friend when one is troubled. . . . I know I've been mad and abominable to you."[51] Repeating Stafford's criticism of Buckman's character in a letter to Dawson, he now called her a forlorn, confused and unhappy child—and assured Dawson that Buckman was no threat to their love. He never told Buckman what had suddenly changed his intense feelings about her, but merely said they were too temperamentally different to get married. Contradicting Lowell's feelings and echoing Schwartz on her own unhappy marriage, Buckman now revised her views and said she and Lowell had never had much fun together.

Lowell told Dawson that when he met Buckman in April 1948 for what seemed like the last time, he had no regrets but she was tormented by the affair: "She was very nervous and tore up bits of paper or played with rubber bands. Several times we were in tears though neither is given that way. . . . 'What happened to us was good, and it was good that it ended, as it had to. But, you're funny, Cal; how could it have passed from you so quietly. It took longer for me to twist it out.' I felt as though I were abandoning my child. I called her up from Boston when I got in, and she said, 'I've been talking to you all afternoon. But you haven't heard me.'"[52] In August he apologized for returning her grace and love with selfish inconsistency. Despite all the pain and suffering (at least on Buckman's part) they kept in touch and occasionally saw each other. When they met by chance in 1970 in London, where the still unmarried Buckman was working for a publisher, he listened to her "brave complaints" about her life and they had a pleasant evening. She'd lived in Rome, and later edited an anthology of poetry, *Compliments* (1980).

Buckman, who'd had a rough time with the self-destructive Schwartz, retrospectively revised her feelings about the affair with Lowell. She truly said that he wasn't "husband material," that permanent involvement with him would have been a crazy thing, and claimed that marriage had never been a serious possibility. During an interview Buckman called him very beautiful, with great talent and a flattering interest in her. He had a strong physique and personality, yet a girlish, dancy manner—like a huge clumsy elf. Generous and utterly seductive, he was diffident yet dominating. She felt he was intellectually passionate but had no real emotions. Childish and immature, he lived in his own world of unreality. He depended on women to take care of him and provide a stable world: wives made his existence possible. All passion spent, Buckman could very simply summarize Lowell and his art: Lowell first behaved atrociously, then felt guilty and finally wrote poems about his terrible experiences.[53]

Buckman stayed with Lowell and Elizabeth Hardwick in both Boston and New York. Hardwick believed that he had mistreated Buckman and felt rare sympathy for her: "He had this thing with Gertrude, and had felt that it wasn't right. I think he broke her heart, I really do, because I think she cared a lot for him. She was a very delicate and unworldly person."[54] According to Lowell's close friend Frank Bidart, the woman in " 'To Speak of Woe That Is in Marriage' " who ties ten dollars and the car key to her thigh so she can escape if her husband becomes violent, is based on Buckman, not Hardwick.[55] When Lowell acquired three young stepdaughters in his last marriage, he named their gerbil "Gertrude Buckman."

IV

The marriage of Stafford and Lowell inspired an autobiographical bounty of two more stories by her and several poems by him. Stafford's ironically titled "A Country Love Story" (1950), based on their life in Damariscotta Mills in the spring of 1946, is told from the point of view of an unhappy wife who fears she is going mad. She has a depressed, solitary and sexually unresponsive husband and an imaginary, elusive and inevitably disappointing lover. The character inspired by Lowell has spent a year in a sanitarium and is recovering from tuberculosis (Stafford's fictional equivalent of Lowell's real-life mental breakdowns). Though they've moved to the country to find peace together and get away from the pressures of the outside world, they create their own disturbing hell. During the gradual disintegration of their once idyllic marriage, the couple move from a second honeymoon to a dreadful physical and emotional estrangement. Their "love, the very center of their being, was choked off, overgrown, invisible."

The husband's obsession with sin preys on his wife and heightens her fear of madness. When he makes vague accusations, she asks, "What have I done?" and he darkly replies, "I don't know. But you've done something." Like Hester Prynne in Hawthorne's *The Scarlet Letter,* "she lived with her daily dishonor, rattled, ashamed, stubbornly clinging to her secret." Like a victim in Kafka, she feels guilty but is unaware of her crime.

The wife cultivates an imaginary lover to compensate for the failure of her marriage, but instead of sustaining her this fantasy threatens her sanity. Her husband's forceful but unsubstantiated threats make her feel as if she were really going mad. He tells her, "you may really have a slight disorder of the mind. It would be nothing to be ashamed of; you could go to a sanitarium"—as if she had caught his disease and were forced to return to his place of confinement. When spring comes, he apologizes for "the hallucinations of a sick man." But it's now too late to assuage the wounds. She's stuck with her cold and distant husband, won't give up her "lover" and wonders "over and over again how she would live the rest of her life." [56]

Stafford's "An Influx of Poets," published twenty-eight years later in 1978, is set at the same time and in the same place as "A Country Love Story." In both works the wife is ecstatic when she buys their first house, and both describe—for different reasons—the end of her marriage. But this time the wife, not the husband, is sick and, as in the previous tale, he advises her to see a psychiatrist. Stafford calls the Lowell character Theron Maybank and reveals his personality with many specific biographical details. He has puritan ancestors who burned witches at Salem, his father was a naval captain who served in the Far East, he has Boston breeding and "totems," including a streak of anti-Semitism, and a trust fund to go with them. The wife is attracted to the "brilliant talk and dark good looks" of the "tall, large-headed genius." They met at a writers' conference and after their wedding moved frequently, from Tennessee and Louisiana to Cambridge, Connecticut and New York. Soon after their marriage, Maybank is seized by religious mania, converts to Catholicism and forces his wife (as Lowell did Stafford) to lead a hair-shirt existence.

Maybank likes "knocking the stuffing out of his bride"; she both loves and hates him. Isolated in rural Maine and with no one else to talk to, Lowell and Stafford welcomed guests to their remote outpost. In this angry but amusing story, written with "the tongue of an adder" and a heart "black with rage and hate," the wife is turned into a household slave for a flood of visiting and intolerably pretentious poets and critics (in real life John Berryman and Delmore Schwartz, R. P. Blackmur and Philip Rahv) as well as for her husband's seductive new mistress Minnie Rosoff (based on Gertrude Buckman). Minnie is a gifted "little minx, raven-tressed, damask-skinned [and] sharp-witted as a critic."

Minnie makes a glamorous entrance by seaplane and immediately

captures the all-too-willing husband. When the wife, just back from seeing a doctor in Boston, is too exhausted to go out, she obediently makes
their picnic sandwiches and they go off without her—presumably to have
sex. Instead of defending her husband from the emotional onslaught, the
wife perversely encourages the outrageous affair in order to escape from
her marriage. She wants to destroy herself by tasting "the vilest degradation, the bitterest jealousy, the most scalding and vindictive rancor."[57]

From Lowell's first to his last book of poems the repulsive and menacing spider imagery recalls Charlotte's web and suggests his unhappiness
and guilt about Stafford and other women. These horrific images were
influenced by Dostoyevsky as well as by the seventeenth-century American
theologian Jonathan Edwards. In *The Idiot* the huge spider symbolizes an
evil and omnipotent God: "someone seemed to lead me by the hand, with
a lighted candle, and show me some huge and horrible tarantula, assuring
me that that was the dark, deaf-and-dumb, and all-powerful creature."[58]
In *Crime and Punishment* spiders symbolize damnation and the torments
of hell: "one little room, something like a bath-house in the country, black
with soot, with spiders in every corner, and that is the whole of eternity."[59]

Combining this recurrent image and one of his dominant themes, and
applying them to world affairs, Lowell wrote in 1943, "Politics is a spider's
web of unreality." In "Mr. Edwards and the Spider" (*Lord Weary's Castle*,
1946) spiders are associated, as in Edwards and Dostoyevsky, with the
slender thread that suspends the sinner over the pit of hell. The image
appears in a draft manuscript of *Life Studies* (1959): "My mind / Moves like
a water-spider."[60] Spiders make a menacing appearance in three poems in
For the Union Dead. In "Fall 1961" he borrows a disturbing image from his
precocious and rather sad young daughter: "We are like a lot of wild / spiders crying together, / but without tears."[61]

In addition to the spider images, which Lowell associated with the
possessive and destructive aspects of Stafford's character, he wrote at least
six poems about her. The subject of "Frederick Kuh, Manx Cat (For Jean
Stafford)" was, rather sadly, "the only friend we never quarreled over, / the
sole survivor of our first marriage," which suggests that neither spouse
had managed to survive that catastrophe. In "Jean Stafford, a Letter," a
nostalgic poem in his last book, he fondly recalled her study at Heidelberg and intellectual achievements: "I can go on imagining you / in your
Heidelberry braids and Bavarian / peasant aprons you wore three or four
years / after your master's at twenty-one." Lowell also recalled the correct

pronunciation of her favorite German author, whose story "Tonio Kröger" had inspired his poem "The Exile's Return": "*Towmahss Mahnn:* that's how you said it. . . / 'That's how Mann must say it,' I thought."

"The Old Flame," using a wasp instead of a spider image, stresses their isolation from friends and from each other in Maine: "how quivering and fierce we were, / there snowbound together, / simmering like wasps / in our tent of books! . . . / in one bed and apart." In "Thanksgiving's Over" the wife bitterly condemns her adulterous husband for not loving her and for committing her to a mental home: "the love I felt the want / Of, when your mercy shipped me to Vermont / To the asylum. Michael, was there warrant / For killing love?"

In Lowell's dark, satanic "Mills of the Kavanaughs" a young widow in Maine remembers with adoration and loathing the mental and physical decline of her husband. He deprived her of sexual pleasure, then descended into insanity and death. Ann Kavanaugh's description of the dream that provoked her sexy husband's jealousy recalls Lowell's violent attack on Stafford:

> You have gored me black and blue.
> I am all prickle-tickle like the stars. . . .
>   Then I was wide
> Awake, and turning over. "Who, who, who?"
> You asked me, "tell me who." Then everything
> Was roaring, Harry, Harry, I could feel
> Nothing—it was so black.

When he attempted to invade her unconscious thoughts and strangle her, she exclaimed:

>   Harry, I am glad
> You tried to kill me; it is out, you know. . . .
> I'll tell you, so remember, you are mad;
> I'll tell them, listen Harry: husband kills
> His wife for dreaming. [62]

In one of her most vitriolic letters, written at the end of their marriage, Stafford condemned Lowell for denying her sexuality and then—amaz-ingly—declared her undying love: "I know this, Cal, and the knowledge eats me like an inward animal; there is no thing worse for a woman than to be deprived of her womanliness. . . . If you had loved me, you would love me now completely as I completely love you so that this is another dreadful truth that I must swallow: these bitternesses that I have tried to swallow still make me retch."[63] Since Lowell's poetry dramatized his own emotional experiences, his women—belonging to a small literary world whose readers knew the real-life people and situations—had to suffer again when the poems were published.

In a final twist of the knife Lowell desecrated the memory of Stafford's beloved brother, killed in a jeep accident in France in September 1944, by suggesting in "Her Dead Brother" that they had practiced perverse sex: "And the pale summer shades were drawn—so low / No one could see us; no, nor catch your hissing word. . . . / O Brother, a New England town is death / And incest—and I saw it whole."[64] Wounded and horrified when the poem appeared in 1947, Stafford sent Lowell another caustic letter. She wrote that publishing the poem in the *Nation,* "with its theme of latent incest, at a time when you have left me and I am in the hospital seems to me an act of so deep dishonor that it passes beyond dishonor and approaches madness. And I am trembling in the presence of your hate."[65]

Lowell's great elegy, "The Quaker Graveyard in Nantucket," whose title echoes Longfellow's "The Jewish Cemetery at Newport," memorializes his cousin Lieutenant Warren Winslow, "dead at sea." This poem caused Stafford more pain by implicitly contrasting the two military men who had both died in 1944. A Harvard graduate and recently married, Winslow was an officer on the destroyer *Turner,* anchored just outside the submarine net that defended New York harbor but did not protect his ship. On January 3, 1944, the *Turner* suddenly exploded and sank with a loss of 140 men. The official cause was the explosion of its own defective ammunition, but the ship was probably hit by a German torpedo. The navy preferred to call it an accident rather than admit they'd failed to protect the vulnerable ship, just off the coast of America, in the middle of the war. Lowell, two years older than Winslow, might have shared his tragic fate if he'd been able to join the navy.

The last line in "The Quaker Graveyard"—"The Lord survives the rainbow of His will"—alludes to God's promise to Noah in Genesis 9:15 not to deluge the earth again: "the waters shall no more become a flood to destroy all flesh."[66] This line, perhaps the most difficult and puzzling in all of Lowell's poetry, has been subject to contradictory interpretations.

Lowell seems to believe that man, not God, is bound by the covenant and that God, not man, is the beneficiary of this destructive bargain. God may even passively stand by and allow evil mankind to exterminate itself. "The Quaker Graveyard," with its wild rhythm and exalted rhetoric, was the greatest poem Lowell wrote while married to Stafford. But it was exactly the sort of successful poem that irritated Randall Jarrell, who disliked his religious conversion and resented his poetic reputation. Jarrell loved to make up wickedly witty parodies of the eccentric trust-fund Lowells and of Cal's favorite morbid-Catholic effects, "full of sabbaths, sermons, grave-yards, ancestors."[67]

By 1946 the Church had served its purpose by inspiring the religious themes and imagery of his early poetry. One critic explained that Lowell "was more attached to the long and august history of Catholicism than he was to the actual church that surrounded him in the 1940s. Thus, he tends to depict the Irish American Catholics in his midst with a condescension that at times borders on contempt."[68] Now that he wanted a divorce, he fiercely attacked the religion that had once set him on fire for its "incompetence, stupidity, cruelty, conservatism, compromise and dogmatism."[69] He also condemned Allen Tate's conversion in 1950 as a fraudulent "Tartuffian dumb show." Lowell was an extraordinary mixture of New York liberal and Southern conservative, of Jew, Episcopalian and Catholic. Emphasizing his vertiginous change of attitude, Stafford mocked the "poem which had begun with the title, 'To Jean: On Her Confirmation,' and finished by being called, 'To a Whore at the Brooklyn Navy Yard.'"[70]

V

Lowell and Stafford had overwhelming problems: their literary competition, psychological difficulties and sexual dysfunction, her depression and heavy drinking, his Catholic fanaticism and brutal violence. Neither marriage nor religion nor psychiatrists could help them. Finally, Lowell's affair ended their union. In a letter of February 1949, Allen Tate analyzed the reasons for Lowell's apparent decline: "As I see Cal over the past twelve years, and no one I think knows him better, three things held him together: the Church, his marriage and his poetry. He gave up the Church; he gave up Jean; and some months ago he virtually gave up poetry. He had been pushed forward too rapidly as a poet and he had attempted a work beyond his present powers; he couldn't finish it." But

Lowell was much stronger, self-protective and emotionally indifferent than he seemed to be. Unlike Stafford, he walked away from the marriage with no deep wounds, continued to write poetry and published *The Mills of the Kavanaughs* in 1951.

In December 1946 Peter Taylor, a close friend of both Lowell and Stafford, tried to act as mediator and to rescue the marriage by suggesting they delay the divorce for a year. But Lowell thought they should have separated in 1944 and saved themselves a lot of bitterness. Stafford felt a delay would only prolong the agony and said that "by this plan he will only be free to reject me in his brutal fashion over a longer period of time than he has done already. Mind you, I would take him back now and I would forgive him because I love him." Though Stafford complained bitterly about Lowell, she still found him beautiful and brilliant, and was willing to absolve him if they could remain married. Her letters vacillate between indignation and pleas for help. With Stafford as, later on, with Elizabeth Hardwick, Lowell's cruel behavior provoked a tender but masochistic response.

Lowell's calm, Olympian stance while Stafford was falling apart made her frantic. As she told Taylor in December 1946, Lowell remained "so immovable, so utterly, so absolutely, utterly unaware of what I might be suffering. . . . He has never shown me anything in any of his letters but cold, self-justified hatred."[71] Lowell wrote Taylor that though Stafford still loved him, she also wanted to punish him and sought revenge: "We had a excruciatingly unpleasant meeting in which she said that she loved me and her one desire was to drive me wild. Something like that—largely subconscious—has been wrong with us for a long time."[72]

Finally Stafford had a mental breakdown and spent a year in the Payne Whitney Clinic in New York. She realized what would happen to her there, but was forced to accept her fate: "I knew the doors would be locked and that they would take everything away from me, that there would be no more whiskey, that I could not get out once I had signed myself in, that the pain of the analysis was going to be excruciating. That first night, I lay perfectly motionless in my bed, fighting off the terror."[73] Her incarceration was all the more bitter since Lowell seemed to have achieved happiness with Buckman as Stafford descended into madness. Overwhelmed by guilt and faced with poverty, she exclaimed, "I do not know what monstrous crime I did when I was a child to merit this punishment. These ghastly months in this ghastly asylum, this ghastly future which I face without *money.*" Charlotte had wished to die when she was pregnant with Bobby, and Stafford now repeated her lament: "I am sick now, I see no end and I wish, I wish, I wish, I wish to die."

When Lowell saw Stafford in the luxurious lockup, she was still mentally unstable. She complained that he had visited her only once and spent most of the time extolling Buckman's virtues. The divorce settlement, like everything else in their life, was acrimonious. In January 1947 Stafford demanded one-third of his income and, after his father's death, one-third of his $33,000 trust fund. When Lowell refused to agree, she increased her demands in September to $7,000 per annum for the next five years, plus $800 a year for life and half of his trust fund. After much wrangling, they finally compromised.

Lowell liked to keep in touch with his women when his marriages and affairs were over. After the financial disputes were finally settled, he later made a conciliatory gesture and accepted some of the blame: "My dear, please never castigate yourself for what you call blindness—how blind we both were, how green we were, how countless were our individual torments we didn't know the names of. All we can do is forgive ourselves and now be good friends—how I should cherish that."[74] The Catholic publisher Frank Sheed, like several other friends, believed that Lowell had wrecked Stafford's life, that she never recovered and that she was a completely different person after the breakup of their marriage.

VI

Just as Lowell's affair with Buckman had ended his marriage to Stafford, so his affair with Carley Dawson ended his liaison with Buckman. Eight years older than Lowell and, like Anne Dick, from the right sort of family, Dawson (1909–2005) was born in Louisville, Kentucky. She was educated after the Great War in London where she attended the first Montessori School. Her father, Avery Robinson, was a composer and treasurer of the Royal Philharmonic Society, and Carley later studied in Paris with the pianist Nadia Boulanger. Her mother, Grace Chess Robinson, founded the cosmetics firm Mary Chess Ltd. in 1932, and Carley took an active part in the business in London, New York and Washington. She married Richard Hope Hawkins in 1931, had a son, and divorced her husband in 1937. She lived in London in the 1930s and returned to America before the war. In 1944 she married Allan Dawson and divorced him a few years later. In the

1950s she wrote three successful books for children, including *Mr. Wicker's Window* (Houghton Mifflin, 1952). She translated the erudite and obscure *Metamorphoses of the Circle*, by the Belgian literary critic Georges Poulet, for Johns Hopkins University Press in 1966. In the 1960s she veered into mysticism and was ordained into the ministry of Divine Science. She died at the age of ninety-six in Williamstown, Massachusetts.

A wealthy, worldly and sophisticated Washington hostess, Dawson liked to entertain the literary elite. She had been the lover of the French poet Alexis Léger, who derived his exotic pen name, Saint-John Perse, from Persia and Perseus. Born on the French Caribbean island of Guadeloupe in 1887, the son of a coffee and sugar plantation owner, he had a high forehead, thin lips and neatly trimmed mustache, and favored polka-dot bow ties. As secretary-general of the Ministry of Foreign Affairs and a leading member of the fallen French regime, the anti-Nazi and anti-Vichy Léger was forced into exile after the German occupation of his country and lived in America from 1940 to 1967. T. S. Eliot had translated Léger's long poem *Anabasis* in 1938, and Léger would win the Nobel Prize in 1960.

Lowell's older cousin Mary Winslow, who moved in the same social circles as Dawson, was not impressed by Léger's political and poetic achievements. She told Lowell, with provincial snobbery, that when Léger addressed her in French, "of course I didn't listen; it's pure affectation for him not to speak American." In fact, she detested Léger and insisted on referring to the great man as "that greasy little Frenchman who dyes his hair."[75]

When Lowell was poetry consultant at the Library of Congress in 1948, he met Dawson at a dinner party at the Georgetown home of Caresse Crosby, widow of Harry Crosby, a wealthy literary man and St. Mark's graduate who'd committed suicide in 1929. In "Modern Muse," an unpublished memoir of Caresse, Dawson entered the literary arena and expressed her ideals by gushing about her friend's talents and forthcoming international journal, brought out by Caresse's own Black Sun Press between 1945 and 1948: "In her dynamic energy, her obstinate faith in and love of people, she has that [imaginative] hammer. Successive numbers of her *Portfolio* should be awaited with respect and interest, not only by intellectuals everywhere, but by all those who sense the world longing for a creative, universal and lasting peace."[76]

As always with Lowell's women, the affair progressed rapidly. Dawson recalled: "Robert later said he'd noticed me because I'd had on dark stockings. This rather intrigued him. I don't remember what happened next—I may have invited him to dinner. And then we went to movies and so on and one thing led to another until we were engaged to be married." Charlotte typically zeroed in on the faults of his latest love. Anne Dick had psychological problems, Stafford was a low-class type from Colorado, Buckman was a Jew from New York—and Dawson was twice divorced. Lowell managed to extract a modicum of praise when his obsessively clean mother conceded that Dawson was excessively neat. But she also offered Dawson a dubious compliment by exclaiming that she "was a very *knowing* person, not a wise person, but a knowing person" who seemed to be acting.[77]

Despite Charlotte's inevitable opposition, the affair continued. Dawson praised Lowell's fulsome flattery, exquisite manners and gracious behavior in a letter to her childhood friend, the English actress Joyce Grenfell. Lowell seemed " 'head over heels in love' with her, had told her he honored her and was even in awe of her. The previous Sunday they'd walked 'along the still frozen canal with sandwiches and apples,' her heart 'in tears at his touching—almost courtly—gesture, of turning back at every step to offer me his hand over the boggy places.' "[78] He also told Dawson that he'd made love to only four women in his life: Dick, Stafford, Buckman and now herself, among the chosen few.

Lowell discussed his divorce from Stafford with Dawson (an expert on the subject) as he had with Buckman. A relatively rapid divorce in Reno would cost him a cool thousand dollars, including travel, food and lodging. He'd just heard from Stafford, who wanted to see him and whom he wanted to avoid. He couldn't convincingly deceive her about Dawson, and if Stafford learned that Lowell wanted to marry Dawson, she'd undoubtedly twist the thumbscrew and increase her demands: "A pathetic letter—she wants to and is afraid of seeing me in Washington. That she will get the divorce looks certain. Who can tell? I don't think she's heard of you, but I don't want to be questioned by her—I won't be able to lie plausibly enough to hide everything."

Always an ardent suitor, Lowell continued to turn on the charm and pour out the praise. When Dawson sent him samples of her work, he recognized her promise and encouraged her: "You're a good writer, I see. Get something of a plot, and write ten or twelve pages as dense as your description of supper—and you'll really have something. World's better than your poems, although they're . . ." He concluded longingly, "How I wish I were with you! . . . Nothing's much fun without you."[79]

Finally confronting the delicate question of marriage, he seemed to declare himself unequivocally but, nervous after the fiasco with Stafford, would not yet commit himself and left her dangling: "I'm writing so that you can hear from me right away, and so that my head can stop milling with the problem fruitlessly—for tonight, maybe. The answer to your three-fold analysis is! I love you with all I have and want you to marry me. But a lot of water is going to flow under the bridge before that happens. Come April, come Jean's divorce, come September. I want to let them come. You're afraid of getting in deeper, and that's just as well. But I'm already in over my head. I'm carried away with love."[80]

Despite her extensive experience with men, Dawson was understandably puzzled by Lowell's behavior and wondered what made that boy *tick*. He was still reluctant to bathe and dependent on her, yet detached and self-absorbed. She described him as "moody, ardent, a kind of captive toy wild pet (and smelling like a badger when she first met him), eager to be sheltered and fed but coming and going as he pleased."[81] It's surprising that the stylish and sophisticated Dawson could become so deeply involved with the badger-smelling Lowell. She told Joyce Grenfell of his disheveled but still divine appearance, and was most impressed by his charismatic performance at a literary conference at Johns Hopkins University in Baltimore: "My dear Robert in grey flannel managed to look, as Allen Tate said in front of him, as if he slept in his clothes. . . . His thoughtful, alert, concentrating face looked like some benign angel come down to study and observe. . . . He thinks and speaks well, impromptu, and was called on frequently by the moderator."[82]

Lowell subjected Dawson, as he'd subjected Anne Dick, to unfair intellectual inquisitions. Though Dick liked the criticism, Dawson was wounded by it. She recalled that early in 1948, "I met Jarrell at a luncheon with a lot of other people who I think were passing judgment on whether I was adequate for Robert. I'm sure I failed completely. I'd just been to the National Gallery and they kept asking which pictures I liked. And I was quite nervous, because I knew why they were asking, that I was being needled. So I couldn't remember any of the things I really liked. I was absolutely terrified." At the Hopkins conference Lowell forced her to attend a breakfast with his high-powered friends—Allen Tate and the critics R. P. Blackmur and Herbert Read—and quietly looked on as they cruelly humiliated his fiancée.

Things got much worse in their tête-à-tête discussion of Shakespeare's plays. Suddenly, as with Stafford, Lowell became violent and Dawson barely escaped injury:

> I had argued something—just really for the sake of discussion, because I don't really know anything about Shakespeare's plays particularly. And all of a sudden Robert . . . swung around and took my neck in his hands and swung me down on to the floor. And I looked at his face and it was completely white, completely blank. I can't describe it. The [real] person inside was not there. . . . I think that if I had struggled at that time I wouldn't be here. But I said, "Robert, it's rather uncomfortable like this. Do you mind if I get back on the sofa?" And then he came back to himself, he was back in his body, and we sat down and continued our conversation. I didn't argue anymore."[83]

As Lowell began to show signs of mania, his character seemed to split between violence and control. Part of him acted irrationally and he didn't quite know what he was doing. Dawson told Grenfell that he behaved "as if he were crazy . . . unstable, infantile, egomaniacal, prone to violence."[84] She was amazed, as Lowell assumed his favorite persona to distance himself from her, that "a man of Robert's intellect should always be talking about bears. I think he really thought of himself as a bear." Her adolescent son, alarmed by Lowell's bear act, was more clear-sighted than his mother and declared, "That man is mad, he's absolutely bonkers."[85]

Lowell then introduced his great friend Elizabeth Bishop into this combustible mix. He asked Dawson to lend her elegant Georgetown home to Bishop, who turned out to be a less than ideal guest. Dawson recalled that Bishop, depressed and alcoholic, "had taken a little of every [bottle] and the vomit on everything all over the house was something to behold. They cleaned it all up. I said something to Elizabeth about it, like 'What had happened about the liquor?' And she said, 'I got feeling sorry for myself one night and I started tasting all the different things. I just started, couldn't stop.' "[86]

Lowell's infatuation with Bishop, despite her behavior, helped to terminate his affair with Dawson. In June 1948 Lowell, Dawson and Bishop drove up to Stonington, Maine, and he began, in his characteristic way, to withdraw from Dawson. She later recalled that after she'd failed her impromptu Ph.D. examination at Johns Hopkins, Lowell refused to take her to meet another group of poets:

There was a question of going swimming, and we drove along the shore—but it was icy cold water, that Maine water. And I noticed that Robert was very different, he was different towards me, and I was extremely uneasy. He didn't seem to be himself at all. And that evening, or some evenings later, there was a question of him going to a group of poets somewhere, near Boston. And I was anticipating going with him, but he said no. And I remember that we talked all night long about this, and I realized something was very wrong with Robert. And so in the morning I went in as soon as I dared and woke Elizabeth and told her that I thought Robert and I were finished. . . . And that was it, I never saw Robert again. [87]

A mutual friend drove Dawson to the train station, and Lowell, relieved at being rescued, told Bishop, "Now that Carley is away, I feel I have been trying to force something that wouldn't work." [88]

Lowell expressed his disillusionment with Dawson, as he had with Stafford, in two satiric poems. The narrator in "The Banker's Daughter," partly based on the rich, well-born Dawson, speaks in the voice of Marie de' Medici, the daughter of a Florentine banker who married King Henri IV of France. Marie (Dawson) describes her uneasy involvement with Henri (Lowell) as if she were a grape being trampled for wine—or blood:

> And so I press my lover's palm to mine;
> I am his vintage, and his living vine
> entangles me, and oozes mortal wine
> moment to moment. [89]

In the unpublished "Two Weeks' Vacation," based on their ill-fated trip to Maine, Lowell calls Dawson "the elfin, blue-blooded / Psychotic bluestocking," though she was far more sane than he was. [90] He recycles the title of "The Old Flame," his poem on Stafford; compares Dawson this time to Madame du Barry, mistress of King Louis XV and victim of the revolutionary Reign of Terror; and criticizes her, though she'd been a good sport on their fishing trip. He also condemns the elegantly dressed woman, whose black stockings had once intrigued him, for trying too hard to be sexually alluring when he was more interested in Bishop. Finally, he portrays himself, not her, as sexually attractive, and says she's the one who abandoned him:

My old flame, Mrs. X—
never left us,
Each morning she met us with another
Crashing ensemble,
Her British voice, her Madame du Barry
Black and gold eyebrows,
She survived a whole day of handline
Deep sea fishing for pollock, skate and sculpin,
Making me bait her hooks.
And wearing a blue silk "ski-suit."
Blouse, trousers, cape and even her gloves matched.
All this, for me! . . .
on my next to last night, the thirteenth
I came down the corridor in pajamas,
No doubt arousing false hopes
And said . . . Well, who cares, my old flame left,
And I never heard from her ever after.[91]

By the 1940s Lowell's marriage to Stafford ended in misery, and he withdrew from his affairs with Buckman and Dawson. Stafford, a physical and
psychological victim, loved him despite everything. Buckman and Dawson were left confused and wounded.

FOUR

Mania,
1949–1976

I

Between 1949 and 1976 Lowell struggled with great fortitude against at least sixteen mental breakdowns, more than one every other year—the most difficult problem his wives and women had to confront. He lived for poetry, writing and teaching, love and friendship, but his recurrent mania ruled his life. Apart from the spells when he was definitely and unmistakably mad, Lowell had periods when he was not entirely sane. There were times when he combined heavy drinking with prescribed drugs. More difficult to gauge were the periods when he was going into and out of madness, before he reached a full-blown debilitating mania. In this confusing halfway state his wives and friends could not tell whether he was sane or crazy, and whether he was responsible for his actions. Some people even thought that this twilight state, when he acted as if he were mad, provided a useful excuse for his violent behavior and sexual adventures.

Though Lowell could not write when he was mad, he did acquire precious experience and insight that he later used in his poetry. He shared the Romantic notion that the poet had a unique role in society and that his madness could be valuable. His suffering inspired some of his most revealing poems, including "Waking in the Blue" and "Skunk Hour." When his British friend Grey Gowrie quoted Winston Churchill who said, "while suffering a bout of his famous Black Dog depression, 'We are all worms,' Lowell suddenly brightened and exclaimed, 'But I do believe I am a glow-worm.'"[1] In fact, Lowell did some of his best writing between manic episodes, in that confusing and terrifying stage when he was entering or

76

emerging from his illness. As he told the poet Ted Roethke, who also suf-fered from mental breakdowns, "All that was lost is returned. We even bring back certain treasure from our visits to the bottom."[2] Lowell's men-tal illness also gave him greater compassion for the suffering of others. The poet Anthony Hecht recalled that when he was hospitalized for depression in a particularly bleak moment of his life, "Lowell was especially kind to me and sympathetic. I was deeply moved and very grateful to him for his understanding. But after all, we seemed to share a common affliction."[3]

Lowell's friends were naturally mystified and alarmed by his behavior in this twilight state. John Thompson said, "We always thought of him as eccentric, but he wasn't crazy. He was odd." The English writer Jonathan Raban added, "The line between Cal at his sanest and Cal at his maddest was a thinner line than one would probably expect with anybody else. In many ways the delusion of mania was so close to the mischievousness of invention which was his sanest side."[4] When the ballet dancer Esther Brooks met Lowell at a New York party given by Jean Stafford after her marriage to him had ended, "he was waltzing around and proudly display-ing the marks of his stigmata." The poet Frank Bidart recalled that "when Lowell was getting sick, he would hurt people by saying something true but cruel. He told a friend to read certain books and when she hadn't read them the next time they met, he exclaimed, "Jackie Kennedy always reads the books I tell her to read and she's much better looking than you." The woman was naturally wounded by this gratuitously harsh remark.[5]

Most spectacular of all the episodes of his half-mad behavior was his breakout from Greenways, a private clinic in London, in 1975. Lowell was supposed to present Seamus Heaney with the Duff Cooper Prize. Despite his illness and contrary to all expectations, Lowell managed to find his way to the proper place and fulfill his obligation to a friend and fellow poet. Heaney recalled the bizarre aspects of the chaotic scene:

He had agreed to do the presentation, but when the time came he was in one of his "high" periods and confined to a nursing home. Then—on the afternoon of the day in question—he disappeared, much to the distress of his wife and friends, who eventually found him in the room in London University where the award ceremony was to take place. It was a sad, mad event. Lowell going about with a jacket over his pyjama tops; Diana Cooper [Duff Cooper's widow] with a Chihuahua on her arm, telling him at some point that the prize was to be presented by some mad American; Lowell, wild-eyed and nodding, "I know, I know!" [6]

In a perceptive letter, Anthony Hecht commented on Lowell's response to the early stages of insanity. Though he feared the end result, he could not resist the joy it brought him: "Though perhaps a little proud of his craziness at times (it became a license for recklessness in his manic moods, and seemed to him sometimes the sign of his genius as well as the frailty of his character) Lowell only indulged it to the extent of not taking his lithium when the first manic signs of an attack came on him, chiefly because he felt so good, and, knowing that all the terrible consequences might, perhaps even must, ensue, he could not bring himself to descend from his exaltation." [7] Lowell's twilight states, between euphoria and madness, and the ensuing deep depression, his need to seize every creative moment, were remarkably similar to Vincent van Gogh's description in October 1889 of his own precarious condition: "I am not strictly speaking mad, for my mind is absolutely normal in the intervals. . . . But during the attacks it is terrible—and then I lose consciousness of everything. But that spurs me on to work and to seriousness, as a miner who is always in danger makes haste in what he does." [8] In "Since 1939" Lowell wrote of his suspension between hope and danger: "we see a light at the end of the tunnel, / it's the light of an oncoming train." [9]

II

Repeatedly, every other year, Lowell took up the Cross of his mania and set out on his *via dolorosa.* Catapulting through the three stages of exuberance, confusion and depression, he remarked that he'd "thought that civilisation was going to break down, and instead *I* did." [10] During the political protests of the 1960s, he made his own madness represent the madness of the modern world. "When Lowell's sanity broke," as Derek Walcott observed, "the evils of our century flooded his brain with horrors." [11]

Edmund Wilson, a close observer, compared Lowell's manic outbursts to "hurricane warnings on the Cape." [12] Even before his first breakdown, he was dangerously irrational with Stafford. He carried Catholicism to fanatical extremes, punched her in the face (a repetition of punching his father) and strangled her. When Lowell lost power over himself, he became obsessed with powerful figures and, a sure sign of his illness, would talk nonstop about the greatness of Hitler. The British critic Karl Miller recalled that "as he plucked down a copy of *Mein Kampf,* said it was very well written and read out some unconvincing drivel about Jews, there was considerable fascination and a heightened sense of danger."[13] Wilson wrote that Lowell would hold forth "to a partly Jewish audience about what a great man Hitler had been." He recalled how his conversations with Lowell accelerated, "going off in all directions, interrupting one another, range of interest and reading, flares of imagination, general freedom of the world. I didn't know that he was getting into his manic phase."[14]

Lowell's sudden bursts of outrageous behavior also warned that he was sailing into stormy seas. The Australian artist Sidney Nolan, who illustrated Lowell's works, witnessed a startling moment at the Metropolitan Opera in New York: "There's a scene in Verdi's *Don Carlos* where a chap is shot in the dungeons. So there is this shot and then dead silence in the opera house, and Cal said in a loud clear voice, 'Oswald' "—the name of John Kennedy's assassin.[15] Lowell's outburst, disturbing to both the audience and the singers, was both funny and macabre. The novelist Flannery O'Connor gave an amusing interpretation of an escapade when Lowell was teaching at the University of Cincinnati: "It seems Cal convinced everybody it was Elizabeth [Hardwick] who was going crazy. Toward the end [of his term] he gave a lecture at the university that was almost pure gibberish. I guess nobody noticed, thinking it was the new criticism."[16]

During one of Lowell's manic attacks he woke up in the middle of the night and suddenly called Jackie Kennedy, whom he had befriended in 1965. Rather surprisingly she picked up the phone, spoke to him and tried to calm him down. On another occasion, Nolan recalled, "Lowell said, 'We'll go and see Jackie Kennedy.' So we went to her flat, overlooking Central Park. And there were the security guards and Cal said, 'We've come to see Jackie Kennedy. Put your guns away. Just do your duty and do what I tell you. Telephone her or I'll have a word with your captain in the morning.' So they called her and she said, 'Come up.' " His eccentric behavior should have warned the Secret Service to keep him away from her, but his personal charisma and imperious manner somehow persuaded them to announce his presence and allow him to pass.[17] Jackie, who admired Lowell, wanted to talk about Baudelaire. Lowell, who had a crush on her, wanted to gossip and flirt.

Ted Roethke once told Lowell about his own breakdown and violence: "it's happened again! Same old routine: 4 or 5 city police . . . dragging me off to the same old nut-bin."[18] Whenever this happened to Lowell, he was fortunate to have a loyal friend who was always willing to rescue him. His old St. Mark's companion Blair Clark would time after time step in, take charge, and clean up the personal and medical mess. Frank Parker said that Clark, a wealthy managerial type who knew how to arrange things, "was always in the middle of everything because he was efficient and orderly and Cal needed all the help he could get. Blair certainly earned his reputation of being the practical man. The trip to South America. The trip to Italy, when Cal's mother died. Blair did that, arranging for the mother to be shipped back. Blair's been in every campaign."[19] Clark "spoke of those times as though recounting World War II battles. Each rescue and restoration had to be planned to the last detail—tactical, legal, psychiatric, emotional."[20] At one perilous point, citing the danger to Lowell's family, Clark tried to appoint a legal guardian who'd be able to commit Lowell if he refused to go into a hospital. Clark told Lowell's lawyer, "his wife and child are by all accounts subjected to risks that so far, fortunately, have not gone beyond the threat of violence. I know, however, that Elizabeth has been badly frightened about the safety of the child and herself."[21]

Several friends left accounts of their unnerving visits to Lowell in mental asylums. When Grey Gowrie was there, "the attendant said, 'Hey, guys, it's ice cream tonight.' Lowell, who loved ice cream, poured hot gravy on it before wolfing it down and exclaimed, 'Now you know I'm crazy.'"[22] When Frank Parker called on him, Lowell "pressed him to sniff his pajamas to see if he could smell the sulfur Cal was sure was emanating from him— 'the brimstone of Hell.'"[23] Ann Fleming, wife of the English novelist Ian Fleming, recalled Lowell lapsing into a robotic depression, self-enclosed and unable to function: "He possessed one torn shirt and never washed; as the anti-depressive drug began to work, his gait became unsteady and the chain smoking lost its aim so the day was spent extinguishing small bonfires, until Caroline Blackwood and the psychiatrist called in a special nurse and he was led away, frustrated, sad and distinguished."[24]

After he'd recovered, Lowell unfortunately recalled all the tormenting details of his madness. His manic phases gave him piercing insight but took away his self-control. His sharp-edged and frenetic descriptions revealed how exciting it was to be crazy—and how boring. In a series of poetic images he likened his sick self to a blind mole, a heedless heart, a man cut in two, a messiah with a bestial glow. After his first breakdown in 1949, he told Buckman that he'd been reduced to a state of terrifying nothingness: "By the time I reached the hospital I was completely out of my head—strange physical sensations—I was a prophet and everything was a symbol; then in the hospital: shouting, singing, tearing things up—religion and antics. Then depression (extreme) aching, self-enclosed, fearful of everyone and everything anyone could do, feeling I was nothing and could do nothing." But even when he seemed better, his recovery was never complete. He contrasted his dreams, in which he seemed invulnerable, with his waking life, when he felt physically and mentally tortured: "For two years I have been cooling off from three months of pathological enthusiasm. I go to sleep now easily, but sometimes I wake up with a jar. In my dreams I am like one of Michael Angelo's bulky, rugged, ideal statues that can be tumbled down a hill without injury. When I wake, it is as though I had been flayed, and had each nerve beaten with a rubber hose."[25]

Trapped in a repetitive cycle, Lowell suffered the degradation of being rescued and committed to the cold solicitude of the locked ward over and over again. Since he could expect no cure for his mania, only remissions, he knew that after he'd recovered from one attack he would have to endure another one. Though he always emerged from his madness, he feared that the cumulative effect of mania, drugs and shock treatments would inevitably make him weaker, make it harder and harder to recover, and finally make him permanently insane. (The fear of permanent insanity was the main reason for Sylvia Plath's suicide.) Walcott noted, "Most of his life had been spent recovering from, and dreading, mental attacks, of having to say early [quoting "Skunk Hour"] 'my mind's not right'. . . . Bedlam, asylum, hospital, his bouts of mania never left him, but they also never left him mad."[26] In "Home" Lowell quoted a sanguine doctor, " 'Remarkable breakdown, remarkable recovery,' " yet noted, "the breakage can go on repeating / once too often."[27]

Using a boxing metaphor to describe a battered fighter who could take only so much punishment, Lowell told Nolan, "I've been sixteen times on my knees. I've got up sixteen times. But if one day I don't get up, I don't mind."[28] Hardwick wrote Blair Clark about the constant menace: "He is profoundly aware that depressive symptoms—fear, remorse, uncertainty, anxiety, chaos—are always threatening him," and added with considerable exaggeration, "and he would truly rather wreck his whole life than have these symptoms for a moment."[29] The very last lines Lowell wrote expressed his own fear of losing his mind: "Christ, / may I die at night / with a semblance of my faculties."[30]

One of Lowell's worst episodes took place in Argentina. In 1962 the Congress for Cultural Freedom, an anticommunist propaganda organization secretly funded by the CIA, invited him to lecture in Brazil and Argentina, and Hardwick and their daughter went with him in early June. Keith Botsford, an Anglo-American writer who knew Lowell and was then on a grant from the Ford Foundation, was asked by the president of the Congress, Nicolas Nabokov, to accompany Lowell and his wife while they visited South America. He told me that the Congress "knew Lowell's mania was risky—Elizabeth Bishop, then living in Brazil, had warned them—but the director, Nicolas Nabokov, wanted him. He thought that Lowell would be a useful tool in opposing the considerable influence of the Chilean communist poet Pablo Neruda. Nabokov felt he would not be all *that* dangerous and was willing to take the risk. But Lowell's incipient mania was obvious from the first day."

In Brazil, Lowell met and declared his love for the beautiful and talented Brazilian novelist Clarice Lispector, a friend of Elizabeth Bishop, who'd translated her stories into English. Though interested in Lowell as a writer, Lispector was heavily involved in her own affairs and did not become sexually entangled with him. At the same time, Hardwick was jealous of Lowell's close, occasionally romantic, but never sexual friendship with Bishop. According to Botsford, when Lowell was very high, Hardwick, fed up with his wild behavior and with the whole trip, left Brazil and returned to New York on September 1st.

When Lowell reached Buenos Aires, Botsford continued, there were scandals beyond repair at the American Embassy. He drank heavily, arrived hours late for appointments and insulted important officials. He then declared himself the Caesar of Argentina, took off his clothes and climbed up several equestrian statues. Lowell frightened all the women, who tried to steer clear of him, but free of Hardwick's constraint he did manage to have a few one-night stands. After a wild party, he locked himself in his hotel room with a woman friend of the exiled Spanish poet Raphael Alberti, who'd agreed to calm Lowell down. When the woman cried out for help and it was clear that Lowell was assaulting her, the hotel manager unlocked the door. Lowell was overpowered by several burly policemen, who tied him into a straitjacket. With his doctor's consent, he was taken to a padded cell in the Clínica Bethlehem, a rundown and poorly managed but profitable private clinic. Lowell's arms and legs were at first bound with leather straps, but supervision was lax and he was later able to bribe his way out a few times.

Exhausted by trying to take care of Lowell, Botsford suddenly returned to Brazil. Nabokov and Bishop were furious that Botsford had abandoned Lowell, and she made him go back to Argentina to help the poet. Soon afterwards, Blair Clark flew down to Buenos Aires and took his friend back to New York. Though the South American trip was cut short, there were even more problems on the way home. Clark recalled that by the time the plane reached its first stop, Asunción, Paraguay, Lowell had fallen in love with the stewardess. Though she managed to elude him, he was terribly keen to accompany her, marry her and begin a *vida nueva* in some remote fastness of South America.[31]

III

Over the years Lowell was confined in five different countries and in fifteen psychiatric hospitals and clinics.[32] Though the time spent in them was certainly not pleasant, these places calmed him after the emotional devastation of his mania. They could not cure him, but provided the security of a refuge and a rest home. He compared his hermetic existence in the asylums to the self-enclosed life of boarding schools and writers' colonies as well as to the close confinement of jails and prisons. As he told William Carlos Williams, who'd also been confined after a mental breakdown, all the patients "are of the opinion that it is better on the outside but all, including myself, agree that we were lucky to have such a place to go to when we needed it."[33]

Grimly joking about a serious subject, Lowell told Bishop, "There's a saying that the true Bostonian has 'a share in the Athenaeum, a lot in Mount Auburn [cemetery] and an uncle in McLean.'" Lowell himself had a family plot in Dunbarton cemetery and was a frequent inhabitant of McLean. With its expansive three-story buildings set amid 240 acres, McLean resembled a college campus and had a number of distinguished New England alumni. Emerson's brother, Henry Adams' wife and even William James had all been treated there. Lowell, with a captive audience, was right in his element, lecturing the patients and haranguing the nurses on the merits of chastity.

Lowell and Marilyn Monroe were fellow inmates at Columbia Presbyterian in March 1961 (though they did not have visiting privileges) just as he and Lepke had been in the West Street Jail.[34] The poet William Meredith, who visited Lowell at the Institute of Living in Hartford, said it had the same luxurious appointments as McLean: "It's for the rich. I don't think they have any scholarship students there. You pay an awful lot of money and you get the amenities of a civilized hotel along with your psychiatric treatment. The thing that struck me about those visits was that he'd get through two pounds of chocolate and two packs of cigarettes a day."[35] Not all Lowell's stays were so comfortable. When Al Alvarez visited Lowell in Greenways in London, it seemed to resemble the Clínica Bethlehem more than a luxury hotel and was "a shabby establishment, more like a boarding house than a nursing home."[36]

Lowell was variously labeled psychotic, paranoid, hypomanic, schizophrenic and manic depressive, and treated with hydrotherapy, electric shock, dynamic psychoanalysis and a potent cocktail of drugs. Nevertheless, his attacks continued inexorably every other year. His most influential analyst was Dr. Viola Bernard, whom he began to see after moving from Boston to New York in 1967. Born in Manhattan in 1907, the daughter of a wealthy German Jewish businessman, she graduated from Cornell Medical School and taught at Columbia, was briefly married and soon divorced. One of Lowell's lovers described Bernard as "a diminutive, red-haired, older woman who looked like a librarian."[37] John Thompson, referring to Bernard, stated that Lowell's "treatment was useless. At one time he had some kind of half-assed analysis."[38]

Hardwick agreed with Thompson that Lowell never cared a fig about psychoanalysis, but followed medical advice and dutifully turned up for his recumbent parleys. He maintained, in a letter to Bishop, that all the thousands of hours of "psychiatry and therapy I've had, almost 19 years, was as irrelevant as it would have been for a broken leg."[39] Caroline Blackwood, speaking of a male doctor in New York, was most vehement that the analytic sessions were counterproductive: "Cal knew it was pointless: he meant it to be pointless. It took him hours to get to this man and it was a waste of working time. The analysts were hopeless at getting him into hospital, because they said it would upset the transference if they took an aggressive line. So they'd hang around, letting him get worse and worse."[40]

In the 1950s and 60s Lowell had electro-convulsive therapy (ECT), a modern version of the shocks that brought Dr. Frankenstein's monster to life. Hemingway endured similar barbaric shock treatments that took place at the same time as Lowell's. In the hospital

the attendants clamped the patients' wrists and ankles, put graphite salve on their temples as a conducent, gave them a piece of rubber hose to bite on, fastened the electrodes to their scalp, turned the dial and released the current that passed through two layers of skin and bone and entered the brain. After a minute or so, the electricity left a sparky smell of burning, corrosion and battery acid.

The power applied ranged from 70 to 150 volts (about the same consumed by a large light bulb) and the electric shock lasted for more than one minute. These "electrical inductions of experimental epilepsy" produced seizures that had "characteristics similar to those of epileptic patients." ECT was supposed to unsettle the brain patterns that were causing psychopathic behavior and allow healthier ones to take their place. [41]

But they intensified instead of relieving Hemingway's depression and didn't help Lowell. In "A Mad Negro Soldier Confined at Munich," Lowell compared the electric current to a "trolley pole sparking at contact."

The French author Antonin Artaud found the effects of this treatment terrifying: "The electric shocks make me despair, take my memory away, numb my thinking and my heart, make me absent and aware of myself as absent. I see myself pursuing my own existence for weeks, like a dead man at the side of a living man who is no longer himself." [42] In addition to this sense of self-alienation, which made Lowell feel as if he were already dead, he feared (as the therapist Eileen Simpson observed), "that the next time, or the time after, he would not recover. Or, if he did, that he would be released with the part of his brain he used for writing poetry burned out by the high voltages of the shock machine. Would his illness finish him as a writer?" [43]

Lowell's shock treatments were eventually replaced by drugs: sodium amytal, a barbiturate antidepressant; thorazine, an antipsychotic; and in 1967 lithium, a chemical salt and mood stabilizer used to combat both depression and mania. But withdrawal from or overdoses of these drugs caused anxiety, tremors and even seizures similar to those induced by ECT. After a few comparatively stable years in which the manic episodes occurred less frequently, the benign effect of lithium—which Lowell usually increased when he felt an attack coming on and often mixed with heavy drinking—began to wear off. He then suffered the same mania with Blackwood in the 1970s as he had with Hardwick in the 1950s and 1960s. At a dinner party in New York in the spring of 1975, Lowell suddenly became unconscious and fell over. He was rushed to Mount Sinai hospital where the doctors found that he'd overdosed on lithium.

In a letter of September 1967, Mary McCarthy, for rather surprising reasons, objected to his taking lithium and felt he'd be better off without it. Lithium, she thought, "has disclosed, by keeping him 'normal,' how mad he is all the time, even when on his good behavior." The doctor had told Hardwick: "The salts will prevent manic outbreaks, but they can't change the fact that he is crazy." McCarthy believed that Hardwick enjoyed the power she had over Lowell when he was sick, drugged and weak. "My opinion," she said, "is that it would be better to let him be crazy once a year, be locked up, emerge penitent, etc., than to have him subdued by this drug in a sort of private zoo—his home—with Lizzie as his keeper. But she prefers it that way."[44] McCarthy preferred the crazy Cal to the drugged one. But she didn't have to suffer as Lowell did, and didn't show much sympathy for his illness or his wife's struggle to deal with it.

Lowell's half-sane condition could sometimes be as painful as his madness. The ironically titled "Home After Three Months Away" suggests a permanent return after a routine absence. But the line "Dearest, I cannot loiter here," is especially poignant. Paroled at home only for the weekend, Lowell has to abandon his beloved daughter, who lathers her own face to persuade him to shave, and return to the close confinement of McLean.[45]

Mixing pride as a poet with humiliation as a patient, and swirling from bewilderment to disgust, Lowell was a phoenix who repeatedly rose from the flames that consumed all those around him. When mad, he had no conscience; when sane, he was guilt-stricken and ashamed. He told Jarrell, who was also mentally unstable, "what's worst, I think, is the groveling, low as dirt purgatorial feelings with which one emerges."[46] Remorseful as he remembered his mad behavior and the pain he'd caused others, Lowell also became deeply depressed and fearful that the tragic pattern would recur. He would behave atrociously, hurt everyone, suffer from his memories, fall into depression, fight his way out and eventually return to anguished delirium. Anthony Hecht, who'd been through it all, recalled: "His vulnerability was touching. Cal would impose himself and demand total affection and support and forgiveness for all the bad things he had done. And yet he was severely critical of himself when he was at the bottom. His Puritanism was most merciless when he was ill"—and his courage most impressive.[47]

FIVE
Elizabeth Hardwick, 1949–1970

I

Elizabeth Hardwick (1916–2007) was Lowell's firm anchor between two turbulent marriages to emotionally unstable women. Though their backgrounds were very different, she reinforced his Southern connections. Lowell's mother and Hardwick's mother both came from North Carolina; and Hardwick—like Allen Tate and Robert Penn Warren, Caroline Gordon and Carley Dawson—was born in Kentucky. Lowell was the unhappy only son of an only son; Hardwick, the eighth of eleven children in a Presbyterian family, grew up happy and secure, cared for by her older siblings as well as her parents. Her father, a plumbing and heating contractor, sent almost all his numerous children to college. Hardwick always maintained her strong family ties, but wanted to keep her two worlds separate. When her Southern relatives visited New York she'd tell her friends, "you don't want to know them."[1]

Lexington is a college town in the Kentucky bluegrass country. Hardwick remembered "Main Street, the ten-cent store, the old cigar store . . . the movie theaters . . . the sandwiches on soft, white Kleenexy bread . . . the July dress sales,"[2] the public library, the hotel lobbies and the red-light district—all characteristic of small town America. The street where she lived was on the way to the Keeneland racetrack, and in her teens she'd sit on the front porch and flirt with the passing jockeys. Exploring religion and politics, she had "fugitive trips to evangelical tent meetings when she was a teen-ager, and a stint as a Communist at the University of Kentucky."[3] In college Hardwick showed some daring and courage when her drunken suitor passed out and, never having handled a car before, she "drove home twenty miles and through traffic."[4]

Just as Lowell had moved from north to south, from Boston to Tennessee, so Hardwick moved from south to north, from Lexington to New York. While earning her master's degree at Columbia University, she led a bohemian life and chastely shared a flat with a homosexual who took her to Harlem jazz clubs. An attractive young woman, she had a pretty heart-shaped face, with hair parted in the middle and wavy at the sides, blue eyes and a delightful Southern drawl. Men recalled "being stunned by how beautiful she was—graceful, slender, animated, fair, wide-eyed, pleasurable to watch and to be with."[5]

Like the hero in John Berryman's story "The Imaginary Jew" who sympathized with the oppressed race, Sylvia Plath who in "Daddy" said "I may well be a Jew" and Lowell himself who was proud of his Jewish ancestors, Hardwick identified with Jews and had the extraordinary ambition of refashioning herself as a New York Jewish intellectual. She admired the Jewish tradition, so different from her own, "of rational skepticism . . . a certain deracination . . . openness to European culture . . . questioning the arrangements of society, sometimes called radicalism."[6] Her mentor in this high-powered world was the prominent Jewish intellectual and editor of the *Partisan Review,* Philip Rahv. He was Mary McCarthy's lover. After she left him for Edmund Wilson, he married McCarthy's Vassar classmate, the wealthy architect Nathalie Swan. Hardwick later succeeded McCarthy as Rahv's lover.

Unlike Hardwick, Rahv had a cosmopolitan, adventurous and politically committed life. Born Ivan Greenberg in the Ukraine, the son of a Zionist shopkeeper living among Gentile peasants, Rahv (1908–1973) invented his pseudonym, which means "rabbi" in Hebrew. After the Russian civil war, his family emigrated to Palestine, where his father opened a furniture factory, and in 1922 they finally moved to America. Rahv went to school in Rhode Island, worked as an advertising copywriter in Oregon, settled in New York during the Depression and became a Marxist. He founded the influential *Partisan Review* with William Phillips in 1933 and broke with the Soviet Party line during the bloodthirsty Moscow Purge Trials in 1937. Though he never went to college, he later became a professor at Brandeis University. While remaking herself, Hardwick admired Rahv's ability to create an identity in a new world and become a driving force in radical literary circles. He was an inspiring example of the *carrière ouverte aux talents.*

Mary McCarthy, still swooning over Rahv long after his death, wrote that "he had a shy, soft voice (when he was not shouting), big, dark lustrous eyes, which he rolled with great expression, and the look of a bambino in an Italian sacred painting."[7] After reading the poems in Lowell's *Life Studies,* Rahv prophetically declared in his strong Russian accent, "Diss is da break-through for Cal and for poetry. Da one real advance since Eliot."[8] In "Man and Wife" Lowell recalled the memorable evening when he was overcome by the heady mixture of alcohol and the ravishing Hardwick, and "outdrank the Rahvs in the heat/of Greenwich Village, fainting at your feet."[9] Hardwick remembered the combative fury of those intellectual encounters that toughened her up: "An evening at the Rahvs was to enter a ring of bullies, each one bullying the other. . . . There was an equality of vehemence that exhausted itself and the wicked bottles of Four Roses whiskey around midnight—until the next time."[10]

More aggressive than Lowell, Rahv had a way with women. He exuded what Irving Howe called "sexual magnetism—'primitive, even animal-like.'"[11] Gertrude Buckman called him "crude, sexually aggressive and unconcerned about rebuffs."[12] Hardwick, who overcame her fear and entered his harem, confessed that she was at first "terrified of the great pasha. Usually described as gruff or grumpy—he was also curious, sly and prying" about her sex life.[13] Rahv's wife Nathalie was listed in the Social Register. Lowell recorded a dream that satirized Rahv's social climbing, snobbery and rejection of his old Marxist principles: "I had a strange dream two nights ago about Philip Rahv, ascending the social ladder rung by rung as I climbed down. I think at the end his two sons were safely in Groton 'de only place to send dem,' while Harriet was graduating from the local public school. We whittle away our inheritance. I think my last words were, 'Is this what *PR* was all about?' And Philip said, 'of course.' Have you ever noticed how snobbish the old rebel bohemians are? No one believes in society now except Mary [McCarthy] and Philip."[14] Rahv inherited a valuable estate from his third wife, Theo Stillman, whom he'd married in 1956 after divorcing Nathalie Swan. At his death in 1973 he left nearly a million dollars.

Hardwick said that Lowell often criticized her infatuation with Rahv's journal: "He sometimes found my *Partisan Review* soul more than a little tiresome. . . . One of his jokes was: 'I am going to put you in a crate with a glass of water and a copy of *Partisan Review,* take the crate to the railroad station and put a big sign on it saying: One Way.'"[15] She sharpened her critical claws in the *Partisan Review* and in 1948, before she knew Lowell, savaged the rather manicured stories of his old friend Peter Taylor. She thought Taylor's cautious reserve ruined his fiction, which could be saved only by a burst of emotion: "He is too serene, too precocious. In his stories one longs, now and then, for harshness, indiscretion, that large, early ugliness a young writer can well afford, a battle with the inexpressible." Wounded by her perceptive review, Taylor complained to Lowell, "How could any magazine print the tripe Elizabeth Hardwick writes for criticism? I had never realized how truly dreadful she is till I saw her mind and her prose style at work on my own dear stories."[16]

While still writing for the *Partisan Review* and deeply involved with its social circle, Hardwick had published her first, rather weak autobiographical novel, *The Ghostly Lover* (1945). In an atmosphere of inertia and dreamy subjectivity, it portrayed a young woman's striving to break free from her Southern origins among the New York intellectuals. In the *New York Times Book Review* of April 29, 1945, Gertrude Buckman (a contributor to the *Partisan Review*) generously called Hardwick "a new writer of great talent and promise." Thus, in the circumscribed literary life of New York, Lowell's future lover reviewed the book of his future wife.

Before her involvement with Lowell, Hardwick felt equally at ease with both the Russian Rahv and the Southern Allen Tate. She advanced her literary career by sleeping with both of them and also published her stories in Tate's *Sewanee Review*. In his most reverent manner Tate declared, "You, as a Presbyterian atheist, have evidently the compassion that we expect only of the Blessed Virgin."[17] Another eminent literary lover was Arthur Koestler, who met Hardwick at a *Partisan Review* party in the spring of 1948, noted her careerism and called her a "charming, nice, calculating Kentucky girl."[18]

Hardwick was talkative and playful, clever and sympathetic in a gracious Southern belle style that went over well in New York. Esther Brooks, her close friend, called her intelligent and opinionated, but nearly hysterical when arguing. Hardwick claimed she had erased all traces of Kentucky from her speech, but actually spoke with a strong Southern accent. Wearied by commonplace conversation, Hardwick would often insist, "Honey, it's just too boring."[19] One observer said that of all the women in that crowd, she was "the prettiest and sexiest and the easiest to have a love affair with."[20] William Phillips, coeditor of the *Partisan Review,* linked her personality to her polemics: "Articulate, witty, very clever, freewheeling, she became a master of the slashing critical style of the politicized literary intellectuals."[21] David Laskin, biographer of the Partisans, added that "Hardwick also had a taste for the quick, barbed exchange, a gift for devastating gossip, a commitment to serious political discourse, and a beguiling gracious modesty that concealed a restless, often brilliantly original mind. She could be quite nasty when she wanted to be."[22] Some of Lowell's friends found Hardwick cocky, acerbic and menacing. The novelist J. F. Powers called her "tough and ambitious,"[23] and she provoked "intense dislike" in the poet W. D. Snodgrass.[24] Randall Jarrell emphasized her insincerity and dishonesty, and (like Mary McCarthy) resented the way she took control of Lowell when he was manic. In "A Well-to-Do Invalid" Jarrell alluded to Lowell as "a natural / disaster she has made her own."[25]

II

Hardwick met Lowell at Rahv's flat in Greenwich Village in 1946, and spent a lot of time with him at the Yaddo writers' colony in 1948–49. At a poetry conference in November 1948, Hardwick and Bishop staggered back to his room with the drunken Lowell. As they took off his shirt Hardwick ecstatically declared, "Why he's an Adonis." From then on, Bishop said, "I knew it was all over."[26] The following month Peter Taylor, still smarting from Hardwick's fierce review, tried to warn Lowell about her. Learning that his brother-in-law, an eligible young man, would be arriving at Yaddo on the same day as Hardwick, he expressed concern about her character and added, "She's dangerous for you too." Lowell replied, "Maybe I can interest them in each other." Taylor then said, "Cal, that would be the most blessed thing in the world for you."[27] In March 1949 Allen Tate, her former lover, also tried in vain to warn Hardwick about Lowell. He wrote that when he heard that Lowell "had fallen in love with you and was trying to marry you, Caroline said, 'Poor Miss Hardwick!' I knew Cal was in one of his manic phases but I could scarcely believe you had lost your reason."[28] Gertrude Buckman, Lowell's former lover, believed that in allowing herself to fall for him Hardwick "had made her pact with the devil."[29]

But Lowell, however diabolical, had a formidable combination of authority, celebrity and potential wealth. Still only thirty years old in 1947, the year before Hardwick fell in love with him, he'd been suddenly catapulted to fame. He won the Pulitzer Prize for *Lord Weary's Castle,* had been awarded $1,000 from the American Academy of Arts and Letters and

$2,500 from the Guggenheim Foundation, was appointed Poetry Consultant at the Library of Congress with a salary of $5,000 and had an offer to teach at the University of Iowa. After an article with his photograph had appeared in *Life* magazine on March 18, 1947, the handsome hunk received an invitation to take a screen test in Hollywood. In contrast to his critical friends, Lowell, excited by his love affair, found Hardwick immensely appealing. In a letter of January 1949 to the still wounded Peter Taylor, Lowell called her "slip-shod, good humored, malicious (harmless) and humorous—full of high spirits, rattling a lot of sense and sheer stuff—very good company," and praised her "marvelous tenderness and humor and a mind that flashes." [30]

The critic Alfred Kazin, who saw Lowell and Hardwick at Yaddo, was enviously impressed by their Scott-and-Zelda glamour. They continued to shine throughout their literary life in Boston and New York, where they knew every important cultural figure in America:

> Lowell and Elizabeth Hardwick were a brilliant couple, but Lowell was just a little too dazzling at the moment . . . wonderful and frightening.
>
> He was not just damned good, suddenly famous and deserving his fame; he was in a state of grandeur not negotiable with lesser beings. He was a Lowell; he was handsome, magnetic, rich, wild with excitement about his powers, wild over the many tributes to him from Pound, Santayana, his old friends Tate and Jarrell and Warren. Flannery O'Connor, who was also at Yaddo, seemed to be attending Lowell with rapture. [31]

Despite his pleasurable dalliance with Hardwick, the mania that Tate had warned about soon exploded at Yaddo. Stifled and rather resentful in the luxurious surroundings, Lowell compared himself to the guests of Shakespeare's misanthropic Timon of Athens, who offered them warm water instead of food and then flung it in their faces: "I guess everyone here feels like Timon's guests, and has to blow off steam." [32] In February 1949, loyally supported by Hardwick, Lowell led a vehement and irrational campaign to fire Elizabeth Ames, the director of Yaddo, for granting prolonged stays and extraordinary privileges to the Communist writer Agnes Smedley. But his putsch failed. Immediately afterward he had his first manic breakdown and spent three months in Baldpate, a private mental hospital north of Boston. Hardwick's letters to him reveal that she knew all about his overpowering, unstable personality and the infidelity that had marked his previous marriage to Jean Stafford. She realized from the start that her relationship with him would be difficult and troubled.

Assuming her Southern belle persona, Hardwick said that she disliked aggressiveness and detested anger. She told Edmund Wilson how frightened she was by Lowell's mania, which reminded her of the deranged characters in a Russian novel. But she was also excited by his madness and confessed, "Once he was in the hospital—unable to harm himself and others with the devastating strain and reckless behavior a manic attack puts upon the sufferer and those around him—I found I could hardly wait to go there for a visit." She described Baldpate as a "quite good small hospital run by an adorable old German doctor, Dr. George Schlomer," [33] and revealed that Lowell's family and friends opposed her as they would later oppose all the women he became involved with: "I went up to see Lowell and I think both Merrill Moore and the family thought that was a very bad idea and got quite mad at the doctor, but the doctor—if I remember—got rather turned off them. He was a very reserved and dignified old man, and he seemed to look on my visits favorably." [34]

Lowell was naturally pleased by Hardwick's appearance in the hospital, which revealed her love and rescued him from despair. He apologized for the trouble he'd caused and felt obliged to tell her about the problems she faced: "your visit was wonderful and *saning*. Hope you can stand me still. . . . I think of you all the time; and worry so about all I have dumped on you." [35] Like Franz Kafka, who asked his fiancée Felice Bauer, "How can you, if you are in your right mind, continue to stay with me? . . . I could very easily feed on some one else's compassion," [36] Lowell showed the worst side of himself in order to test Hardwick's ability to endure him. He gave her fair warning, which she bravely ignored.

But Hardwick, then and later on, was always amazed by his powers of recuperation and found them almost as jolting as his breakdowns. She suffered herself and suffered with him during his manic periods, and waited for the good times to return. She recalled that when he was released from Baldpate "he was in a very depressed state about what had happened, saying, 'No one can care for me. I've ruined my life. I'll always be mad.' So he literally had no place to go. He couldn't go home. . . . So we got married"—and *she* cared for him. [37] Mary McCarthy was bridesmaid and lent Hardwick her Balenciaga dress for the occasion.

Lowell's family was present in July 1949 at his wedding to Hardwick, though her family was absent. She warily recalled, "So we got married, in his parents' house. He wanted to do it, and I wanted to do it. I don't think it was a very happy occasion for anybody else. He had just come out of an illness and here he was taking on something else. One doctor at the hospital said: 'He certainly needs someone, but if I were you I wouldn't do it.' Well, we did."[38] Marriage to Lowell, when he was mentally ill, both tested and proved the depth of her commitment. She admired his genius and wanted to protect him. She remained faithful to him, through all his travails, out of pity, charity, faith, masochism and love.

When they married, Charlotte expressed her usual hostility and asked Blair Clark "whether I thought Elizabeth was 'suitable' and would 'take good care of Bobby,' the same questions she had put to me about Jean."[39] Charlotte thought Hardwick was opinionated (that is, didn't agree with everything Charlotte said), but conceded that she had good manners and played the role of dutiful daughter-in-law. Lowell and Hardwick both found the strain of Charlotte's criticism unbearable. Hardwick complained that "the horrid reality of Mrs. L. battered and crushed us."[40]

Theirs was a union of opposites: the Massachusetts, Episcopalian, upper-class, trust-funded, only child of a naval officer and the Kentucky, Presbyterian, lower-middle-class, hard up, eighth child of a plumber. Yet she was personally ambitious and impressed by the New England aura surrounding him, and treasured the prestige and power that came with being Mrs. Robert Lowell. By marrying him she climbed higher than she had ever dreamed, from provincial obscurity to a glorious lineage, with all its privileges and accoutrements. He arranged her entry into the *New York Review of Books,* which supplanted the *Partisan Review* as the leading intellectual journal, and greatly enhanced her literary reputation. But the prospect of marriage put an intolerable burden on Lowell, making him tense and fearful. He felt threatened by permanent insanity, fell into a deep depression and spent his honeymoon in the Payne Whitney Clinic—the alma mater of Jean Stafford. For the next twenty years Hardwick's identity would be intimately bound up with his, for better or usually for worse.

III

Hardwick, Lowell's match in many ways, provided sympathetic encouragement, praised his work and capably managed the practical affairs of her impractical husband. When he was ill, she corrected his student papers at

Boston University and Harvard, attended the premieres of his plays, and told him about the performances of the actors and response of the audience. The poet Donald Hall, invited to dinner with the Lowells, found her amusing and charming. When Lowell mentioned a man who'd slept with "everyone," she demurred and replied, "I've searched my mind. . . ." [41]

Richard Wilbur found her chatty and amiable. He said she held her own with Lowell and did not defer to the Master. Wilbur noted that "she knew from the beginning that Lowell was different—self-indulgent, self-absorbed with his career, which always came first—but took this on. Unlike most couples, they were part of the same stream. Both were writers and the world of arts was very important to them." Wilbur believed her ambition strengthened her emotional bond with Lowell: "Her marriage tremendously advanced her career. She would not have walked out of the world in which Lowell was a distinguished member and *the* name." [42]

They had a marriage of true minds and each valued the other's intelligence. In her *Paris Review* interview, Hardwick praised the thrilling quality of Lowell's mind and emphasized that "Cal had a great influence on every aspect of my life. In literary matters, his immense learning and love of literature were a constant magic for me." [43] The equally admiring Lowell—slovenly himself and scattering random compliments—wrote that he loved "your varied interests, your refreshing teaching, your neat clothes, your capacity for keen conversation and argument." [44]

The poet William Meredith remarked that Hardwick always handled Lowell like a Southern mother. He quoted Lowell emphasizing her hidden, sensitive side and describing her "as delicate and as frightened as a hare. And when I hold her sometimes she trembles continuously from being held." [45] Hardwick often had to control her rowdy guests as well as her husband. Dwight Macdonald, a critic in the *Partisan Review* circle, was notorious for his frequent outbursts of ridicule and contempt. When he arrived at a party at the Lowells', "Hardwick shepherded him through the room with a quiet plea: 'Now Dwight, don't raise a row, don't cause a ruckus, don't be rude.'" [46]

On other social occasions, especially when Hardwick had too much to drink, she could be aggressively rude to her own guests. When they met his old Kenyon friends, the David McDowells, in Rome in 1952, Lowell reported that Hardwick had told them "for ten minutes, with devastating charm and mobile face, that they talked too much, until they dramatically strode into the Roman dark and out of our lives." [47] Amused and almost pleased by her offensive performance, Lowell didn't seem to mind the loss of a an old friend.

A friend's wife witnessed Hardwick provoke another quarrel in the Lowells' New York apartment. They invited the eminent Italian novelist Giorgio Bassani, whom they hadn't met before and who came with the Italian consul. Hardwick, who'd been a theater critic, declared ex cathedra that Luigi Pirandello had changed the theater forever. Bassani, a gentle and courteous man, claimed that many modern playwrights had also done this, and she got into a terrible argument with him. She shouted at him, and he got so upset that his English failed and he shifted into Italian. Lowell, enjoying the spectacle (as he did in Rome), remained a silent witness. Bassani then abruptly announced that he had to leave. After he'd gone Hardwick, exasperated by his refusal to agree with her, exclaimed, "Well, he was pretty disappointing." A guest thought Hardwick was pretty hard to please.

Another extraordinary incident (unnoticed by writers on Lowell) took place, with Hardwick present, in their New York apartment in January 1961, when Allen Ginsberg gave Lowell a psychedelic drug. Ginsberg told his accomplice Timothy Leary that Lowell needed special handling:

> "We're not dealing here with a Dionysian fun lover. He's a good guy with a psycho streak. We should be cautious about the dose."
>
> "Why are we giving psilocybin to Lowell?," asked Peter [Orlovsky].
>
> "We hope to loosen him up, make him happier," said Allen. "And on the political front, if Pulitzer Prize–winner Robert Lowell has a great session, his product endorsement will influence lots of intellectuals." . . .
>
> Three hours later, Lowell was beaming. According to Leary he shook his hand and said, "Now I know what Blake and St. John of the Cross were talking about. This experience is what I was seeking when I became a Catholic." Allen, however, remembered a less enthusiastic reaction. At the door, leaving, he said [quoting Chaucer's Prioress' tale], "*Amor vincit omnia*," to which Lowell replied "I'm not sure." . . .
>
> [Leary thought they should have given him a heavier dose and taken him all the way.]
>
> "That could have been risky for us," Allen said. "I wouldn't want

to be known as the guy who put America's leading poet round the bend."[48]

Already heavily medicated, Lowell wanted to try the drug, and Ginsberg, exploiting him to generate good publicity, was glad to oblige. Hardwick let him take the sacred mushroom, though a bad trip would have propelled him into a risky manic episode.

Lowell and Hardwick often had violent quarrels that escalated from her criticism of his defective driving to his wounding insults—and worse. He noted that when she got drunk, she'd ask ignorant questions like, " 'Did Pascal live before Plato?,' then vanish to read the *New York Review of Books*."[49] Sometimes, when completely exasperated or trying to put her down when he was courting another woman, Lowell would remark, "Everybody has noticed that you've been getting mighty dumb lately."[50]

But Hardwick, far from submissive, sharply retaliated. Referring to her personal attacks as well as to her literary criticism, Lowell said, "I have a razor-sharp critic in my household."[51] Alcohol always loosened her tongue and released her anger. He recalled that after drinking a formidable number of martinis, she "began sotto voce an amazingly frank and detailed reappraisal of our entire marriage" that went on for an agonizing ninety minutes.[52] As with Stafford and Dawson, Lowell, when drunk or manic, became violent. Hardwick would gently remind him, when he calmed down, that "other men don't hit their wives."[53] Obsessed by the fragility of their marriage, a kind of *folie à deux,* Lowell worried that he'd break down again while Hardwick wondered how much longer she could stand it.

A revealing (and again unnoticed) incident, subject to various interpretations, took place in Boston in November 1956. It featured an unnamed Hungarian American student in his Boston University class, who wrote him bad love poems. Edmund Wilson, who had a soft spot for Hungarian women, recorded in his diary: "He had a pretty little girl in Cambridge, who wanted to write poetry and with whom he had been going to bed. He told Elena [Wilson] and me both about her: 'She looks like a Renoir'— and when I met her, I saw that she did. . . . After dinner Elizabeth went upstairs to her room and burst into tears, and the mistress remained with the younger crowd and stupidly tried to play hostess."[54] Most wives, instead of retreating, would have ordered the girl out of the house. But Hardwick, instead of attacking the girl with her caustic tongue, was reduced to flight and tears.

Hardwick associated Lowell's affairs with his mania. But it's quite possible that Lowell, when completely sane, behaved cruelly by inviting the girl without telling Hardwick who she was, and Hardwick was shocked to discover that Lowell was sleeping with her. Though in alien territory, the young girl had a distinct advantage. Enthralled by her sensual beauty, Lowell ignored his wife's feelings. Most significantly, Hardwick, seven months' pregnant and dressed in maternity clothes, was then more prone to tears, more anxious about Lowell's affair, more fearful of his possible desertion. Hardwick put up with Lowell's infidelities for longer than most women ever would. So it's not surprising that she sometimes reached the limit of her tolerance and broke down under the strain. Esther Brooks recalled that on other occasions, when Lowell's mania got absolutely out of control, Hardwick would send him from New York up to Cambridge to stay with her and phone Brooks to declare, "Honey, I can't cope. He's on the way!" [55] Lowell would then storm around town and collect a train of people, former and would-be students, who were amused and enthralled by his mania and ended up in Brooks' living room. She'd then have to clear them out and drive him to McLean.

Despite their quarrels and Lowell's mania, Hardwick's letters to him were kind and forgiving, devoted and loving. She was always careful, after their numerous fights, to leave the way open for future reconciliation. *Seduction and Betrayal,* the title of Hardwick's book of essays, expresses one aspect of their marriage. It helps explain her unusually tolerant attitude toward Lowell, whose superiority she always acknowledged. In her chapter on Zelda Fitzgerald, whose novel rivaled her husband's works, Hardwick wrote that the less talented partners of great writers not only had to submit to the interests of the more talented ones, but even had to sacrifice themselves:

> In the case of artists these intense relations are curiously ambivalent, undefined collaborations—the two share in perceptions, temperament, the struggle for creation, for the powers descending downward from art, for the reputation, achievement, stability, for their own uniqueness—that especially. Still, only one of the twins is real as an artist, as a person with a special claim upon the world, upon the indulgence of society. . . . The presence of an intelligent, sympathetic, clever sensibility, always at hand, always bright and somehow creative, is a source, even a source of material. [56]

The wife as a "source of material" would later become an extremely contentious issue when Lowell published extracts from her letters in *The Dolphin*.

In "Easter 1916" W. B. Yeats wrote, "Too long a sacrifice / Can make a stone of the heart,"[57] but Hardwick's heart continued to beat in sympathetic rhythm with Lowell's. Their surprised and baffled friends tried to explain her capacity for suffering and tolerance of his destructive behavior. John Thompson remarked that "Elizabeth's fidelity and sacrifice is so great that I think it puzzles even her."[58] Yet Stanley Kunitz hit the mark by observing that "Hardwick loved Lowell's name and prestige, was willing to put up with any humiliation to keep it and retained considerable power from Lowell long after his death."[59] Hardwick admired, respected and loved Lowell's humor, his brilliance, his love of writing, his dedication, his inspiration and his genius. She even said, like a Graham Greene character making a pact with God, that she'd be willing to "kill myself if it would cure you."[60] She called Lowell "the most extraordinary person I have ever known, like no one else—unreplaceable, unaccountable."[61]

IV

From October 1950 to December 1952 the Lowells lived in Europe, first in Florence, then for seven months in Amsterdam (so that Lowell could study Dutch history and art), and also traveled widely, from England to Turkey. Though Europe was culturally stimulating, the experience also put additional strains on their marriage. When they were moving from Italy to Holland and temporarily separated, Lowell seemed lost without her. After all their bitter fights, he promised to be more kind and regretted the clash of egos that threatened to destroy their marriage:

> The unmarried life is too much for me—a whirl of impressions around one's bruised pulp! Try not to get all nerve-wrung and hysterical. . . . Nothing matters so much as our own lives—we need each other so desperately—at least I need you, and I am really going to be more considerate from now on and take care of you and myself in doing so. . . .
>
> I am knotted in my nerves and keep asking myself where the Hell we are going. Where is there any help for either of us to give, or to take? . . .

I miss you, I need you, I need sympathetic, level-headed encouragement. I want to give it. We've got to stop this state of "sauve qui peut."[62]

When they traveled together Hardwick found Lowell exhausting. "Cal just loved it," she said, "he was the most tireless sightseer. We'd get up at 7 and walk all day and come back to wherever we were at 5—seeing everything." In 1951 she also traveled without Lowell, sent ahead to find a place to live. She took an exhausting train trip from Florence to Amsterdam, and told him that taking care of all the practical details during the frequent moves of the last two years in Europe had been a tremendous burden. She felt anxious, miserable and close to a nervous breakdown. She later recalled, "I went to Holland alone to look for a place. I found it absolutely terrifying—I didn't know anyone there, I didn't know what to look for and so on. I was full of complaints—it all seemed so dour and hard to manage."[63]

Once settled in Amsterdam, they became close friends with Huyk van Leeuwen, a psychiatrist and literary critic. A year older than Lowell, whom he'd met at the Salzburg Seminars, he was engaged to his future wife Judith Herzberg (born 1934), then a promising and now a distinguished poet. In a recent letter, Herzberg illuminated the tensions in the Lowells' marriage, their contrasting characters and their animated talk:

> They were never calm, they were always intense in whatever they expressed. I do remember that Cal was very irritated when they had planned to go out and Elizabeth wasn't ready. He couldn't get used to the procrastination.
> I found her frighteningly severe and intellectual. They had a totally different style of conversation. Like a bear and a bird, even when they talked at the same time, which they often did.
> I was fascinated not only by what he said, which I only understood parts of, but by the waving of his hands as he spoke. The movements resembled the puzzling ones of a duck's feet under water. He could go off on a tangent, but his erudition was overwhelming.[64]

As miserable in cold and uncomfortable Amsterdam as Stafford had been in Baton Rouge, Hardwick wrote, "I think only of leaving the Netherlands, my only thought, in fact, for the last seven months." Though longing for the sunny Mediterranean, she had to submit to Lowell's wishes.

She felt battered by living with him and wrote, "by now Cal has me so well trained I sometimes feel as if I were failing in all my school subjects."[65] Lowell knew that she found Holland completely dull and depressing, but they stayed on through the winter and paid the price. He admitted that during those " 'rain-every-day months' in Amsterdam the two of them had 'both suffered from the spleen and mastered . . . every wrinkle of domestic argument and sabotage.' "[66]

When their money and patience ran out, they returned to America. In the fall of 1953 Lowell took up a job at the University of Iowa, where he'd taught before the journey to Europe. The principles of New Criticism—which he'd learned from Ransom and Warren—stimulated the study of literature. Iowa City then had a population of about fifty thousand. A literary biographer wrote that "the downtown consisted of owner-run stores, second-floor law offices, taverns with pool tables in the back, and restaurants that served meat-and-potato meals."[67] After living in the cultural centers of Europe, Hardwick found it pretty depressing. "It's so flat and ugly," she lamented, "and somehow has the air and look of a temporary town. Actually, anything over fifty years old is a landmark."[68] Lowell agreed with her, but said the place was redeemed by a few good students and one highbrow movie house. He proudly told J. F. Powers that Hardwick was taking Greek and auditing his course (co-taught with a classics professor) on Homer and Pindar.

In 1955 Hardwick published her second novel, *The Simple Truth,* based on a sensational murder trial, which she'd seen in Iowa City as an accredited reporter. Her novel emphasized the responses of two people involved in the event: a graduate student on the G.I. Bill and an older woman married to a chemistry professor. The defendant is acquitted when the jury decides that the victim had not been strangled, but fell and choked to death. W. D. Snodgrass—whose confessional *Heart's Needle* had the same impact as *Life Studies* (both published in 1959)—described Hardwick's odd behavior when she was working on the novel. Clearly depressed, "she was apparently ill quite often" and received guests in her bedroom. But she could be roused from torpor to animation when urged to put on an act and do one of her theatrical performances: "Usually languid and exhausted, she could occasionally be encouraged to don a robe, get up and 'do' some well-known, eccentric acquaintance. These imitations were delicious, crackling with energy, so that even a lowly graduate student never wanted to leave the room."[69]

Domestic and house-proud, Hardwick was always eager to settle into a permanent home. Despite Lowell's trust fund, royalties, teaching salary and lecture fees, and her own modest earnings, she constantly worried about money and feared they would not have enough to pay their basic expenses. But the money Lowell inherited after Charlotte's timely death in 1954 enabled them to move from shabby flats like the ones in Amsterdam and Iowa City. In the fall of 1955 they acquired a grand house at 239 Marlborough Street, Boston, near the Charles River and the Public Garden. Lowell proudly told William Carlos Williams, "We've just bought a house in Boston a block from where I grew up. It's an unimpassioned, darkish, bricky, Londonlike street, still the mirror of propriety, but lately filling up with rooming houses and cramming schools. . . . This is the first year since 1940 when I have spent two successive autumns in the same city."[70] Expressing a certain irony about their suddenly exalted status, Hardwick said they'd become very pretentious and sociable. But living in Boston revived distressing memories of his childhood. When Lowell took one of his girlfriends to see a play in Boston, he said, "this beats going to the theater with my mother."[71] He could never shake off her pervasive influence. On another occasion, in a Boston theater with Frank Bidart, Lowell was amused and disturbed when an older woman seated behind him tapped him on the shoulder and asked, "aren't you Charlotte Winslow's son?"[72]

After six years the Lowells got tired of the provinciality of Boston and the ghosts of his past, and in 1961 moved to New York, the center of intellectual life. They sold the Marlborough Street house and bought a duplex apartment at 15 West 67th Street, just off Central Park and conveniently near the newly built Lincoln Center. The main room had a baronial fireplace, a twenty-foot-high beamed ceiling, a two-story window and a sliding ladder to reach the highest bookshelves. There was a balcony and bedrooms on the upper floor, and Lowell used an old servants' room on the top floor as his study. He later said they ought to put up a blue plaque to commemorate all the famous people who'd slept there.

Beginning in 1957 the Lowells spent summers in Castine, on the coast of Maine, an upmarket reprise of Damariscotta Mills, about eighty-five miles northeast of it. In 1964 his favorite cousin, the unmarried Harriet Winslow, died and left the more responsible Hardwick her house on the Castine Common. The Lowells' neighbors included Mary McCarthy and the poets Richard Eberhart (his old teacher) and Philip Booth, both of whom owned sailboats. Lowell described Castine, the senescent setting of "Skunk Hour," as "an ailing little town with one admiral, two retired Episcopal bishops, and a population fifty percent over 75." [73] His productive routine was, after breakfast, to pick up his mail at the post office, write in his converted barn-studio, eat a late lunch, take a nap, play tennis, and then go back to work before drinks and dinner. Outings in Castine included sailing along the Maine coast with Ted Kennedy. Hardwick, satiated with "those jet-set Kennedy women in their tight pants," refused to join the excursion, but changed her mind about the women after meeting and being charmed by Jackie Kennedy. [74]

V

Several writers close to Lowell—Stafford and Bishop, Roethke and Jarrell—had no children. Lowell was more concerned with continuing his dynasty, and Harriet's birth in January 1957 surprised their friends. Sarah Stuart, Lowell's distant cousin, noted that "for so many years they had been trying everything to have a baby, seeking help from innumerable doctors, until finally they had given up—only to go off on vacation where a few hasty embraces had resulted in Harriet." [75] Hardwick was forty years old when she gave birth to their child, who brought a new kind of tenderness into their highly intellectual life. Lowell told J. F. Powers that he was amazed at his wife's transformation: "You wouldn't know Lizzie, cooing, blasting the skin off nurses, talking a whole new baby language." [76] As Harriet grew older, Lowell called himself her boyfriend and (always literary) compared her child's headgear to Charles Bovary's absurd hat. He loved the way she lathered her own face when he shaved, and liked to quote the small child as if she were as clever as Oscar Wilde and much wiser than her father.

Keith Botsford, who met the Lowells at the airport in June 1962 when they started the ill-fated trip to Brazil and Argentina, recalled that the five-year-old Harriet "was the most objectionable child I ever met, a real pain in the ass. A first-class whiner, she hated the climate, food, being with her parents, everything. She always wanted her own way and the parents allowed her to manipulate them. She was their cherished one and only, and Lowell played the devoted father." [77] Toni Kern, a Radcliffe undergraduate who took care of Harriet on that trip, gave a completely different account of her behavior. As Lowell began to crack up, Harriet was fortunately unaware of the tragic events and had a pleasant holiday with the young nanny, who liked being with her. When Harriet was away from her parents and had settled into her new routine, she was amiable, not difficult, and enjoyed going to the beach and watching people fly kites.[78]

Lowell's friends also had contrasting views about his role as a father. Gertrude Buckman felt he "had no understanding of or interest in children, and was both whimsical and unnatural when he tried—and failed—to amuse them."[79] Karl Miller said that Lowell seemed very attached to Harriet, who was responsive, and that he developed a close relationship with her.[80] Ann Adden noted that "he loved Harriet with a purer love than for anyone else, but felt no responsibility for her as a father."[81] Frank Bidart observed that Lowell and Harriet had a sweetness and intimacy, and that Lowell was very sorry for all the pain caused by his mental illness, infidelities and fights with Hardwick. Lowell was enchanting, but incapable of the practical aspects of fatherhood, and all the responsibility rested with Hardwick.

Lowell liked to make silly jokes. When Harriet asked, "Who's Julius Caesar?," Lowell replied that he was the "first man to land on the moon." Harriet knew he was joking, but Hardwick exploded, claiming that Harriet would repeat this in her class and look foolish. As Harriet grew older, she adopted a sceptical and ironic attitude toward her parents. But when they quarreled, she'd sometimes be drawn into their disputes and forced to take sides.[82]

Esther Brooks thought Harriet's two dynamic parents made it very hard for the timid girl, who had no proper childhood. When Harriet played with Brooks' children and Hardwick sat in the living room, she'd anxiously scream up the stairs—but not actually get up to see what was happening—"Harriet, are you all right, honey?" Like most children, Harriet preferred to be left alone and allowed to play with her friends. While they were traveling in Spain, Hardwick said that Harriet, who had asthma, was not able to climb the tall Giralda tower next to the cathedral in Seville. Nevertheless, Brooks climbed up with her and Harriet, pleased with her feat, was fine. Lowell called Harriet "the sanest and most solid of us all." But he told her, "just don't find a husband who wants to talk to me about sports."[83] Lowell recorded Harriet's amusing and penetrating remarks: her put-down of Tate, "if you are still alive," and her tragic comparison, like "spiders crying together / but without tears," which suggested her own sadness.

Hardwick wrote a fictional account of her marriage in *Sleepless Nights*

(1979), published after Lowell's death. The ecstatic praise of the novel by many eminent authors testified to the power of Mrs. Robert Lowell in the New York literary world. Lowell emerges from the shadows of the novel and enters the dreams of Elizabeth, the autobiographical heroine. The romantic figure in her life also "bore a great name whose dignity extended throughout our county." His family history includes documents: "The license, the will, the property rights, income tax, the cousins, the funerals, the photographs!" and the Naval Academy plates he inherited from his father. She gives a surprisingly sympathetic portrait of the parents Lowell satirized in "91 Revere Street," writing that they dressed for dinner every night and "were in marvelous shape, very careful and prudent." She also mentions (by her initials) his favorite cousin, Harriet Winslow, who gave her name to their daughter and her house in Castine to Hardwick.

Elizabeth wants "to rescue a smart, sulky man" but is, paradoxically, always "looking for help from a man." [84] In a bitter, self-reflective moment she observes, "It is better to be exploited by the weak than by the strong. Submission to the powerful is a redundancy and very fatiguing and boring in the end. There is nothing subtle or interesting in it, mainly because the exercise is too frequent. . . . She found, with her ineluctable ill-luck, a nightmare of betrayals, lies, deceits, shocks, infidelities, dismissals."

She mentions their homes on Marlborough Street in Boston and on West 67th Street in New York. He observes that in Holland "the coziness of small countries could not always be expropriated by an invader" and that the striking Belgian place-names, Antwerp and Ghent, were (in a nice pentameter line) as "hard as the heavy cobbles in the square." But in Holland she complained, "How cold the house is. How we fight after too much gin."

She gives her fullest account of Lowell's politics and writing, mental condition and favorite animal persona when they move back to Boston: "perhaps in the end this city will interest him as it did when he was young. Now, a lot of people seem to think he's an anarchist . . . and he does often have the preoccupied look of a secret agent. Just as always he reads and writes all day, here in this house on the top floor, drinks quarts of milk, smokes cigarettes. He hates for me to play my jazz records, but sometimes I do late at night and then he dances around, off the beat, like a bear. His health? All right"—for the moment. [85] Though Elizabeth tries to suppress her late husband, he keeps resurfacing in her wandering thoughts and stylish pages, and she persuasively reveals what it was like to live with him.

VI

Hardwick hinted at Lowell's work habits in her novel, but later gave a more complete description: "All day long he lay on the bed, propped up on an elbow. And this was his life, reading, studying and writing. The papers piled up on the floor, the books on the bed, the bottles of milk on the window sill, the ashtray filled. . . . The discipline, the dedication, the endless adding to his *store,* by reading and studying—all this had, in my view, much that was heroic about it." [86] The bed brought him, a Freudian would say, close to the land of dreams and the unconscious, the milk compensated for the nursing he never had from his mother.

Lowell himself compared the chaotic condition of his study to the wrecked offices at Columbia University during the student riots in 1968. [87] He briefly cut down his smoking to a mere twenty cigarettes a day, then told J. F. Powers, "I've stopped smoking—scared to death by an article in *Time,* but after a day I know I'd rather have cancer." [88] This was sheer bravado. He expected to die (like his father) of heart disease. To rest from the intense demands of writing Lowell recharged his batteries at endless literary conferences, poetry readings and arts festivals. He could earn money and adulation, seek stimulation and hear the latest gossip, go to parties and have sexual adventures with literary groupies.

Lowell and Hardwick once planned to write a high school literature textbook for Harcourt, Brace, but found it too difficult to work together and never really got started. But she suggested the well known, tell-the-truth line in the Epilogue to *Day by Day,* "why not say what happened?" She also explained why Lowell's absolute self-absorption in his own writing prevented him from helping with her work: "His suggestions were always wonderful, but so general I couldn't make much use of them. And he was always revising his own work and showing it to me and to his friends. He was revising something the moment he got up until the moment he went to sleep, if only in his head, and so much of the time when you were alone with him was spent in reading and talking to him about what he had done during the day." Asked if Lowell's character and work had overpowered her own, Hardwick replied, "I should hope so. I had great regard and admiration for it. Learned from him and it, got pleasure from it. . . . The quality of his mind—quite the most thrilling I've known." [89]

In 1963 Lowell helped found the *New York Review of Books,* which turned out to be a spectacular success. He took out a $4,000 loan, backed by his trust fund, and convinced wealthy friends like Blair Clark to invest in the journal. Hardwick took an active role as adviser and contributor. Lowell suggested that her excitement about the new journal was similar to her response to the new baby and, in a sense, it was her new child: "I've never seen anything like Lizzie and the magazine. Instead of her somewhat murky Kentucky Scottish reserve, all is smiles, flutter and superlatives."[90]

Lowell did not publish a book between *The Mills of the Kavanaughs* (1951) and *Life Studies* (1959). His two great poems on Hardwick are best understood in the context of *Life Studies,* brought out when they'd been married for a decade. This innovative and influential book, which made most contemporary poetry seem pale and tame, had intellectual authority, contemporary relevance and tragic dignity. The cape work of his imagery and emblems of adversity fed the modern passion for pathological details. Strikingly different from the Catholic angst and religious symbolism of *Lord Weary's Castle* and *The Mills of the Kavanaughs, Life Studies* transformed his style from the baroque to the demotic, from the rhetorical to the colloquial. Finding it impossible to sustain his previous intensity, he said, "my old way of writing wore out for me, and it seemed Sisyphean to continue." He included the brilliant prose chapter, "91 Revere Street," and explained, "I found by reading aloud that I wanted more humor, more immediate clarity, fewer symbols, more of the good prose writer's realistic direct glance."[91]

Though Lowell's confessional poetry seemed new, similar shocking revelations had appeared not only in Whitman's "Calamus" poems, but also, more obliquely, in both Yeats and Eliot. Yeats' biographer Roy Foster related that "he turned into poetry his family and his past, his friendships and alliances, his enmities, his quarrels . . . his storm-wracked love for Maud Gonne" and her daughter Iseult.[92] Contrary to the tenets of the New Criticism and to his insistence on the impersonality of the poet, Eliot's work was filled with personal emotions and intimate disclosures. He wrote, more covertly and allusively than Lowell, about his own crack-up and the breakdown of his marriage. In one of the great sleights-of-hand in twentieth-century poetry, Eliot portrayed his own private misery as the universal condition of modern man. In 1923, the year after *The Waste Land* appeared, his mother recalled, "Tom wrote me before it was published that he had put so much of his own life into it." He also said that in that poem he had "crucified himself."[93] While breaking out of his puritanical carapace, Eliot was cunningly confessional; Lowell was more openly demonstrative. Clearly recognizing the personal aspect of Eliot's work, he wrote that "*The Waste Land* is sex gone haywire—trembling incapacities, [self]-disgust, and the brute compulsion to seduction. . . . Eliot in this poem has stabbed very deeply and cruelly."[94]

Written in clear, imagistic language, *Life Studies* has the characters, plot and action of a novel. Poem leads to poem, section to section, and his best book becomes a unified whole. The title suggests both paintings from live models and biographical studies from life—and from death. Part One is historical, and portrays Lowell as an exile in Europe and outsider in America. Part Two, the confessional prose in "91 Revere Street," sets the tone, makes the transition from the historical to the personal, and provides the essential background for the poems on his parents and family. Part Three, in contrast to the satire on his parents, contains affectionate elegies of four writers—Ford Madox Ford, George Santayana, Delmore Schwartz and Hart Crane—who came to sad or tragic ends. Part Four-I portrays the disease, death and graveyard of his family, his father's decline and mother's death, his own breakdowns and confinement in mental asylums. Part Four-II describes his confinement in jail and marriage problems, and ends with the equivocal mitigation of pain in "Skunk Hour."

Life Studies is emotion recollected in emotion: the worse the life and more extreme the pain, the greater the authority of suffering. The dominant theme—as in Conrad, Mann, Joyce, Kafka and Nabokov—is loss: loss of faith, friends, parents, sanity, freedom and love. Like the philosopher Santayana whom he quoted, Lowell could say, "I have enjoyed writing about my life more than living it."[95] Like Eliot, Lowell made his personal chaos symbolize the disintegration of the modern world.

The closing couplet of "Beyond the Alps"—a poem about Lowell's loss of faith and rejection of the Catholic Church—is one of his perfect and most impenetrable images: "Now Paris, our black classic, breaking up / like killer kings on an Etruscan cup."[96] In this densely allusive poem, Lowell contrasts Apollo and Minerva, Ulysses and Cyclops, classical and modern, pagan and Christian, emperor and poet, Rome and Paris, Caesar and Mussolini. Lowell's reference to "Paris, our black classic" alludes to Baudelaire's "Parisian Dream," in *Les Fleurs du Mal* (1857). Baudelaire contrasted the phantasmagoric landscape of his dream vision, in which "everything, even the color black, / Seemed polished, clear, prismatic," with the horrible reality of his gloomy Parisian garret and "the sky that poured darkness / Over the sad lethargic world." In his essay "In Praise of

Make-Up," Baudelaire explained the power of blackness: "black lines give depth and strangeness to the expression, and to the eyes they give a more specific appearance of a window opening unto the infinite."[97] Black, the color that defined Paris, not only heightened the eyes, but also (following Neoplatonic thought) made them the window of the soul.

The third stanza of "Beyond the Alps," omitted from *Life Studies* but restored when the poem was reprinted in *For the Union Dead*, also elucidates this enigmatic couplet. Alluding to Ovid's banishment from Rome to the distant shores of the Black Sea for offending the emperor Augustus in his *Ars Amatoria*, Lowell mentions "black" three times. He calls Ovid's successors—Lucan, Tacitus and Juvenal—"*black republicans*" and, conflating the Black Sea and the Mediterranean, speaks of "black earth by the black Roman sea." Baudelaire's modern Paris is now "*our* black classic." For Lowell, traveling from Rome and over the white Alps to Paris, the city is breaking up, like a precious, "polished, clear" black Etruscan vase, incised with battling warriors, which crashes to the ground and symbolizes the destruction of European civilization. He cannot accept the dogma of Mary's bodily assumption, a "miscarriage of the [Pope's] brain" that has forced him to leave the church. The killer kings, specified in the poem as Caesar and Mussolini, both ruled from Rome. In the classical period Caesar broke up and exterminated his weaker Etruscan rivals. In modern times Mussolini invaded Abyssinia and Albania and slaughtered their people. Lowell arrived at "black" through a dense series of literary and historical allusions. His closing couplet brilliantly conflates his own spiritual crisis with two millennia of human history.

Lowell was caustic about his parents, tender in his elegies about his four lost friends: Ford and Santayana were father figures, Schwartz and Crane were examples of self-destruction. Lowell's attitude toward Schwartz was very like the anxious attitude of Jarrell and other friends toward the dangerous Lowell: "I felt frightened to be with him for years—needlessly, in a way, but I was sure it would lead to confusion and pain."[98]

"Skunk Hour" is filled with images of decay, death and madness. Lowell's "my mind's not right" comes directly from James Boswell's anguished assertion after witnessing David Hume's burial, "My mind was not right."[99] The "dark night" of St. John of the Cross ends in the soul's union with God; Lowell's ironic parallel, "One dark night," ends in the poet's union with skunks.[100] The female skunk jabs her wedge head into the refuse as if imitating the sexual act but also, by dropping her tail, refuses to have sex and reproduce her kind. The skunks reflect the poet's dismal state of mind yet, perversely, seem to inspire him. They stink and eat garbage but, unlike the anxious poet, they are not afraid. Moving from the consolation of religion to the affirmation of the symbolic skunks, the poet is fortified by their united family, single-minded search for food and resolute determination to survive.

The title of "Man and Wife" is ironic: "Man versus Wife" would be more accurate. Set in the marital bed, with neither sex nor sleep, Lowell's poem reveals the horrid gulf between past love and present torment. The puns in "*lie* on Mother's bed" and "war paint *dyes* us red" suggest duplicity and death in a quasi-incestuous setting. The luxurious "gilded bed-posts," which offer no comfort, recall Pope's "gilded Chariots" in "The Rape of the Lock" and Eliot's "gilded shell" in *The Waste Land.* The ominous Charlotte is a cause of Lowell's madness, which was both inherited from and incited by her. The blossoms of the magnolia tree, reflecting the burning intensity of the estranged couple, explode into color and soon die. He recalls that Hardwick had often confronted his madness and saved him. Now, driven beyond the limit of her patience, she condemns his behavior. Yet he still addresses his wife as if she were his savior:

> All night I've held your hand,
> as if you had
> a fourth time faced the kingdom of the mad—
> its hackneyed speech, its homicidal eye—
> and dragged me home alive.

But she turns her back on him and, unable to sleep, regressively clasps the pillow instead of the poet. She still cares enough about him to tell the absolute truth, but he can no longer bear her scorching words. He's destroyed by his madness and cannot be saved by his wife. His self-condemnation ends as "your old-fashioned tirade—/ loving, rapid, merciless—/ breaks like the Atlantic Ocean on my head." [101] (He might have used more precise and less gigantic images of destruction: breaks like "shattered glass" or "pounding waves.")

The title of " 'To Speak of Woe That Is in Marriage'," written in couplets and narrated by the embittered wife, comes from Chaucer's Prologue to the lusty Wife of Bath's tale. Lowell said that his second poem on Hardwick "started as a translation of Catullus. I don't know what traces are left, but it couldn't have been written without the Catullus." [102] Two poems by Catullus illuminate his poem. Number 85, the famous *odi et amo,* also portrays the torments of love: "I hate and love. / And if you ask me why, / I have no answer, but I discern, / can feel, my senses rooted in eternal torture." Catullus' number 11 describes similar anger and doubt, separation and loss. In this condemnation of Lesbia, the poet rejects the faithless woman and asserts, despite her abundant lovers, that she will never find true love:

> Live well and sleep with adulterous lovers,
> three hundred men between your thighs, embracing
> all love turned false, again, again, and breaking their strength,
>   now sterile.
>
> She will not find my love (once hers) returning:
> she it was who caused love, this lonely flower,
> tossed aside, to fall by the plough dividing blossoming meadows.[103]

In Lowell's poem the wife complains that her drunken husband is unfaithful, stays out all night with whores and is impotent when he returns to attempt clumsy sex with her: "Gored by the climacteric of his want, / he stalls above me like an elephant."[104]

The older English critic I. A. Richards, Lowell's colleague at Harvard, disliked the shocking innovations of *Life Studies.* In a letter to Lowell he accurately predicted that Lowell would become the subject of doctoral dissertations, but criticized the use of obscure allusions that Lowell had picked up from Pound and the personal revelations that he'd found in Yeats and Eliot: "the form, the tone, the address, the reiteration, the *lacunae* in connexity, the privacy of the allusions, the use of references which only the Ph.D. duties of the 1990s will explain, the recourse to contemporary crudities, the personal note." But Richards also recognized the merits of the poems that were quite alien to his temperament and taste, and praised "your immense vividity, your phrase-encapsulated explosiveness, your creative originality of slant, your triumphantly compelling cadences."[105] Edmund Wilson, more perceptive and enthusiastic than Richards, declared that Lowell's "poetry never ceases to be noble, and the imagery, which is spiky and dark, is also in its way rich and brilliant. He is, I think, the only recent American poet—if you don't count Eliot—who writes successfully in the language and cadence and rhyme of the resounding English tradition."[106]

Lowell was rather surprised at the favorable response to the book that became the cornerstone of his reputation. He lamented that poets "are little read, cause no sensation and live on grants."[107] But *Life Studies* was precisely the opposite: widely read, vividly sensational and written by a wealthy poet. Trying to explain why his work was esteemed, Lowell observed that readers identified with his personal weaknesses: "It may be that some people have turned to my poems because of the very things that are wrong with me. I mean the difficulty I have with ordinary living, the impracticality, the myopia. Seeing less than others can be a great strain."[108]

For Lizzie and Harriet (1973) was published the same year as the contentious *Dolphin*. In "No Hearing 1. The Dialogue" Lowell uses military and bullfight metaphors to describe, in a third poem, his domestic conflicts with Hardwick. She's an old campaigner who, at 6 p.m., the hour of the *corrida,* won't surrender. Husband and wife fight *mano a mano,* face to face. Unlike the teetotal, uxorious monologist Samuel Johnson (mentioned in the poem), who talked for victory, Lowell and Hardwick, fuelled by Old Fashioneds, fight for survival. Lizzie and Harriet suffered first in Lowell's poems and then in the reviews. In a harsh judgment, Marjorie Perloff wrote that Lizzie is depicted as "Super-Bitch par excellence" and (agreeing with Keith Botsford's estimate of the child's character) "poor Harriet emerges from these pages as one of the most unpleasant child figures in poetry."[109]

VII

Lowell's painful disengagement from Hardwick, his own manic periods that terrified his third wife, Caroline Blackwood, and Blackwood's acute nervous depression—as well as their marriage and the birth of their son—were the subjects of his penultimate book, *The Dolphin* (1973), which he wrote while living through and inspired by this emotional chaos. He compounded his past cruelties by describing the private disintegration of his marriage to Hardwick in his public poetry. He contrasted his idealized portrait of Blackwood (soon to become another casualty) to the bitter interjections of his discarded wife, and used passages from her harrowing personal letters—sometimes in italics, sometimes not—in the text of his poems. Though he felt guilty about publishing the poems that would torment Hardwick, he was more ruthless than remorseful.

Other writers had used the breakup of their marriages as the subject for poetry. As early as 1862 George Meredith published an ambitious fifty-sonnet sequence, *Modern Love,* which moves from the husband's illusory confidence to his cruel disappointment. With novelistic episodes and emotions, it portrays the disintegration of a marriage that ends in discord and misery. Lowell's book could have been called, to paraphrase the title of D. H. Lawrence's account of his marital conflicts with Frieda and their triumphant life together in exile, *Look! We Have NOT Come Through!*

Gabriele D'Annunzio wrote a novel that turned the Italian actress Eleanora Duse—when both were celebrities—into another literary victim. Her biographer William Weaver wrote that "D'Annunzio's fleeting infidelities, his open admiration of other women, were not the only source of Duse's unhappiness. . . . She knew that *Il Fuoco* [1900] was largely about her, and must have suspected that it would reveal parts of her life she wanted to keep private." Duse had read the novel as D'Annunzio was writing it and had clear warning of the wounds it would inflict. But she raised no objection to publication and generously said, "I thought it was true art; I tried to defend it."[110] In Henry James' story "The Lesson of the Master" (1888) the young disciple who plans to marry asks the older writer, "Are there no women who really understand—who can take part in a sacrifice?" To which the Master replies, "How can they take part? They themselves are the sacrifice."[111]

Closer to home, Eliot used the nerve-shattering words of his mentally unstable wife Vivien in *The Waste Land* (1922). Lowell's mentor and friend William Carlos Williams infuriated his young friend, Marcia Nardi, by using her love letters in the early books of *Paterson* (1946–48). In a letter to Bishop in July 1948, long before he published *The Dolphin,* Lowell defended Williams with the same justification he would later use to defend himself. The letters made the poetry vivid and the poet condemned his own behavior: "I think of their effectiveness in two ways 1) so terrifyingly and typically real, and yet I don't think I'd want to read many of them straight—too monotonous, pathological. Yet in the poem they are placed and not pathological, the agony is absorbed. 2) Aren't they really hardest on Williams himself, a damning of his insensitivity? She's mad, but he, like Aeneas [with Dido], can't handle her and shows up badly."[112]

In *The Dolphin* Lowell carried the practice of using real-life words and situations to a new level. From the beginning of his career Lowell appropriated the words of wives and friends, put them in quotation marks (always worth noting when reading his work) and wove them into his own poems. He took not only the words and letters of Hardwick, but also of Charlotte, Stafford, Bishop, Mary McCarthy and Blackwood. A particularly egregious example occurred in Lowell's poem on the accidental death of one of Allen Tate's twin sons, born during the poet's third marriage, when he was sixty-eight. Tate wrote Lowell that the ten-month-old infant "fell face down and choked to death, the toy being forced down his throat. . . . The Negro nurse panicked and forgot where we had gone for dinner. She wasted half an hour trying to locate *us,* instead of calling the hospital or doctor."[113] In "To Allen Tate 3" Lowell publicized the ghastly death by writing, "and Michael Tate / gagging on your plastic telephone, / while the new sitter drew water for your bath."[114] Tate was hurt and angry at Lowell's appropriation of his personal tragedy. As McCarthy told Hardwick, criticizing Lowell's selfishness and echoing the Jamesian theme, "Cal is not a sacrificing man, least of all, I suppose, where his poetry is concerned, which means more to him than any people. People in fact are sacrificed to *it,* to keep the flame burning."[115]

Lowell took the dominant symbol of the dolphin (which he contrasted to his recurrent spiders) from many different sources: myth, book, film, aquarium, natural history and statues. In mythology the dolphin, known as the guide and savior of drowning men, admired the verses of the Greek poet Arion and carried him safely ashore. Lowell was charmed and fascinated by Robert Sténuit's *The Dolphin, Cousin to Man* (1968), which emphasized their affinity to human beings. He saw the popular film *Boy on a Dolphin* (1957), starring Sophia Loren in a clinging wet blouse and written by Blackwood's lover Ivan Moffat. Lowell loved to visit the London Dolphinarium on Oxford Street to see the performing dolphins, and learned that the warm-blooded mammals were intelligent, vocal, friendly and even therapeutic. Jonathan Raban recalled that the dolphins seemed to reproduce in Lowell's London house: "To Caroline's intense horror he took to going down the Kings Road and buying incredibly expensive stone dolphins, from places like the Antiques Hypermarket. . . . There were dolphins at either side of the front door, dolphins in the garden, dolphins as hat stands."[116]

Lowell agonized about the use of Hardwick's words and letters, and consulted several writer-friends about it. Everyone advised against it. The playwright William Alfred, his colleague at Harvard, said "the poems will tear Elizabeth apart." Frank Bidart, who helped Lowell revise the poems, foresaw the damage they would cause: "it had to give Lizzie pain, he was very aware of that." Ian Hamilton commented that it was agonizing for Hardwick "to have these intensely private torments paraded in a poem, to see herself portrayed as the ousted, vengeful wife, to have snatches of her letters, telegrams, phone conversations used as the all too raw material for Lowell's lightly fictionalized drama of *his* indecision."[117]

The intensely private and reserved Elizabeth Bishop, Lowell's moral and artistic conscience, was absolutely opposed to his punishing revelations. Until now, they hadn't dared to wound each other with frank judgments. She needed encouragement rather than criticism, and his harsh words might have prevented her from writing. But after decades of mutual praise, Bishop finally and honestly told Lowell that she disliked *The Dolphin*. Deeply upset by the poems, which she thought were cruel, she exclaimed in her most Episcopal manner: "Lizzie is not dead, etc.—but there is a 'mixture of fact & fiction,' and you have *changed* her letters. That is 'infinite mischief,' I think. . . . One can use one's life as material—one does, anyway—but these letters—aren't you violating a trust? IF you were given permission—IF you hadn't changed them. . . . But *art just isn't worth that much.* . . . It makes me feel perfectly awful, to tell the truth—I feel sick for *you.* I don't want you to appear in that light, to anyone—Elizabeth, Caroline—me—your public! And most of all, not to yourself." Responding to Bishop's objections, Lowell softened the original version of "Voices," in which he'd quoted the overwrought Hardwick referring to herself and Harriet. Making her worst accusation, Hardwick had confirmed that she now found her brilliant husband tedious: "your clowning makes us want to vomit—you bore, / bore, bore the friends who wished to save your image."[118]

W. H. Auden, even more censorious than Bishop, refused to speak to Lowell after *The Dolphin* appeared. The poet Thom Gunn called it "a brutal violation of personal trust."[119] Grey Gowrie regretted that Lowell "hurt people he loved, and did so in the most public way."[120] Stanley Kunitz, a close friend, lamented, "there are details which seem to me monstrously heartless. . . . Some passages I can scarcely bear to read: they are too ugly, for being too cruel, too intimately cruel."[121]

But Lowell believed his art was worth her pain. His forte had always been to turn shocking revelations about himself, his family and his friends into poetry, and many readers were eager for his confessions. Though Lowell was willing to soften Hardwick's words in *The Dolphin,* he knew the personal disclosures were the main interest in the poems and—despite well-intentioned pressure from his friends—was not willing to eliminate them. Unconstrained by threats of libel suits, loyalty to Hardwick and the condemnation of his peers, he was desperate for catharsis and had no fear of exposing himself as well as her. In these poems, as Lowell takes pleasure in portraying Hardwick's unequal rivalry with Blackwood, Hardwick insists it's not a question of which woman Lowell wants, but which one can take the most punishment and remain with him: "*You say you'll remarry, you can't take none or two*. . . . / Do you really want / to live in the same room with anyone? / . . . . Agony says we cannot live in one house, / or under a common name." Estranged from him when he was writing the poems, she couldn't judge his mental condition or know if he was responsible for his behavior. She also wonders if he's truly serious about Blackwood, if his "*manic flight to London*" was sane or mad, and suggests that his real self is with her, his deranged self with Blackwood.[122] In January 1965 she wrote that she dreads his letters and hopes they will not contain anything too disturbing. Otherwise, she looks forward to receiving them. In the poems Lowell has her say, "I despair of letters. . . . I wait for your letters, tremble when I get none, / more when I do."

In the poetry Hardwick's persona then becomes wounded and furious: "*I can't tell the things we planned for you this Christmas. / I've written my family not to phone today, / we had to put away your photographs*"—which were too painful to look at.[123] She accuses him of trying to bribe Harriet and buy her affection with gifts: "My daughter knows no love / that doesn't bind her with presents, letters, visits." Though they've tried to love and care for him in every possible way, she warns that she and Harriet "*can't stand much more of anything, / they are so tired and hurt and worn. . . . / it's impossible for anyone to help you*." She also condemns him for wavering between herself and Blackwood, for being a hypocrite and for not real-izing the suffering he's caused:

> *You can't carry your talent with you like a suitcase.*
> *Don't you dare mail us the love your life denies;*
> *do you really* know *what you have done?*

She particularly objected to these lines, which Lowell invented and attrib-uted to her. But in the poem Hardwick, despite her anger, was (like Staf-ford) still in love with him. She reverts to her characteristic kindness and admits, "I have never denied I miss you. . . . I love you, Darling, there's a black black void, / as black as night without you."[124]

The last and title poem in *The Dolphin*, confronting Lowell's betrayal, brilliantly summarizes Hardwick's role in his life and his poetry. He calls her his "collaborating muse," admits that he's appropriated her life for his poetic plot and adopts his familiar confessional tone. He echoes both *The Book of Common Prayer* ("avoid injury") and "The Battle Hymn of the Republic" ("Mine eyes have seen"). He begins the poem by idealizing Blackwood as a dolphin and ends by portraying Hardwick as a menacing sea snake. In his letters he called Hardwick "the eel I try to ensnare and release from the eelnet, but she will feel bruised by the intimacy":[125]

> I have sat and listened to too many
> words of the collaborating muse,
> and plotted perhaps too freely with my life,
> not avoiding injury to others
> not avoiding injury to myself—
> to ask compassion . . . this book, half fiction,
> an eelnet made by man for the eel fighting—
>
> my eyes have seen what my hand did.[126]

Lowell's last words, seething with self-accusation and remorse, suggest a dissociation of head and heart, act and thought, and echo several of his notable lines: "I saw your eyes / Looking in wonder at your bloody hand"; "I think of all the ill I do and will"; "Are we so conscience-dark and cataract-blind?"[127] He sadly told Hardwick, "the distance [between us] is farther than a hand can reach or mind can perhaps attend."[128] He's now seen his error, cannot deny his guilt and wants to punish himself for mistreating her.

As their friends had predicted, Hardwick was devastated by *The Dolphin*, which hurt her more than anything else in her entire life. She then fired off a barrage of what Lowell in his correspondence called "boiling messages" and "stinging cables,"[129] and told him in her first bitter reaction, "I never want to hear from you again."[130] Emphasizing his egoism, she informed his friend Blair Clark: "I do not want Cal back under any circumstances. This is the last time he will see me. . . . In all the months he has been gone . . . he has never answered one question I have put to

him, or discussed really anything, me or Harriet or practical things or
Caroline—except himself."[131] She also emphasized, with a rhetorical question, the disastrous consequences of his slaughter of the innocents: "Did
he *realize* the damage he had done?"

Then, in a furious letter to both Lowell and Blackwood, she excoriated
their utter selfishness. Hardwick and Harriet had planned to join him in
England; Harriet had given up her place in the Dalton school and Hardwick had given up her precious teaching position. Financial stress added
to the emotional onslaught: "I want to add my absolute horror that you
two people have taken away something I loved and needed. My job at Barnard, which I tried to get back, but it is filled for this year and the budget
is filled. . . . My utter contempt for both of you for the misery you have
brought to two people who have never hurt you knows no bounds."[132]
Friends reported that when *The Dolphin* appeared Hardwick became
depressed and suicidal, and that they had to drop in and telephone frequently to make sure she didn't take too many pills. Lowell made her a
famously betrayed woman and (like Sylvia Plath) a feminist icon.

In her essays on self-destructive writers, Hardwick obliquely criticized
Lowell's character and his use of her personal letters. Her 1974 chapter
on Zelda Fitzgerald emphasized the guilt in both crazy people and those
close to them, and drew a clear parallel with Scott Fitzgerald's damaging
use of his wife's deranged letters in his novel: "sick persons create guilt of a
mysterious kind, whether by their own wish or merely by the peculiarities
of their often luminous fixity. The will to blame, to hold them to account,
soon appears futile to those closest. Instead the mad entwine their relations
in an unresolved, lingering, chafing connection, where guilt, exasperation
and grief for the mysteries of life continue to choke. . . . If there is any
culpability on Fitzgerald's part it may lie in his use of Zelda's torment to
create the destructive, mad heiress, Nicole, in *Tender Is the Night*."[133] Like
Zelda with Scott, Hardwick felt trapped and exploited by Lowell.

In *A View of My Own* (1962) Hardwick also wrote about Dylan Thomas,
who died of alcoholism at the age of thirty-nine, as if she were writing
about Lowell: "Here in America the approbation was extreme, the notice
sometimes hysterical, the pace killing. . . . His last months, his final agonies, his utterly woeful end were a sordid and spectacular drama of broken hearts, angry wives, irritable doctors, frantic bystanders, rumors and
misunderstandings, neglect and murderous permissiveness.[134] She added
that he was "undeniably suffering and living in the extremist reaches of

experience. . . . Behind his drinking, his bad behavior, his infidelities, his outrageousness, there was always his real doom. . . . He had delirium tremens, horrors, agonies, desire for death, and nearly every physical and mental pain one can imagine."[135]

Responding to the thunderstorm of criticism, Lowell at first tried to justify what some reviewers called his hijacking of Hardwick's words and feelings. Explaining that he'd misquoted her letters for dramatic effect, he alluded to Shakespeare's *As You Like It*—"the truest poetry is the most feigning" (3.3.18–19)—and told Hardwick, "one neither does or should tell the literal or ultimate truth. Poetry lies."[136] More concerned with Bishop's feelings than with Hardwick's, he tried to answer Bishop's objections by defending his method in two exculpatory and rather self-contradictory letters. If his poems were awful and wounding, they could not also be sympathetic and poignant:

> Lizzie's letters? I did not see [the poems] as slander, but as sympa-
> thetic, tho necessarily awful for her to read. She is the poignance
> of the book, tho that hardly makes it kinder to her. I could say the
> letters are cut, doctored part fiction . . . (I attribute things to Lizzie
> I made up, or that were said by someone else. I combed out [some]
> abuse, hysteria, repetition). The trouble is the letters make the book,
> I think, at least they make Lizzie real beyond my invention. I took
> out the worst things written against me, so as not to give myself a
> case and seem self-pitying. . . .
>
> The problem of making the poem unwounding is impossible, still
> I think it can be made noticeably milder without losing its life. It
> might be much better, for who can want to savage a thing. How can
> I want to hurt? Hurt Lizzie and Harriet, their loving memory?[137]

While considering Bishop's criticism, Lowell told Bidart, "I do think Elizabeth is mostly right, though she is peculiarly (almost unintelligibly) sensitive to private exposure."[138] But exposing his private life in public was his particular specialty. Despite his doubts, he'd forged ahead with *The Dolphin*. He assured Eileen Simpson that Lizzie and Harriet were fine, and compared himself to Marsyas, who was flayed and torn apart by Apollo. Simpson recalled that Lowell thought "it was he, the one who was asking for the divorce and planned to remarry as soon as it was final, who was suffering. 'Being in New York again makes me feel as if the skin on my back is being raked.'"[139]

After *The Dolphin* was published and reviewed, and the damage was done, Lowell finally changed his mind and admitted his guilt. He wrote Hardwick, "I swear I never in all this business have wanted to hurt you—the very opposite. . . . I'm sorry I brought this on you. . . . I regret the letters in *The Dolphin*. The only way to make a narrative was to leave a few."[140] He told the political philosopher Hannah Arendt that "having deserted [Hardwick] would haunt him until his grave."[141] In this confession, the former Catholic convert seems to have reverted to his old beliefs. He had committed the sin, repented and (despite his protestation) felt absolved of guilt.

Forty years after publication, when the pain Lowell caused has subsided, *The Dolphin* seems morally wrong but artistically right. Following the tradition of the dolphins who saved the Greek poet, of Shakespeare's description of "a mermaid on a dolphin's back" in *A Midsummer Night's Dream* (2.1.150) and of Milton's noble line in "Lycidas," "And, O ye dolphins, waft the hapless youth," Lowell portrays Blackwood as his dolphin-savior.[142] His dramatic and novelistic love story has a fascinating plot and characters—including the birth of their son and the accidental scalding of her little girl—and portrays both intense passion and extreme suffering. His poetry endures, vivid and convincing. Many of Lowell's readers now treasure the revelations and feel (as Lowell did) that his art was worth her anguish.

VIII

In June 1970, Hardwick's close friend Mary McCarthy (who had a similar literary career) told Hannah Arendt that Lowell had left Hardwick and planned to marry Blackwood: "He broke the news to Lizzie by telephone. She apparently suspected something since she hadn't heard from him for a long time. The affair has been going on about two months. What Lizzie's reaction has been is not exactly clear. I gather that she realizes that this isn't just another girl; there've been many in recent years." But McCarthy, who thought the marriage was hopeless and Hardwick well out of it, saw the positive side of the break: "His finding another wife could be a blessing for Lizzie. . . . Seeing her as I've done so exhausted, beaten, and unhappy, one couldn't have much hope for a miraculous improvement of the marriage. . . . [Cal's madness] more than anything else has *bored* her the last few years, to the point of excruciation."[143] Hardwick did not view the prospect of divorce in the same way. She felt Lowell's rejection would be publicly humiliating, and feared that she'd lose personal influence and literary prestige when he abandoned her.

When *The Dolphin* was published and Hardwick's wounds were still raw, she sent off another "stinging cable" in response to Lowell's query about his rights to the Castine house. Harriet Winslow had left the property to Hardwick, whom she felt was more responsible than Lowell. Defending her interests, Hardwick informed him that his claim to one-third of the Maine property would not stand up in court because of their separation agreement and insisted, "Your books leave the house tomorrow I beg you." A year later, however, after he'd visited her at Christmas, she reverted to the conciliatory mood of her early letters. She apologized (yet again) for her "misunderstanding" about *The Dolphin* poems, lamented Hannah Arendt's recent heart attack and mourned the loss of their dead friends. She was saddened by the disappearance of an entire generation, the greatness of their learning and their lives. She concluded, in a rather elegiac tone, that she was surrounded by death and loss: "So I write in that spirit of forgiveness and honor all that we have touched in our lives."[144]

In their divorce settlement Lowell lost his $20,000 annual trust fund, the apartment in New York, the house in Maine, even his books and family silver. Hardwick's "writing income was supplemented by a combination of Lowell's trust, the considerable profits from the sale of her share in the *New York Review of Books* and, until she retired in 1985, her teaching of creative writing at Barnard College."[145] Her closest friends were Barbara Epstein and Robert Silvers, the editors of that journal. Hardwick, who lived thirty years longer than Lowell, had a few minor affairs, but never remarried.

Lowell rarely took care of any practical details. But in 1970 the distraught Hardwick told McCarthy that she was having trouble coping on her own (and could never hope to reach McCarthy's standard of perfection): "The phone rings all day, plays one is urged to go to in the freezing night, an occasional unwanted invitation, the malignant growths of mail, bills, anxiety about the cost of things, the look of things."[146] A few friends gave glimpses of her later life. After Lowell left her, she continued to entertain colleagues from the *New York Review.* In February 1976 the Harvard historian Arthur Schlesinger recorded, "Last night we went to Elizabeth Hardwick's for dinner—a small party, Mary McCarthy, Susan Sontag, Bob Silvers, and an uncommonly pleasant evening. . . . I have had ups and downs through the years with Liz Hardwick, though recently we have been restored to the mood of the fifties when she and Robert Lowell briefly lived in Boston."[147]

As Hardwick got older her temper got fiercer. As her career rocketed from *Partisan* and *Sewanee* through marriage to Lowell and the *New York Review of Books,* she aggressively maintained the role of literary celebrity. She was well known for her malicious gossip, and Lowell could justly declare of Hardwick, as he did of Stafford, "Here comes the black tongue!"[148] William Styron, a fellow Southerner, named her "the Boss-Lady intellectual of New York."[149] Katherine Anne Porter called her "a hatchet man. . . . Hatchet woman sounds too gentle for her."[150] Fanny Howe found her overbearing and scary. At a literary party Hardwick pushed her way through a crowded room and rudely told Howe, "I hate your novels. You should stick to poetry!"[151]

Joel Conarroe, president of the Guggenheim Foundation, felt Hardwick was crushingly disdainful: "[Colleagues] often found her charming but somewhat mandarin, a Blanche Dubois with a steely will. . . . She could diminish people when she didn't agree with them. She sometimes made fellow jurors feel as if they had no literary judgment whatsoever."[152] An academic colleague, who'd also served on committees with Hardwick, called her intimidating and nasty: "You didn't want to make a remark before she did, because of course she would demolish you. . . . It was just being mean for the pure exercise of it. . . . She was devastating in her remarks about other writers."[153]

The novelist Mary Gordon, her friend and colleague at Barnard, cast a cold eye on Hardwick in later life, on the dyed hair, makeup and flashy apparel which, in her seventies, seemed like a desperate attempt to look young: "Lizzie had Lucille Ball red hair, arranged in ringlets and deliberately unnatural-looking. She wore mascara, which was smudged by the end of the day, and dark lipstick. Her clothes were excitingly designed, and she wore high heels with interesting bows and buckles." Hardwick had spent a year in Rome and Florence, but when she and Gordon attended a literary conference in Sicily in 1986 Hardwick could speak no Italian. Her unwillingness to be contradicted and appetite for malice erupted when she "praised a writer and Gordon said, 'I don't think her sentences are very interesting.' Lizzie had had a lot to drink; she was drinking more and more as she aged. 'What would you know about it?' she said to me. 'You've never written an interesting sentence in your life' "—a remark that severed their friendship for the next twenty years.[154] Hardwick's tolerance for Lowell did not extend to others. After decades of taking punishment from him, she'd become embittered and also liked to dish it out. Like the power-hungry Lillian Hellman, she felt the need to assert her authority and to make cruel judgments in order to maintain her position as literary dictator.

IX

Like Hardwick's essays on Zelda Fitzgerald and Dylan Thomas, her last book, on Herman Melville (2000), illuminates her attitude toward Lowell's attractive heritage, dedication to art and rebellious nature as well as to her own ability to take punishment. She sees Melville's life and character through the prism of Lowell: "The atmosphere of gentility arises . . . from the remembrance of things past created by birth, prosperity, an honorable reputation, even charm. . . . He was animated by a need for a mirror reflecting his own struggle to honor his vision, his experience in the battle with words. . . . He has about him, even in settled married life, much of the renegade, the scars of knowing, choosing, the bleak underside of life."[155]

Most significantly, her negative view of Melville's overbearing mother and description of his tempestuous character and insane behavior, which almost drove his wife (also called Lizzie) to a nervous breakdown, clearly reflect her own marriage:

> Elizabeth Melville was seen by family and friends to be living in a nightmare. Melville was consumed by rage, breakdown, misery uncontrolled, given to violence in the household. He appeared to some to be insane. . . . It is very hard to live with one so desperately stretched, pummeled, weary, frazzled and fractious, but more dreadful to live *in* such a state than to live *with* it. . . . She is on occasion said to be "prostrate" and near collapse; among other tribulations she had to wait until fifteen years later for the death of his lashing-overseer mother. . . . After twenty years of her husband's frenzy, his bad temper with too much to drink at night, Lizzy seriously considered a separation.[156]

It's now more difficult than it was in the 1950s and '60s to understand how Hardwick could suffer so much abuse in her Elizabethan tragedy and still remain loyal to Lowell. A friend observed that Hardwick—tough and censorious—never struck her as a woman who could tolerate much abuse. But she closely identified with Lowell as husband and writer, and felt there was no one else like him. He really was *It* for her, the great love of her life, and she remained devoted to him till the very end.

Though Hardwick had suffered greatly, she had no regrets and believed their marriage was the best thing that had ever happened to her. "I didn't know what I was getting into," she said, "but even if I had, I still would have married him."[157] She adored and idealized Lowell as a heroic artist and moral witness to his times. Her mission in life was to support and save him. Since he was usually manic when he fell in love with young women, she felt such infidelities didn't seriously count: the real, sane Lowell always remained loyal to her. She also accepted and forgave a lot for Harriet's sake and for the sake of her own literary career. Like Antigone with the aged Oedipus, she was willing to sacrifice herself to rescue him. Her selfless fidelity, dedication merging into martyrdom, humiliating masochism, unlimited capacity for suffering and stoic endurance made Hardwick the tragic heroine of Lowell's life.

SIX

The Heedless Heart, 1954–1970

I

Like a good commander, Lowell always secured his rear before advancing. He held on to his current wife—Stafford when he was with Buckman and Dawson, Hardwick with all the others—before starting a liaison with another woman. His serious marital problems with Hardwick, graphically described in "Man and Wife" and " 'To Speak of Woe That Is in Marriage,'" spurred his search for compensatory affairs. Again and again—whether manic, sane or in-between—he would suddenly fall in love with a young woman. He would threaten to divorce Hardwick and marry her latest rival, break down and enter a hospital, then regain his reason and return to Hardwick.

Lowell found lovers wherever he met women—from Salzburg to Cuernavaca—and his nine most significant attachments formed a truly diverse rainbow coalition: Protestant, Catholic and Jew, American, Italian and Baltic. Anne Dick and Carley Dawson were wealthy socialites and upper-class WASPS. Gertrude Buckman and Sandra Hochman were New York Jews, college graduates and literary types. Giovanna Madonia, an Italian musician, later married a prominent poet and an important painter. Ann Adden and Martha Ritter were exceptional students at Bennington and at Harvard. Vija Vetra was a well-known Latvian dancer. Mary Keelan, a disciple of the priest and educator Ivan Illich, worked for him in Mexico.

His early girlfriends, Anne Dick, Buckman and Dawson, like Stafford and Hardwick, were older than Lowell. But as he got older he chose much younger women and the difference in age became a major theme in his love poetry. His sexual relations with his lovers varied with his physical and mental condition. He was sexually inept with Dick and Vetra and was impotent with Adden. But he was also a passionate and pleasing lover with Hochman and Ritter and, apparently, with Buckman, Madonia and Keelan. Lowell never suggested living together without proposing marriage, and wanted to marry Dick, Dawson, Madonia, Hochman and Vetra. He never impregnated any of his lovers, though Hochman, for one, did not use contraceptives. All the women were single at the time, but he never managed to marry any of them. Before he could get a divorce, the affairs suddenly ended.

Anne Dick, Buckman and Keelan never saw Lowell's mania and despite dark hints, thought that he was of sound mind. But he was violent with Dawson and Hochman, first met Adden when he was in a mental hospital, and was committed to asylums when involved with Madonia, Hochman and Vetra. Ritter knew the extent of his illness and saw him after a breakdown in England. Lowell's friends and wives suffered when they became enmeshed in his amorous adventures. He wanted them to endorse and strengthen his relations with his current lover, and relied on them to rescue him and pick up the pieces when he veered out of control.

Most of the women in Lowell's life moved in literary and artistic circles. Some of them later became interested in the New Age ideas that were fashionable in the 1960s. Dawson was ordained in the Ministry of Divine Science, Adden studied the Tao Te Ching, Vetra absorbed Indian religions and Ritter qualified in Chinese medicine. At a time when divorce was fairly unusual, except among movie stars and the jet set, seven of Lowell's nine lovers got divorced. Dawson, Madonia and Hochman were divorced twice; Vetra never married. Lowell's passion had a powerful impact on these women's lives: Dick and Dawson were wounded and scarred; Buckman and Vetra were angry and bitter; Madonia and Hochman were devastated. But Ritter had no regrets and Adden, the only one who did not have sexual relations with Lowell, had fond memories.

Lowell enjoyed his power to attract, delight and dominate. He won his women with the subtle strategies of duplicity and charm, and was rather like a sultan choosing the most promising candidates for his poetic harem. Like Hans Castorp with Clavdia Chauchat in *The Magic Mountain,* he delighted the women—Hardwick, Madonia, Adden and Vetra—by playing records, especially operas with romantic themes. Their surge of emotion complemented his refined sensuality. He idealized the women and encouraged their artistic talent in music, poetry and dance. He seemed completely serious when proposing marriage and easily persuaded each woman to sleep with him. But with all his experience, Lowell didn't really understand a woman's deepest needs and feelings, and always conducted his frenetic affairs entirely on his own terms. His harsh treatment of women was, in some ways, a form of revenge against his mother. He not only wanted to secure the love that Charlotte had denied him, but also was determined, by dominating them, to expunge the memory of her oppression and compensate for his father's submission.

Lowell told Stafford, who was more fragile and less tolerant than Hardwick, "I don't want a wife, I want a playmate." His poetry is saturated with sexual longing, with the struggle to free himself from the constraints of his puritan heritage and to recapture the romance of his youth:

> O to break loose. All life's grandeur
> is something with a girl in summer.
>
> to meet the second overflowing of Eros,
> himself younger in each young face.
>
> our clasped, illicit hands
> pulse, stop my bloodstream as if I'd hit rock.
>
> nothing lovelier than waking to find
> another breathing body in my bed. [1]

Even the most devoted wife could not possibly match the new woman's youthful adoration and romantic excitement, her rejuvenating powers and sexual thrill, her eagerness to have her teacher and lover form her still undeveloped character and mind.

Despite the clear danger signs—Lowell's nonstop talking, demonic energy and erratic behavior—it was difficult to tell if he was sane or crazy. Each of these women fell almost instantly in love with him, agreed to marry him and allowed him to suddenly transform her life. Though most women would have been frightened by the symptoms of his mania, his lovers were attracted by the mixture of sexual desire and unnerving fear. Lowell needed to be taken care of. When he became manic Dawson, Adden, Hochman and Vetra had the uncanny power to calm him down, alleviate his illness and even persuade him to enter a mental hospital. They wanted to rescue, protect, nurse, cure and inspire him. Powerful in the literary world, Lowell could do a great deal to advance the careers of adoring and aspiring writers. These women revered his poetry, fell in love with the poet and were ecstatic about the poems he wrote for them.

Two anonymous women shed light on the positive and negative aspects of Lowell's character. A beautiful young poet less than half his age said, "His depressions generally disappear with his second drink, and reappear with his fifth. From that moment on, it's all downhill." Another woman praised his intense interest in her and his constant, tangible affection. He had that "extremely strong instinct for focusing on you and what you're about and what you're trying to do. He did that more than anyone I've ever known. . . . He was very cozily physical. He liked to hold your hand, or if he walked with you, he liked your arm linked in his. The times I slept with Cal he wasn't crazily sort of sexy at all. He was very huggy. He'd hug you all night, the minute he woke up he'd hug you. But I think he was quite panicked by thoughts of impotence."

There was no need for Lowell to "lie to his wife and wait six months," as he'd once advised John Berryman to do when his friend was engaged in an illicit affair. Lowell tried to be discreet, but felt free to pursue young women, knowing he had a secure bolt-hole. Hardwick would always take him back if things didn't work out—and they never did. Frank Parker said that Lowell, assured of his charisma and able to evoke the most profound feelings his women had ever experienced, "had a way of thinking about anyone he'd once had a relationship with: he only had to walk back and the door would be open. And it always seemed to be. I mean Anne [Dick] always wanted to see him, and it was the same with Jean [Stafford]."[2] Like Odysseus—who escaped emotional entanglements with Nausicaa, Calypso and Circe—Lowell would finally find his way home to his faithful Penelope.

Lowell's women sowed the wind and reaped the whirlwind. His lover was thrilling as long as he was with her. But when they were physically separated, he suddenly broke with her and remained silent. Then, years later, he'd find her and unexpectedly reappear. Covering a vast geographical area, he left Anne Dick in Tennessee, Buckman in Manhattan, Dawson in Maine, Madonia in Salzburg and in Milan, Adden in Boston, Keelan in Mexico, Ritter in England. When he had manic breakdowns and went into mental hospitals, he left Hochman in New York and Vetra in Connecticut. Lowell ended his intense, glamorous affairs abruptly and painfully, rather than gently and tactfully, both disrupting his lover's life and destroying the one she hoped to have with him.

Lowell's affairs were an emotional and sexual reward for the suffering he'd endured during his previous mental breakdowns. They were sparked by fantasies of rejuvenation and rebirth, and by a deep need to have his wives and lovers competing for his favor. His women, still deeply in love, were like wounded victims on a battlefield; he was the sole survivor. Like a driver who'd caused a car crash and driven away from the accident, he left a trail of desolation behind him: a dozen infatuated women and two wives (Stafford and Blackwood) driven to alcoholism and mental breakdowns. These women, like maidens fed to the Minotaur, were drawn to his genius and madness. They succumbed to his charm, were eager to get emotionally involved with him and became the sacrificial muses who inspired his poetry.

II. Giovanna Madonia

In July 1952 Lowell, who did not speak Italian, and Giovanna Madonia, who could write but not understand much English, met in Austria. He was lecturing at the Salzburg Seminars in American Studies, which were held in the romantic Leopoldskron Castle in Mozart's native town. Madonia (1927–2008) was born in Forlì, near Ravenna and the Adriatic coast of Italy. Her mother was Milanese; her father, who owned a felt factory where her brother also worked, was Sicilian. Though strongly influenced by her emotional Sicilian background, she also tried to reject it and told Lowell, "I hate these uncivilized stories of blood: the opera I hate most is *Cavalleria Rusticana:* every evil Italian characteristic is concentrated in this opera. Blood, adultery, male conceit, false Catholic piety. But you need to understand that this is the climate in which I grew up."

After studying at the music conservatory in Milan in the 1950s, Madonia became the assistant to Walter Legge, the classical records producer at EMI. She recorded and edited opera tapes of many singers at La Scala, including Maria Callas, who befriended her and appeared with Madonia on the cover of the EMI recording of *Tosca.* Madonia's job took her on extensive travels in France, Spain and other European countries.

In Salzburg, when Madonia fell in love with Lowell, Hardwick's presence had cramped his style. But he was much freer when he met Madonia in Milan two years later, in February 1954, and Blair Clark ran interference. His second meeting with her took place immediately after one of the most traumatic events of his life, Charlotte's sudden death in Rapallo, and just before he sailed home with her corpse. Lowell gave the Catholic novelist J. F. Powers a sanitized version of his cultural tour of Milan: "I saw [Leonardo's] *The Last Supper* and heard Elisabeth Schwarzkopf sing *Figaro* at the Scala."

Blair Clark recalled that he and Lowell went from Rapallo to La Scala, where Madonia appeared with her new husband, the prominent Milanese poet Luciano Erba, whom she called the "weakling Cal made her marry" because Lowell was already married. With Clark's assistance, Lowell and Madonia managed to evade Erba and slip away to a nearby hotel. Clark gave an amusing account of their love tryst: "Giovanna came to the opera and there was a lot of dodging around the pillars of La Scala to avoid the husband, and I saw some of it, like an Orson Welles movie [*The Third Man*]. I don't quite know what happened that night. Somehow the husband was spirited away—maybe I had something to do with it—and they had some time together, a couple of hours." Lowell must have enjoyed plotting his opera-buffa strategy with Clark, and been pleased that he'd managed to persuade the impulsive Madonia that her marriage was over and to abandon her husband for him. The following month Madonia wrote Clark that they preferred lovemaking to conversation: "Cal's love for me is more phissical than anything else (actually we talked very little, also because it is hard for me to understand his English)."

Lowell's liaison with Madonia, though stretched over two years, was the briefest and saddest of all his affairs. Their letters were mainly confined to March 1954, after Lowell had returned to America. But Madonia didn't realize, at least at first, that Lowell had suffered his third manic breakdown and was sending his passionate declarations, which gave her precious hope for the future, from inside the Payne Whitney Clinic. Madonia's letters were emotional, melodramatic and operatic; confused, abject and defiant; she threatened to retreat to a convent or to destroy herself. She submitted to Lowell's chameleon plans and desires. At the same time, she stated all the reasons why she could not comply: the fear of scandal and sin, her Catholic beliefs, the opposition of her father and husband, the objections of her boss and loss of her precious job, her lack of money, and the difficulty of obtaining an Italian divorce and getting an American visa. Despite or because of her overwhelming love, she was far too unstable to take care of Lowell, and warned him that "my father is my second God (after you, of course, after you) and he will suffer enormously because of this unclear situation: you, Luciano, Elizabeth and me."

On February 22, on the ship taking him back to New York, Lowell initiated their correspondence and described the longing for his Madonna-Madonia: "I live only in you too, your heart beats in mine, I feel you heavy in my arms—all this voyage I seem to have been carrying you—every bone in my body, every drop of blood, every nerve and sinew in my mind, are yours! . . . I'm very devoted to Elizabeth and don't want to hurt her, But O my Giovanna, I am not alive without you." As T. S. Eliot wrote of John Donne, Lowell, in his life and his poetry, "looked into a good deal more than the heart," he looked "into the cerebral cortex, the nervous system, and the digestive tracts."

Madonia, responding with equal intensity and declaring her love, urged Lowell to listen to Callas singing the mad scene from Donizetti's *Lucia di Lammermoor*: "*Alfin son tua, alfin sei mio*" (At last I am yours, at last you are mine). On March 11 Madonia, echoing Lowell's words and increasing the emotional heat, condemned her marriage (to a surprisingly tolerant husband) and stated that even her boss was acting like a Sicilian Mafioso:

> Darling, I think too much of you, far too many things in my mind, in my heart, in my nerves. . . . You are my life, my blood, my hands, my future and my past. You are God. . . . Luciano never thought that I loved him.
>
>   . . . He knows quite well how much this Sicilian pride works in me. (If I do something [except her marriage] it must be all-right for ever.) But now I have told him that sometimes I will go, that I will not live with him for ever. . . . It has always been hell, just hell. . . .
>
>   It will break my father's life, if I will not be able to live in Italy any more. . . . My *boss* simply told me that if I would go away with a man I love he would kill somebody, or me, or this man, or himself. . . . They would not bear me making love to anybody. I suppose it is my Sicilian body that makes people so furious. . . . I want you: I am yours, you are mine. If I cannot have you, better to stop living now. . . . [Your letters give me] a wonderful sensation of huge happiness, something I never felt before, except in Salzburg, under that tree, where I kissed you

—and where he turned her life upside down.

Like an operatic hero, Lowell expressed his eternal commitment to

Madonia—"together, together forever"—and swore that he would leave Hardwick just as she would leave Erba. At the same time, he was torn between confusion and commitment, between his wife and his lover: "There was a swelling tension between me and Elizabeth. . . . I said I wanted to marry you. Well, a seething night. . . . I realized that I loved E. and wanted her with me, and she realized that I was *in* love with you. . . . I am yours undeviatingly forever. Insieme, insieme . . . per sempre! . . . I am undressing you. WE are together, our mouths are together, our hair is together. Ah, there! I speak of mysteries." He planned to extricate her from the tensions of marriage in Milan and repossess her Sicilian body. He fantasized about importing her, "with perfect propriety," as his Giovanna-of-all-trades, demoting her from recording artist to her predetermined roles as housekeeper, secretary, music teacher, Italian instructor and pupil of English. He then added that he couldn't bear spending any more time with the intolerable Hardwick.

Madonia, naïve, optimistic and blinded by love, continued to take him seriously. Reveling in her guilty passion, she imagined holding Lowell when Erba tried to kiss her, and again shifted into her exaggerated Sicilian-operatic mode: "I think it would be much more simple for me to commit suicide or to become a nun [a veiled threat], or do any of these silly things that people used to do in my case (at least in my country)." Madonia exclaimed that she'd suffered more than a normal woman would suffer in two lifetimes. She was tormented by her marriage to Erba who, alone with his poetry all day and eager for conversation when she returned, bored her to death with his endless talks (Lowell's frenetic talks would have been just as exhausting): "Luciano lives through words, in this sense he is a real man of letters, and every day when I get home from work I am forced into conversations with him that last for hours and hours, conversations that leave me completely exhausted. . . . [I am] immensely happy now that you are alone [without Hardwick], only now, are you mine. I love you and you are mine and that is enough for me. That's all. Nothing other than you binds me to life. I want to live with you and for you. I want to have your child."

By March 26, at the end of the tumultuous month, Lowell planned their exotic honeymoon, repeated his wish to see Madonia in her designated role as housekeeper, and strained for an eternal vow in Latin and in his limited Italian: "We can honey-moon any where—England, France, Austria, Palestine, Greece—except behind the Iron Curtain. . . . If you were here tomorrow, it would be late for my desires. Are you sure your silly Sicilian head can handle such things as negotiating for a visa? . . . Dear heart, mia Venus, O Magna Mater, puella: I love you, I love you, I love you. Also I want to get you to work housekeeping, so I can have the leisure to write love poems to you. Il tuo Cal." The following day he imagined himself kneeling at her feet and exclaimed that their love transcended their different languages: "Now I am only il tuo, your friend who waits only for you. It seems so close now, and nothing else exists. . . . You are the best woman in the world. I want to be worthy. I want to kneel and hold you. . . . [We'll be] talking to each other in our separate languages, our separate voices, forever understanding and loving each other more and more, forever and forever. I don't think we differ on anything—it's only that we keep understanding each other better." No woman could resist this emotional onslaught.

Two months later on May 23 Madonia, regaining some grasp of reality, told their intermediary Blair Clark, "before taking decisions we have all to be well—I am not dreaming. I want to spend my life with Cal, that's all." Nevertheless Lowell, still manic, continued to declare his love and make plans for the future. On June 21 Madonia assured him, "I want to have you next to me, calm, without shaking with desire and fear. . . . I beg you, never think, for one second, that I, while alive, could cease to love you."

Meanwhile, Hardwick was wounded, shocked and repelled by what Lowell had done to her. His old friend Randall Jarrell, who'd been conscripted to secretly receive and forward the letters from Madonia, made things even worse by entering the fray. Jarrell, who disliked Hardwick's abrasive manner, enraged her by congratulating Lowell for deciding to marry Madonia. As Jarrell told Elizabeth Bishop in September 1956: "While he was in the hospital I had to do quite a bit of difficult corresponding with the Italian girl, since he'd named me, in letters, as the American friend to correspond with; also he'd shown Elizabeth Hardwick my letter saying I was glad he was being divorced—presumably also saying to her, 'Yah, yah, you see what he thinks of you!' We saw them a little last summer; she was very cordial, poor disingenuous thing!"

After five years of marriage to Lowell and three of his manic episodes, Hardwick continued to show forbearance and tact. But she was also torn by trying to serve the best interests of both Lowell and herself. She told the father-confessor Blair Clark that, like Stafford with her second husband Joe Liebling, "I wish to forget the whole marriage and start all over. I want

to marry a nice, sleepy old man who snoozes in front of the fire all day."
She couldn't say, "Cal wants to leave me, therefore he's crazy." But she
didn't want Lowell "to come with Giovanna at the docks, a not unlikely
happening because if what he says is true, she's moving fast." Encouraged
by Lowell's urgent telegrams, Madonia was leaving her husband, getting
her visa and promising to start, posthaste, for America.

By July 7, however, the dust had settled. Lowell, emerging from his
mania and with insight acquired during his confinement in Payne Whitney, was jolted back to reality. In one of his emotionally shattering letters,
he told Madonia—despite all his past avowals of forever—that he now
needed Hardwick, who had a deeper understanding of his character and
illness, more than he needed her. Though he'd hoped that Madonia might
help cure his mania, he didn't want to burden her with his mental problems: "I see more and more clearly that I will never be over my disturbance
and back to my health and work again without Elizabeth. That is I've got
to be (and above all now) *with* some one and living a life that I understand
already and feel master of. Except for you, Elizabeth has always been a
good wife, and one who understood my disease far better than I myself.
On the whole, even in this, she hasn't been interfering."

Lowell's contagion of desire had compelled Madonia to confess her
affair and leave her husband, only to be abandoned by Lowell when he
regained his sanity and no longer needed her. In a letter to Blair Clark—
who'd been through it all from Rapallo to Milan and back to New York—
Lowell confessed that he had been, paradoxically, both crazy and honest.
He now felt guilty for causing Madonia so much humiliation and suffering: "The whole business was sincere enough, but a stupid pathological
mirage, a magical orange grove in a nightmare. I feel like a son of a bitch."

Madonia left Erba, after her short-lived marriage, in about 1954 and
went to work for EMI in Paris. She married the distinguished Italian
painter Leonardo Cremonini in 1963 and in December of that year had
a son, Pietro, who is now an architect in Paris. Madonia returned to her
Sicilian roots when she and Leonardo bought a holiday house in the island
of Panarea, off the north coast of Sicily. But her second marriage didn't
last and she divorced Leonardo in 1970. Madonia's son remembered her
speaking of her "difficult encounters and a tormented life" with Lowell.
He kept in touch with all his women and, true to form, did not entirely let
go of Madonia. Pietro remembers that in May 1974, when he was ten years
old, his mother took him to England to see the operas at Glyndebourne

in Sussex and to visit Lowell at Blackwood's house in Kent. Welcoming her visit, Lowell wrote, "I know we think of seeing each other again with excitement of course and surely fear. . . . May we be gay and gentle when we meet."

Lowell did not write poems about Madonia, but made two intriguing allusions to her. In "A Mad Negro Soldier Confined at Munich," about the man he encountered after his breakdown in Salzburg at the American military hospital in Munich, he wrote, "Who but my girl-friend set the town on fire?" In "Dante 3. Buonconte," Count Buonconte poignantly refers to his widow and Madonia's namesake by lamenting, "No one prays for me . . . Giovanna or the others."[3]

III. Ann Adden

Ann Adden was born 1938 and grew up in Concord, Massachusetts, near Boston. Her grandmother came from a New Bedford whaling family who'd lost their fortune long ago. Lowell, strongly influenced by *Moby-Dick*, was greatly interested in her background. Her nearly blind father was a furniture maker, and her happy childhood gave her a solid psychological foundation. After a year at Connecticut College she transferred to Bennington in Vermont. She then thought of becoming a psychiatrist. Between colleges she took a semester off to work as an attendant in Massachusetts Mental Hospital, which trained Harvard medical students and allowed her to attend doctors' meetings about patients.

Adden met Lowell in January 1958, when she was nineteen, on the floor of the mental hospital where men and women patients were housed separately but allowed to socialize during the day. She knew who Lowell was; and though he was manic, he was still brilliant and charismatic. The mania, in fact, was part of his attraction. Adden recently wrote that she was more a seeker than a thinker, "I wasn't intellectually sophisticated or clever, just extremely intense and passionate in my budding, thought-filled eagerness. It was the intoxication of ideas, the obsessive puzzle. That's what drew me. It was heady stuff, plus the fame, for a nineteen-year-old young girl/woman." She fell in love with his exciting personality and ideas, but remained remarkably level-headed and self-possessed.

Adden's character and insight enabled her, though young and inexperienced, to help Lowell in times of crisis. She recalled, "Mostly I still see those hurting eyes, like the eyes of an animal in the headlights of an oncoming car, a desperate cry for grounding in the oncoming chaos of things careening into madness. In the extremity of his falling apart, like a child, he projected onto me some 'still-point' at the center of his whirling vortex." Quoting Lowell's "Summer Between Terms," she recalled that "his soul was stripped naked and his mind had 'branch-lightning forking through [his] thought and veins.' He was screaming, threatening to throw furniture through the [barred] windows. The medical staff would then send out a call for me, which certainly seems unprofessional today. Would I come and quiet him down? And I would, with a few words of calm reassurance. He would then become tranquil, malleable—even peaceful. I never doubted that inexplicable capacity to return him to some bedrock of calm." She was never afraid of Lowell and had the ability to make him sane: to help him, save him and make him "wanted," as he'd never been wanted by his mother. His line, "I mad, you mad for me" was a plea for help that suggested their powerful bond.

While recuperating at McLean, Lowell as usual combined romantic infatuation with high-brow tutorials to prepare his young, eager disciple for her future role as his intellectual companion. Following his strict instructions, the penalty clause for emotional involvement with Lowell, Adden was told to read and respond to a heady mixture of Dante's *Inferno*, Kant's *Critique of Pure Reason* (an apt title in view of Lowell's current condition) and—one of his weird favorites—Hitler's *Mein Kampf.* Departing from his rigorous program and following her own taste, she also read Rilke and Robert Graves, took German and piano lessons, and started to paint.

When paroled from the hospital Lowell chose and played his favorite records for his select audience. In "1958," one of his poems to Adden, he asked, "Remember playing / Marian Anderson, Mozart's *Shepherd King, / il re pastore?,*" with its quartet of dubiously faithful lovers. In order to train her "to like the unlikeable," he subjected her to the trial of Alban Berg's atonal opera *Wozzeck,* with its medical experiments, betrayal and murder. They browsed in bookstores and went to the Boston Symphony. Lowell talked about his friends, describing his meetings with T. S. Eliot and emphasizing that Eliot's second wife was thirty-eight years younger than the poet.

They also spent a therapeutic weekend at a ski resort in Franconia, New Hampshire. Adden recalled her exuberant glide down the mountain, and the striking contrast between her robust health and Lowell's debilitating illness that accentuated their twenty-one-year age difference: "Skiing down with the full athleticism of youth and coming to a stop, I'm sure my cheeks were ruddy, my body brimming with the cold winter air and full of the exhilaration of floating down a mountain. Lowell just stood there watching me descend and then exclaiming over and over again something about rosy cheeks, the joy in my face, my health running over, but never once did he try to touch me as another might have done." Lowell didn't ski, but stood at the bottom of the slope to observe her impressive descent, which he later portrayed in "For Ann Adden 1. 1958": "at the Mittersill, you topped / the ski-run, that white eggshell, your sphere, not land / or water." Though he was attracted to and excited by Adden, they had no physical contact or sexual relations. She explained that "Lowell was, of course, heavily drugged during our brief time together, which left him, by his own admission, sexually incapable."

Lowell gave Adden compensatory gifts and love tributes that were meant to bind them together. She recalled that "he ordered a large print of an early Picasso for me, and I think his wife discovered it and cancelled the order or kept the print for herself. He felt very chagrined having to tell me that, like a small boy acknowledging who really ruled the roost." In fact, she got the contentious print before the order was cancelled. She wasn't quite sure how to return it and asked Lowell, "What should I do concerning the Picasso? If you want it sent to Marlborough Street you better say something to Lizzie. I don't know where you ordered it or what you want me to do."

In his manic state, Lowell was more impulsive and committed than Adden. He announced his plans for a new life and his intention to change his will and leave everything to her. He actually saw his lawyer to make it all official and called Adden's father to exclaim, "I'm planning to marry her." Adden's uncle, Francis Brown, editor of the *New York Times Book Review,* knew Elizabeth Bishop, who (as with Carley Dawson) became involved in Lowell's affairs. Like a mother hen, she called Adden's parents and tried to sever the relationship. Nevertheless, and to seal their "engagement," Lowell bought Adden an expensive gold ring. But once again, she cast a cold eye on the expensive present: "As for 'that twelve-carat lump of gold': the gold wedding ring was archetypal—not worldly—nor did I ever take it to be anything else. I think there was something written inside it, but I don't remember what it was. My parents 'disappeared' it while I was living in Europe, hopefully dismissing what was for them a traumatic event with a young and headstrong daughter." Adden had no desire for sex and no thought of marriage—even if Lowell had been well—and was much too young to become permanently involved with him.

On January 31, 1958, as their heated relations cooled down, Adden began to withdraw from Lowell. She knew that Lowell—"both there and not there"—projected his romantic fantasies on to her but had never left his real life with Hardwick. She tactfully wrote to console and encourage him: "It's so hard not to be able to see you. This time you must get well and I must not interfere, much as I would like to. And it will come from within you, a fact we women find hard to believe. I don't let myself believe it, fearing you will be able to find peace without me. Anyway, it's there and you'll make it. I only ache in the knowledge that staying away is the mature way to back you up. Again, all my love and I'm sorry I can't see you but from all sides it appears wisest."

Their brief, intense encounter came to an end when Lowell, under pressure from his family and friends, doctors and lawyers, suddenly stopped communicating with Adden. Hardwick, in a difficult position, described the end of the affair from her not entirely accurate point of view. She called Boston her own "inferno of suffering" and wrote, with a certain sympathy: "These damned girls complicate everything; they keep me from acting in his best interests, often because I don't want to seem pushing or jealous. . . . After completely dropping the poor girl, not even telephoning her when he got out of the hospital, not answering her calls—all of this seemed good when I heard it even though the girl, who had told everyone Bobby was in love with her and only needed to be rid of me to be well and happy, was described by a friend as in a 'basket case condition' due to all the disappointment."

Adden now throws new light on Hardwick's recollections:

I don't ever remember telephoning Lowell, certainly not in his home, and I don't ever remember him "not calling me back." . . .

The last thing I was was in a "basket case condition." McLean Hospital called me and pleaded with me to come talk with him so that he would cooperate. After our conversation, which was really only about that, I felt enormous relief watching him walk off calmly to be readmitted. It was a perfectly natural conclusion.

I don't really think I ever was in love. For me there was never any thought of clinging to the relationship. And despite what a gold ring is thought to signify, I don't think there was any thought of clinging on his part. I was a "passing unreality" but a very powerful element of souls crossing in the night, which had no grieving.

Adden was not sad. "I felt real relief," she wrote, "at being let off scot-free from something that in my own youthful spinning of drama, illusion and fantasies had taken on disproportionate and unmanageable dimensions. I had created an unreality that was much larger and potentially more harmful to many than I had ever imagined." Her departure for Europe ended their involvement, and she was relieved to hand over the burdensome and all-consuming responsibility to Hardwick.

Fascinated by Rilke, Adden spent her junior year in Europe. In 1958 she adventurously set out from London to Vienna on a red Triumph motorcycle and stopped for an intensive three-week German course in Munich. After a streetcar hit her motorcycle and broke her leg, she couldn't get to Vienna in time and enrolled instead in the University of Munich. She did not return to get her degree from Bennington, but stayed in Munich for eight years and earned her doctorate in philosophy. Her dissertation, "Das Weltproblem in den Frühwerken Martin Heideggers und 'Sein und Zeit'" (The world problem in Heidegger's early work and *Being and Time*, Munich, 1968) explored, she said, "in Heideggerian German the breakdown of the concept of 'value' at the turn of the 20th century." During her decade in Europe, Adden fell in love with a man named Constantine, whose father was mayor of Athens. She spent a lot of time in Greece, where she worked on her dissertation, and almost married him. She then became pregnant by her brother's friend, an English architectural student named Nicholas Kuhn. She had a son, Marcus, and a daughter, Melanie, and remained married to him for eighteen years.

Adden said that Lowell "was always listening to catch a line of poetry, the way an alcoholic always searches for a drink." His beautiful muse inspired five fourteen-line, unrhymed "sonnets": "1958" and "For Ann Adden 1–4" as well as the draft of a twenty-five-line poem that traced the course of their friendship and had many personal allusions that only she could explain. "Adden 4" describes his treatment and panic in the insane asylum, with its "swaying wall, / straitjacket, hypodermic, helmeted / doctors, one crowd, white-smocked." "1958," which refers to the year they met, mentions the gold ring, record playing and ski trip, his temporary escape from the madhouse and fear that she will escape from him, his feel-

ing of vertiginous dislocation, and his comparison of Adden to a leaping
rainbow salmon and to the heroic Joan of Arc:

> Remember standing with me in the dark,
> escaping? In the wild house? Everything—
> I mad, you mad for me? . . .
>   no circumference anywhere,
> the center everywhere, I everywhere,
> infinite, fearful . . . standing, you escaped.

"Adden 1," a variant of "1958," ends by paraphrasing the poignant vow in
Psalm 137:5, made by the Jews during their Babylonian exile. Substituting
"Ann" for "Jerusalem," Lowell writes, "if I forget you, Ann, may my right
hand . . . [forget her cunning]."

The longer draft poem includes lines specifically addressed to Adden
that Lowell deleted from "Waking in the Blue," his poem about confinement in McLean. He praises her beauty and character, and says her absence
makes him feel like a speared whale or the tortured victim in Franz Kafka's
"In the Penal Colony":

> Like the heart-toughening harpoon,
> or steel plates of a press
> needling, draining my heart—
> your absence. . . .
> Ann, what use is my ability
> for shooting the bull
> far from your Valkyrie body,
> your gold-brown hair,
> your robust uprightness—you, brisk
> yet discreet in your conversation! . . .
> you loom back to me, Ann,
> tears in your eyes, icicles in your eyelashes,
> bridal Norwegian fringe
> on your coat.

Her family did not come from Norway but, she explained, "I was wearing
my favorite Norwegian ski sweater which at the time was a great luxury."

The long draft poem also describes Adden's tawny hair and tanned complexion, the charm bracelet that girls then wore, and his vain wish to return to the time when he was about her age—a teenager still in prep school:

> Your salmon lioness face is dawn.
> The bracelet on your right wrist jingles with trophies:
> The enameled Harvard pennant,
> the round medallion of St. Mark's School.
> I could claim both. . . .
> Ann, how can I charade you
> In a lioness's wormy hide?—
> massive, tawny, playful, lithe? . . .
> You are 19,
> see me still a St. Mark's sixth former,
> my symbol the Evangelist's winged lion!

Adden was naturally thrilled by Lowell's love tribute and didn't at all mind the use of her personal letters. In January 1958 she wrote him, "I feel *most* inadequate at expressing the love I have for the poems you sent me. Liked especially 'Your salmon lioness face is dawn.' Your poems fill me with inexpressible warmth—All my love, Ann."

"Adden 2 and 3" describe their chaste encounter in Cambridge when she returned to America in 1968 and taught philosophy at the University of Maine. The first poem refers to her German doctoral thesis on Heidegger, quotes Maxim Gorky's *Reminiscences* on Lenin's brutal response to Beethoven's "Appassionata" piano sonata, and mentions "a rattling stress of cherry-stones" when a robber broke her window, entered her house and then fled.

"Adden 3," in quotation marks like the previous poem, is a close transcription of her lively letter to him in October 1968. Her retrospective, nostalgic letter mentions that she was a virgin when they first met ten years earlier and, picking up the Norwegian theme and her Valkyrie body, that she now has a "Viking son," born in 1965:

My father is building a house on the edge of a cliff overlooking Penobscot Bay [in Maine]. Returning from Europe after ten years, we came here to wait for emigration papers, work permits [for her husband] and here I chanced upon your book *Near the Ocean*.

Your work has grown tremendously these past years—or maybe I've just grown a bit older. It seems to have taken on much greater strength in health, an extending potency. Actually, I'd like to say humanity.

This particular book thundered me through my present and then dropped me suddenly in 1958. What a beautiful remembrance of someone, of you, to hold and looking all the way through to that seemingly virginal time when I fled America. I have a Viking son of three.

After divorcing Kuhn, Adden married an American in 1981 and, after their children had left home, they spent five years living on a boat. During this time many of her possessions, including Lowell's letters, disappeared.[4]

IV. Sandra Hochman

Sandra Hochman, an only child, was born in New York in 1936. Her father, Sidney, who had never gone beyond the third grade in school, was the wealthy owner of Ace Builders Supply, a brick manufacturing company, and of the Dryden Hotel on East 39th Street near the United Nations, where many diplomats stayed. Her parents got divorced and fought bitterly over her custody, but Sandra was unable to live with either of them. Her mother, who resided in the upscale New York suburb of Scarsdale, won custody. But her jealous second husband didn't want Sandra in his house and her mother didn't want Sandra to be brought up by her vulgar and materialistic father and his various lady friends. So from the age of eight to seventeen Sandra was sent to the Cherry Lawn boarding school for Jewish children, in Darien, Connecticut. Many of the teachers were refugees from Nazi Germany, and the headmistress, a Swedish Lutheran, taught a mishmash of world religions. Despite her privileged childhood—with speech lessons, piano lessons, riding lessons, psychotherapy and summer trips to Europe—she was miserably unhappy. She and Lowell were both only children who'd been rejected by their parents.

At Bennington College (two years before Adden), Hochman never dated, drank or took drugs, but studied hard, wrote her thesis on Elizabeth Bishop and planned to become a writer. After graduation in 1957, she had a bit part in Eugene O'Neill's *The Iceman Cometh* and then studied at the Sorbonne in Paris. The self-styled, youthful "art tart," who'd met

Anne Dick and Frank Parker, 1941

Lowell and Jean Stafford, 1946

Gertrude Buckman and Delmore Schwartz, 1943

Carley Dawson, age 16, 1925

Lowell and
Elizabeth Hardwick,
1977

Giovanna Madonia,
c. 1950

Ann Adden, 1960

Sandra Hochman, 1974

Vija Vetra, 1962

Martha Ritter, 1970

Elizabeth Bishop, 1964

Lowell, Caroline Blackwood and her two daughters, c. 1970

Saul Bellow in 1959 "on the pretext of interviewing him for a magazine, claimed that he talked about marriage on their second date." She slept with Bellow but, after he dumped her, gave him low marks as a lover and claimed "he didn't know a clitoris from a kneecap."

She also had a brief affair with the American composer Israel Citkowitz. He frequently complained that his wife, Caroline Blackwood, had left him with three children and that he had to spend his whole life being a mother. He was very handsome, but narcissistic and neurotic. Hochman was turned off when he wore a black mask at night, which made her feel she was sleeping with the Lone Ranger. She thought it was strange to have had affairs with both the father and stepfather (Robert Lowell) of Blackwood's children.

Hochman met the Israeli concert violinist Ivry Gitlis, who was fourteen years her senior, while she was still in high school and married him on Mount Carmel in Israel in 1959. She traveled with him on his concert tours, lived with him in Paris and, as "full-time baby nurse and manager," took care of all his needs. But Gitlis, who'd been a child prodigy, had been dropped by the impresario Sol Hurok, was trying to make a comeback and had trouble getting concerts. So they were always short of money.

While in Paris her first book of poems, *Voyage Home* (1960)—later annotated by Lowell—was published in a small-press limited edition by the expatriate writer Anaïs Nin. But when Hochman discovered that Gitlis, with more than one string to his bow, was having many love affairs, she returned to New York. She moved into her father's apartment at 929 Park Avenue, attended the Actors Studio Playwrights Unit and studied literature in graduate school at Columbia University.

In February 1961 the novelist James Farrell, a tenant in her father's hotel, gave Lowell's telephone number to Hochman. He never mentioned Lowell's illness, but suggested she interview him and promised to help her publish the piece in *Encounter*. Her affair with Lowell—which started fast and ended fast—had the same pattern as with Bellow: a putative interview, followed by talk of marriage and a sexual liaison. Lowell immediately agreed to talk and they met in the Russian Tea Room, next to Carnegie Hall on 57th Street. She'd just separated from Gitlis and Lowell announced he was leaving Hardwick. They took a cab to the Brooklyn Bridge, he read Hart Crane's poem about the bridge to her and impulsively exclaimed that he wanted to marry her. He announced that they'd have servants and would pay the maid top wages, and (rather prematurely) that they would be buried together in his family plot in Dunbarton cemetery. They fell instantly in love, registered in the Gotham Hotel on Fifth Avenue under the names of Mr. and Mrs. Hart Crane, and slept together that night. She didn't use contraceptives then or later on, never thought about them and wasn't afraid of getting pregnant. She may have felt that Lowell would marry her if she were going to have his child.

Hochman described herself as "five foot three, with an athletic body, green eyes, blonde and brownish hair." She was slightly chubby and didn't mind when Lowell affectionately called her Butterball. She was struck by Lowell's "beautiful cat eyes, yellowish green, his high cheek bones and drawling voice." She wrote that "we both took off our clothes without any embarrassment. I looked at Cal nude. He was sculpted perfectly. I loved his tall body with curly black hairs on his chest. I loved his very white skin." She recalled that he was "a fabulous and considerate lover. . . . We were sexually perfect for each other. . . . Our lovemaking was heated, passionate and beyond the boundaries of anything I had ever experienced sexually."

According to Hochman, Lowell was also enchanted. He told her she was his ideal: " 'You're exactly the woman I've been looking for all my life and never could find. You're a poet. You're young. You're beautiful. . . . We have a new life without arguments, without tears, your face lights up when you see me. . . . Not a line on your face. Not a slash on your soul. I see you smiling and looking so fresh and enthusiastic about everything.' . . . Cal could mold me any way he wanted. As a genius he had me enthralled."

Lowell rented a flat at 85 East End Avenue, a posh address on the East River, and Hochman spent most of her time there. He set up two desks with Olivetti typewriters in the same room and treated her as a fellow poet. She helped him cut down on his drinking, gladly assumed all the domestic duties and even prepared his first Passover Seder. They listened to music, attended "happenings," rode the carousel and rented rowboats (which capsized) in Central Park. They dined and danced in the Rainbow Room in Rockefeller Plaza, and painted watercolors, including his masterpiece "Sandra Sunrise of Creation." He bought her an expensive riding outfit and admired her horsemanship (as he'd admired Ann Adden's skiing). They set out in a rented car for Oyster Bay on Long Island, but got terribly lost and wound up on Fire Island without reservations. Unable to find a room, they spent a rough night sleeping on the cold beach. Lowell used his shoe to carve out a slight concavity.

She went to his classes at the New School and he revised her poetry. On separate occasions, he met her all-too-suspicious parents. She also met Lowell's psychiatrist, Dr. Viola Bernard, who encouraged him to leave Hardwick and begin a new life with Hochman, and the poet Stanley Kunitz, who gave her a warm reception. At a dinner party the editor Jason Epstein, a close friend of Hardwick, told Hochman that her poetry was terrible. He disliked her affair with Lowell, and tried to break it off by insulting her and forcing Lowell to take sides against her. But Lowell became furious, defended her and later apologized for subjecting her to Epstein's rudeness.

After two blissful months Hochman began to question her conflicting roles as student, younger sister, new buddy, best friend, sex object and mommy. On March 3, 1961, Lowell surprised her with an "engagement" party at Blair Clark's townhouse in Turtle Bay, near the United Nations. Though she'd attended Lowell's classes at Boston University, where the students gossiped about him but he seemed perfectly normal, and had carefully read *Life Studies* ("My mind's not right"), she thought he'd recovered and that his mania was a thing of the past. She'd lived with him, met his friends, talked to his psychiatrist (in those days everybody had one) and was acquainted with many writers who knew him, but she "was the only one at the party who knew *nothing* about his madness." Later on, she was amazed at "how naïve and foolish [she] was at twenty-five, not to have seen the signs of Cal's insanity," which suddenly erupted that evening.

As the guests realized that he was manic, they became afraid of his violence and suddenly left the room. Lowell began to click his heels like a Nazi and goose step toward her, lunging at her throat and throwing her on the ground. " 'I'm Hitler and you're a Jew and I'm going to kill you,' he said, putting his strong hands around my neck"—as he had done with Jean Stafford and Carley Dawson. She thought, "If I hadn't stayed perfectly calm until he got off my body and then passed out, he would have murdered me."

Blair Clark recalled, "I didn't know Sandra Hochman existed before then. Cal was in terrible physical shape, shaking, panicky, God knows what he was taking in the way of drugs. He was sweating, lighting cigarettes, talking nonstop. They both stayed overnight in my house. I locked my door and in the middle of the night she started beating on it; I think it was not so much that he was attacking her but that she was worried about him, because he was breathing badly and drinking. So I spent the rest of the night trying to calm everything down, trying to get him to sleep." The next day Clark took him for a six-week stay in the locked ward of Columbia Presbyterian hospital.

Hochman now realized their engagement had been a terrible hoax, and was angry that he'd hidden and even denied his mental illness. She was frightened and repelled, felt he'd polluted her idyllic dreams and decided she would never again risk her life with him. She didn't love him enough to take responsibility, see him through his mania and live a precarious life with him when he got well. Kunitz also changed his mind about their affair. After seeing Lowell ranting in the hospital, he realized that Hochman was too young and inexperienced to deal with his madness. He wanted to save her and warned her to stay away from Lowell. Kunitz now believed Lowell would never recover and marry her, and agreed that it would be best if he returned to Hardwick.

Sad and shattered, Lowell regretted the devastation he'd caused. In letters to Elizabeth Bishop he explained what had attracted him to Hochman and what he'd learned from her. She'd rejuvenated him, but it had all been a terrible mistake: "Once more there was a girl, a rather foolish girl but full of a kind of life and earth force, and once more a great grayness and debris left behind me at home. . . . I also thought she was very pretty. . . . The whole business is a slightly malarial memory for me. She has surprising energy and freshness, a slice of the new age, full of references, interests and rhythms that are strange to me, a bit of what one once was or might have been at that age. . . . I am glad it is all clear now, and I did feel considerable sympathy for her, and curiosity." He also told T. S. Eliot, who'd had a nervous breakdown himself when writing *The Waste Land,* that he was trapped in a kind of Nietzschean eternal recurrence from which he might never escape: "Our troubles are over and Lizzie and I are together again. The whole business has been very bruising, and it is fierce facing the pain I have caused, and humiliating to think that it has all happened before and that control and self-knowledge come so slowly, if at all."

In her novel *Endangered Species* (1977) Hochman said Lowell was her favorite poet. He told Bishop that Hochman's poetry certainly had "bounce and unexpected images, though I don't know how much order." Hochman wrote several poems about Lowell. "On the Island of Mull" (using a place in the Inner Hebrides of Scotland to represent Fire Island), she described the uncomfortable night when they were forced to sleep on the beach:

> But there was not one bed.
> Not one house. And remember this?
> We found white sand dollars
> Under the very white sand.
> And we slept in the sand.
> The fireflies scared us to dig
> Deep and make our hole for sleeping in.

In "Heroes" she admitted, "It is absurd / To look for you in the / Marriage bed." Echoing "Mad Ireland hurt you into poetry" in Auden's "In Memory of W. B. Yeats" and changing what actually happened, she wrote in "Reading a Copy of *Life*": "Your / Trap dropped me into / Insight. I walked with you through all that madness / Singing, 'He is not mad. He knows what he is doing.' / Until our bridges started burning."

In 1964 Hochman's father died and left her the interest on a million dollars. That year, after her break with Lowell and divorce from Gitlis, she married Harvey Leve, a lawyer who worked for the U.S. Consulate in Hong Kong, and spent two years there. In 1968 they had a daughter Ariel, now a journalist in London, and in 1970 Hochman divorced him. Leve was unhappy when they returned to New York, where he had no clients and few job prospects. He was eager to return to the Orient, she wished to stay in America. The divorce, which she really didn't want, was bitter and her settlement poor. Soon after, she had a nervous breakdown. But she'd won the Yale Younger Poets award for *Manhattan Pastures* (1963); published several novels and books of poetry with Viking and Putnam in the 1960s and 1970s; made a documentary film, *The Year of the Woman,* in 1973; taught poetry to children at the Metropolitan Museum of Art; and wrote many musical plays for staged readings and workshops.

Hochman felt that Hardwick hated her, never allowed reviews of her books to appear in the *New York Review of Books* and tried to ruin her career. But in the 1970s, after Lowell's marriage to Blackwood, Hardwick unexpectedly invited Hochman to tea. Filled with venom, unable to mention Blackwood's name but alluding to her notoriously messy household, Hardwick exclaimed, "I hate the one who's with him now. I hate her. I wish he'd stayed with you. Cal told me you are a wonderful person and very clean. This one is a filthy pig. I couldn't believe when I went to visit, how filthy she is." Later on, Lowell wrote occasional letters to keep in touch with Hochman. When her book of poems, *Earthworks,* was published in England in 1971, Hochman (like Buckman, Madonia and Ritter) saw him when he was married to Blackwood. The couple seemed uneasily civil in front of her, and Lowell seemed strange and withdrawn.

When she first met Lowell, Hochman could scarcely believe that she was having an affair with her hero, the man she most admired in the world, the greatest poet (she believed) in the twentieth century. She has never known, since then, the intense happiness she had for a month with him. She had hoped to marry him, thought they'd be like Robert and Elizabeth Browning, and planned to have a happy life together. When the affair suddenly ended, she didn't think, "Oh, well, on to the next one." Lowell became a sad memory, left a terrible wound and broke her heart. She never got over him. But she continues to admire his poetry, which strongly influenced her own work. Like Martha Ritter later on, she deliberately married an apparently solid man who was a great contrast to Lowell, and hoped to lead a normal life with him. But, as disillusioned as Ritter would be with her supposedly solid husband, she found that "he turned out to be as crazy as Lowell." [5]

V. Vija Vetra

Ian Hamilton described Lowell's relations with Vija Vetra from Hardwick's rather distorted point of view, but the turbulent events look quite different from Vetra's perspective. Born into a Lutheran family in Riga, Latvia, in 1923, she had (like Madonia) dark hair, eyes and complexion, and the exotic looks of an East Indian. After graduating from high school, she studied dance in Vienna and experienced the bombing of the Axis city during the war. Unable to return to postwar Latvia, which was occupied by the Russians, she became a refugee and spent three months in a German camp for displaced persons. She emigrated to Australia in 1948, spent eight years each in Sydney and Melbourne, and established her own studio and dance group. A choreographer as well as a dancer, she performed Indian, flamenco and modern dance throughout the world for seventy years. She spoke eight languages, including Russian and Greek. Devoted to her career, she never married or had children. She was closer to Lowell's age and more sophisticated than his young Boston students. But—far from her country, language and family—she was also more alone and more vulnerable.

Vetra first came to America in 1964 and performed on a coast-to-coast dance tour. When offered a job, she decided to stay on. In December of that year she introduced a sacred dance, accompanied by the music of Bach, as part of the services in St. Clement's Episcopal Church in Manhattan. Dancing under a hanging crucifix, she first wore a billowing white gown and then an elaborate Indian costume. Lowell's play, *The Old Glory,* was also being performed there. Just before the religious service, when she was in her costume, he introduced himself by saying in a rather British manner, "I'm Robert Lowell." He seemed like a child, so eager to impress her, and expected her to crumble with awe or squeak with delight. But she'd never heard of Lowell or his family and had no idea who he was. Intrigued by her lack of response, he was determined to win her esteem.

After the service, Vetra and Lowell joined a group of people for dinner in a Greek restaurant. When he discovered that she was from Latvia, he questioned her closely about the Communist takeover of the Baltic countries. She'd just returned from the Caribbean island of Aruba and had a bad cold. He noticed that she was ill and was very attentive, offered her hot tea and took her home by taxi. He visited every day and gave her copies of his books to show that he was an important poet. He was kind, brought her food and his wife's record player, and said she'd get well more quickly while listening to music.

Lowell was eager for Vetra to see *The Old Glory.* A few days later, at the reception before the play, he introduced her to Hardwick and unwisely said, "Vija knows all about T. S. Eliot." Sensing danger, Hardwick was glacial. Frank Parker was the only one of Lowell's friends who spoke to his guest. Playing off the rivals during the performance, Lowell sat comfortably between Hardwick and Vetra. When he went backstage to greet the cast, Hardwick told his friends, "Make sure Cal comes home tonight."

Instead, he took Vetra home and announced that he was going to stay. When she begged him not to complicate things by involving her in his marriage, he threatened her by exclaiming, "All right, then, would you like me to run under a bus? I have all this sedation. Anything can happen." She was then sharing the flat with a Hungarian doctor, and made a bed for Lowell on the couch. She expected him to leave the next day, but he stayed for a week or two: "That was Robert." Using a euphemism for sexual intimacy, he immediately wanted her to become "amiable." Though there was strong attraction on both sides, she temporarily put him off but aroused expectations by saying, "You will get my cold. Not yet. The time is not right."

When Lowell called Hardwick and told her to send some of his clothes, she asked to speak to Vetra and launched an attack on this new threat to her marriage. Vetra said, "I was called every imaginable awful word that was under the sun. She has quite a big mouth. She's a Southerner, you know. And, my God, she called me all kinds of names"—even comparing her to a whore. But Vetra felt Lowell was not a prisoner and stayed on of his own free will.

Lowell treated Vetra, like Hochman, as a fellow artist. They went to restaurants, to the theater and to a poetry reading, where he introduced her to Stanley Kunitz as his next wife. She danced for him, like Salomé dancing before King Herod or King David dancing before the Lord. She read Lorca to him in Spanish and talked about her favorite poet, Rabindranath Tagore. But she was also troubled by Lowell's emotional insecurity. When she went to the kitchen to prepare lunch, he'd call out, "Vija, Vija, where are you for so long. I am lonely without you." She said, "He had to have me all the time, to touch and be near. He hung on to me like somebody who could save him, like an anchor. I became to him something like an image of strength." Vetra was not strongly interested in sex. Lowell—always up and down, overexcited, distracted or exhausted—was not at all good as a lover. Their sexual relations were unsatisfactory and they gave up after trying a few times.

At first, Vetra (like Hochman) didn't know that Lowell was manic and became alarmed when she found out the truth. He also took her to see his psychiatrist, Dr. Viola Bernard who, for obscure reasons, encouraged Hochman but disapproved of Vetra. Bernard insisted that Lowell must be crazy if he was interested in Vetra and that he had to go back to Hardwick. But Lowell stayed with Vetra and she ended up as his nurse. She made him take his medicine and, since martinis mixed with drugs had terrible effect, tried to keep him from drinking. When he suddenly became weak, almost fainting on a bus, she held him and gave him her seat. A normal life was impossible and she had a very hard time with him.

When she realized he was crazy, it was difficult for her to believe anything Lowell said. But his brilliance and charm compensated for everything. She felt compassion and sorrow, as well as love, and suffered with him. Though he concentrated on himself and lived in his own world, he also included her in his emotional life and made her feel she was important to him. Though she couldn't fathom his motives, she became greatly attached to him and recalled, "I wasn't so sure of his health, and I wasn't sure if he really meant what he said—or if I were just a passing phase in his slightly dazed state. But he was very lovable. And he was very helpless. So my heart went out to him for that reason too. He was sort of lost at times, quite lost in the world of reality."

As he'd done with Hochman, Lowell secured a flat to show that he was serious about Vetra. He leased a studio in the Chelsea Apartments at 16 West 16th Street and signed the agreement as "Robert and Vija—Mrs. Robert—Lowell." They began to buy furniture, some of which she still has, and set up the flat. Jean Stafford, in an account of the latest crisis, told the astonished Edmund Wilson that Cal "is living somewhere in a basement with a Lithuanian [i.e., Latvian] ballet girl from Australia whom he met in a church where his play was performed. He said that she hadn't read as many books as Jean and Elizabeth had but had something that they didn't have"—exoticism, novelty, adoration, tenderness. Vetra fell in love with him and thought living in the flat would strengthen their relations. She "felt that having come to America, it would be wonderful to have a new life with someone I could really love and cherish. I felt very lonely at that time."

Lowell never spent any time in the studio. His friends, who wanted to rescue Lowell from Vetra, convinced her that it would be best for him to be placed in a mental asylum and he was taken to the Institute of Living in Hartford, Connecticut. She didn't think that falling in love with her meant Lowell was crazy. She knew that she risked losing him, but thought she should help him and hoped things would work out well. Lowell hesitantly said, "I really don't want to go, but if you think. . . . And of course as soon as I come out we will marry." They embraced, he asked her to wait for him and swore he would never leave her. A mouse, which she'd never before seen in her flat, peeped out to witness his oath. Later, she asked him, "Do you remember the little mouse?" "Oh, yes, I do." "It will come back as a lion," she predicted. Thinking of himself, he replied, "It already has." She thought that when he came out and was well things would once again be normal.

They spent the night before going to Hartford in separate rooms in Blair Clark's house, where the playwright Lillian Hellman interrogated and accused Vetra, as if she'd committed a crime. The next day Vetra came along in the rented limousine because (as with Ann Adden) Lowell wouldn't listen to anyone but her. He sat quietly between Vetra and Clark, as he'd once sat between Vetra and Hardwick, and held her hand all the way. He seemed like a lion brought to the altar for sacrifice and it was a very sad trip for her. Dr. Erik Linnolt at the Institute was Estonian and joked that there was some kind of "Baltic conspiracy" between them.

She returned to the flat, which seemed like a hospital waiting room, expecting his release and hoping they'd remain together. Though she heard nothing from him for two weeks, he wrote to her every day, exclaiming, "Please don't change your mind, mine only grows more set in determination to marry you. Dearest Love, Love, Love, you wanted letters, but I only want to return to you as soon as possible." But the Institute sent his letters to Hardwick, not to Vetra, who recalled, "I thought I would take my life, that's how down I was."

On February 9, 1965, still torn between the two women, and expressing himself in negatives and suppositions, Lowell wrote Hardwick from the Institute: "If you and Harriet want me, I am yours. Vija is coming up here tomorrow, and I ought, I suppose, to make no decision till after then. Still, I now know for certain that I can't avoid returning to my two girls, if they'll have me. I am sorry from my heart for having put us all through the hoops."

Vetra (not Hardwick) was the only one allowed to visit Lowell in Hartford. He had probably been given shock treatments. He was so unsure of himself, looked like a vegetable and seemed as if he had been "walked on." The doctors had changed him and persuaded him to return to his family. "Well," he said, "I guess it will be best if I went back home." He felt guilty and suffered greatly when he told her. She thought it would be the last time she'd ever see him. She asked, as a sad keepsake, for the shirt he was wearing. He offered to give her a clean one, but she wanted the one on his back.

Vetra, who'd given up her own flat, was summoned by Lowell's lawyers and given two days to get out of the studio. She felt their behavior was "heartless, absolutely heartless. That's the American way. Very ugly." Hardwick recalled, as if Lowell owed nothing to Vetra, that Vetra retaliated by sending him "a lot of bills with demanding notes." Lowell ignored them and Hardwick paid up.

Once released from Hartford and forbidden to see Vetra, Lowell was spirited away on a trip to Egypt. After he returned to America, she had an awkward encounter with him on a Fifth Avenue bus. Still confused about his motives, she asked about the missing letters he'd sent from the Institute. He was enraged at being deceived by the doctors, and asked Hardwick to return his letters to Vetra.

In 1971, when Vetra was going to perform in London, she heard that

Lowell had left Hardwick and would be there at the same time. Kunitz told her how to get in touch with Lowell through his publisher Faber and Faber. She wrote to him from New York, giving her London address and phone number, and Lowell phoned as soon as she arrived. He was very excited and wanted to see her immediately. She had an appointment, but agreed to come right away. In a final twist of the knife, Lowell appeared with his new wife, Caroline Blackwood, who was pregnant with Sheridan. They had a glass of wine and a chat, and Lowell said, "Now Lizzie will understand why I left her for Caroline. I wanted you to know before I told Lizzie." Shocked and humiliated by his behavior—she's still angry about the way he treated her—she wished them well and left. Playing one woman against the other and enjoying their rivalry, he first showed off Vetra to Hardwick, then showed off Blackwood to Vetra.

Hardwick claimed that she did not consider Vetra a formidable rival and that it was "the only affair I know Cal to have been truly, honestly ashamed of; there was regret sometimes, but not shame of choice." But the talented Vetra was worthy of his love. He was not ashamed of his choice, but of his own behavior. Vetra loved Lowell and, with no experience of mental illness, had to deal with his drinking and mania, and confront a formidable phalanx of opposition from Hardwick, Lillian Hellman, Blair Clark, Viola Bernard and Lowell's doctors and lawyers, all of whom made her feel suicidal. Lowell had suddenly abandoned her, destroyed all her hopes and forced her to reconstruct her shattered life.[6]

VI. Mary Keelan

In December 1967–January 1968 Lowell spent ten days at the left-wing Center for Intercultural Documentation, sixty miles south of Mexico City in Cuernavaca, an elegant, cosmopolitan town with a good climate. While there he met the twenty-seven-year-old Irish American Mary Keelan, an assistant to Father Ivan Illich at the monastery of Emmaus. The innovative Center—founded in 1961 by Illich, a tall, thin, Austrian Jesuit priest—emphasized the study of Latin American culture and the teaching of Spanish (the economic basis of the Center) to missionaries and volunteers. The students, both old and young, came from all over Europe and America. Shepherd Bliss—a Vietnam veteran and social activist with a theology degree from the University of Chicago—visited the Center several times. Bliss described Illich as a European intellectual who spoke many languages, had an early interest in multicultural studies, and

wanted to reform education and "deschool society." He found Illich pleasant, energetic, rigorous and scholarly. Bliss had been at Chicago and at
Harvard, but found the Center the most intellectually stimulating place
he'd ever known. Paul Goodman and Jonathan Kozol had also visited the
Center, but neither Bliss nor Kozol remembered Keelan.

In January 1968 Lowell discreetly wrote Elizabeth Bishop that he had a
"marvelous stay in Cuernavaca with a radical priest friend of mine, Mon-
signor Ivan Illich. . . . Queer gathering; at one moment I'd be talking to
heavy Chicago nuns, and the next to Brazilian refugees with forty year
sentences waiting for them. Lots of climbing Toltec ruins, New Year's
midnight in the market." But the real thrill was satisfying his "unlimited
desire" and having sex with Keelan in the monastery packed with well-
fed nuns.

On January 8, 1968, the day he flew back to New York, Keelan accompanied him to the airport. The next day she wrote to express her maternal
concern, recalled their "fierce moments" together and made a sentimental
symbol out of the flower she wore: "Yesterday I waited till after your plane
lifted . . . did you fly safely? I hope you slept, you seemed tired, but also
a little happy, and so I was happy. I wanted to run over and give you the
blue flower I was wearing. But then I thought how it would begin to die
and wither on the way home, and I didn't want you to have anything but
a sense of life, not withering." In the same letter she said how much she
missed him, had been reading his poems and had injured herself when
dreaming about him: "Walking by your room is hell. . . . I read *Life Studies* past midnight. The nuns scolded that I go to bed. I bumped into the
iron staircase in my *cell* going to bed thinking of you—in *Life Studies* and
now—and have a gashed lip and puffed eye. . . . I look to see you soon. Let
us clasp and not grasp what's life, and fragile. But strong too, as the hills,
and colored too as the flowers."

When Keelan returned to visit the monastery eighteen months later,
she noted that the rules had become stricter (and might have constrained
them) and remembered their joyous time together: "Gates—locked
ones—and signs and rules and hierarchies all about. . . . When we were
here it had a flavor that it will *never* have again—and I am *very very* happy
that that is what I experienced and what you have captured for all time.
Everything here now is *so* relevant."

Ian Hamilton observed that the twelve "Mexico" love poems about
Keelan "have a candor and clear-sightedness which Lowell has never

before allowed himself when writing of his 'affairs'; for the first time, the 'girl' has a real dramatic presence." Lowell contrasts his age, fame and married state to her natural, childlike innocence. His theme is similar to Andrew Marvell's in "The Definition of Love":

> My Love is of a birth as rare
> As 'tis for object strange and high:
> It was begotten by despair
> Upon Impossibility.

In "Will Not Come Back (Volverán)," Lowell's first poem about Keelan, he changes the Spanish "*will* come back" to a less promising negative. The swallows "that stopped full flight to see your beauty / and my good fortune" will not return. But he insists, with religious solemnity and romantic hyperbole, that his love for her is greater than any she will ever have with another man: "as men adore God at the altar, as I love you—/ don't blind yourself, you'll not be loved like that." In the "Mexico" poems he celebrates her youth and beauty: "you, some sweet uncertain age, say twenty-seven, / untempted, unseared by honors or deception," and mourns her absence: "When you left, I thought of you each hour of the day."

In some of his most voluptuous lines, he recalls their Blakean mixture of innocence and experience, the magical experience of undressing her and their sexual encounters when there's room for only one in bed: "We're knotted together in innocence and guile. . . . by some hallucination of my hand / I imagined I was unwrapping you. . . . You curl in your metal bunk-bed like my child, / I sprawl on an elbow troubled by the floor."

As the emotions intensify, he worships her body, reflected in the luscious landscape, from breast to vulva, "a cleavage dropping miles to the valley's body," and records their heights of passion, "the hours / of shivering, ache and burning, when we charged / so far beyond our courage." Calling her child once again and echoing *Hedda Gabler*'s "vine leaves in his hair," he refers to the flowers she wore when they said farewell at the airport. Evoking the shivering coolness after the heat of sex, he apologizes for the rough strife of their lovemaking and describes their pillow talk:

> Poor Child, you were kissed so much you thought you were
>   walked on;

yet you wait in my doorway with bluebells in your hair. . . .
Our conversation moved from lust to love,
asking only coolness, stillness, intercourse.

In the penultimate poem, "Eight Months Later," he claims he'd assumed godlike powers through sexual exultation with a young woman: "did anyone ever sleep with anyone / without thinking a split second he was God?"

When Frank Parker asked Caroline Blackwood which woman had meant most to Lowell, "she thought this girl about whom he wrote those poems on Mexico was important." As usual, Lowell kept in touch and saw Keelan again in New York in 1968. The painter Sidney Nolan recalled, "There was the Mexico girl. She was a nice girl. Cal liked her. He called her 'lace-curtain Irish.' She was a medievalist, I think. Irish-American—in her 30s. We went out to dinner a few times. . . . There are very touching poems about her. I really liked her. I met them both once on a sunny street and they sat down on the steps outside the place where she was teaching. They were like a couple of kids. She was a serious girl and she wished him well."[7]

VII. Martha Ritter

Martha Ritter could spin yarns about her family to match Lowell's and (as with Adden) he was fascinated by her background. Her ancestors were both reformers and adventurers. One was minister of the *Mayflower* congregation; another, a murderer, was the first man to be hanged in the New World. Her parents were restless idealists and activists, dedicated to improving society. Her father, a graduate of Yale Law School, served in the Connecticut legislature. He fought against segregation, worked for civil rights with Eleanor Roosevelt and Jackie Robinson, and was a legal adviser to Martin Luther King. Her mother, who earned an FBI file while still in college, attended Yale Divinity School, sang in nightclubs on Saturday nights and preached on Sundays.

Ritter was born in New Haven in 1948 and had four younger brothers. She grew up in Hartford and attended the Chaffee School in Windsor, Connecticut. Intellectual and idealistic, with long, striking red hair, she entered Harvard in 1966. She planned to major in history to prepare for a political career, but later changed to English literature. She had an adventurous visit to Czechoslovakia during the Russian invasion of Prague in August 1968, and was a summer intern at the *Hartford Times* in 1969.

In the fall of 1969 Ritter, who wanted to take Lowell's poetry class but hadn't read much of his work, slipped three of her poems under his locked door and was admitted to the select circle. She found his teaching marked by stimulating but cryptic statements. One student poem, he said, "sounds like Dickens having just read Tennyson." And he would exclaim to a puzzled class, who may not have read either poet, "Marvell is bonier but more electric than Horace"—leaner, that is, but more exciting.

Ritter decided to write her senior thesis on Lowell's latest poems, *Notebook, 1967–68* (1969), and he agreed to an interview. She recalled, "He said I could come and sit in on sessions he had with Frank Bidart. Every week the poems he had written that week were gone over by Frank and Cal. He told me, in that funny way he had of being sardonic and friendly at the same time: 'If you keep quiet in the corner, you can listen and take notes.'"

She helped Bidart with the typing, sometimes made suggestions (as Lowell had done with Ford) and—since Lowell was always open to advice—even had a few of them accepted. Instead of following Lowell's example of endlessly revising, she did the opposite with her own work: she would either finish her poems or abandon them. Lowell encouraged her by saying, "You have remarkable capabilities. If you can learn to appreciate the poignant moments, you will be a remarkable person." Bidart, who liked Ritter and found her attractive, said she was not self-important, not trying to advance her career as Lowell's girlfriend and not interested in breaking up his marriage. He described her as sweet, decent, nice and sincerely fond of Lowell.

Ritter was intrigued by Lowell's unusual combination of dazzling intellect and childlike personality. His wife and daughter remained in New York, and he felt rather lonely at Harvard. She said, "I would go to his rooms at Quincy House and spend a lot of time with him. Yes, I fell in love with him: gradually during that fall. We developed these very secret kind of domestic interstices. I would go and cook things and type up poems and make typographical errors and invent new words." They talked about many subjects besides poetry: the secret lives of Caesar, Ovid and Nabokov, the domestication of dogs, different religions, the history of art and the definition of love. She found him considerate and focused, gentle, calm, courtly and surprisingly funny, and never saw him in a manic state.

Ritter recalled that during the period of intense sexual activity among college students after the social and political upheavals of 1968, she behaved quite differently from the others and was saving her body for a special man who understood and appreciated her. In the taxi on the way back from his favorite restaurant, the Athens Olympia in Boston, Lowell—thirty-one years older than Ritter—held her hand. A couple of weeks later, after one of their dinners at Quincy House, he stroked her bright hair. He then kissed her and declared she was that other life outside of his real life—his marriage.

She was, she said, "worldly in my head in some ways, but very inexperienced in terms of men and love. One of the attractions was that I was quite untouched." Her innocence fascinated him and inspired literary talk about scenes of lost maidenheads in Elizabethan drama. Conveniently forgetting his relations with Anne Dick to intensify Ritter's mystique, Lowell said he'd never slept with a virgin. She observed that Lowell's mixture of longing and guilt, usually accompanied by a breakdown, made him start and suddenly end his affairs:

> I think for him women were somehow distant, mythological, as if they were to be studied—as if he was watching them, like a child. Yes, he was conscious he was treading on dangerous ground. He would talk about it and was upset about it—almost ashamed. But we couldn't keep away from each other. He said something to me, acknowledging that my love was greater than his. He said that most people can say that they love, but very few people can say they have been loved. And the fact that I loved him so deeply was an incredible thing to him.

Even in middle age, Lowell still felt disturbed about being unwanted by a mother who had never held or loved him. Again and again he sought compensatory love from other women.

When they made love for the first time, Lowell was a delicate, caring teacher. Ritter wanted to use the pill, but birth control was then illegal for unmarried couples in Massachusetts. Two Boston doctors turned her down, and a third one finally agreed when she told him she planned to marry her fiancé. When the hard-won pill caused nausea and chest pains, she tried to get a diaphragm at the Harvard health clinic. But the female doctor—severe and moralistic at a time that sexual activity on campus was volcanic—exclaimed: "I can't give you that. It's illegal. Have you thought of what you're doing? What will your future husband think?" So Ritter once again found help in Boston.

When Lowell was in Cambridge, he and Ritter spent many days and most nights together from October 1969 to March 1970, when he left for Oxford. They had dinner, sometimes with Bidart and the Harvard professor William Alfred, went to plays and museums, and drove around in a rented car. When Lowell was in New York, he called her on the phone in his upstairs study. He was fascinated with what he considered the bizarre demands of the women's liberation movement and was amazed by the innovation of co-ed showers in the student dormitories, which would have been inconceivable when he was a Harvard undergraduate. He loved to concoct weird combinations of unlikely couples in the showers: a slovenly waitress with a fastidious Harvard professor.

Their routine changed in January when the term ended and Lowell had to move out of their love nest at Quincy House. He also had to invent reasons for continuing to commute from New York to Cambridge. He and Ritter stayed in cheap motels to avoid discovery—though there must have been many people at Harvard who knew about their relationship. She'd lie in bed at night, while Lowell slept, listening to the heavy trucks thundering by on the highway.

Another crisis occurred in the spring term when Ritter got pneumonia and languished for a week in the Harvard infirmary. Lowell called to express his concern and fortified her by echoing Deuteronomy 31:6: "Be strong and of a good courage." He insisted, rather cryptically, "The best thing you can do is to completely give into it. You are strong." After her recovery and still only twenty-one, she realized that she would never be able to marry Lowell. She noted, "I knew intuitively that such intensity could not last. I knew there was an unreality to our days."

When Lowell left for All Souls College, Oxford, in April 1970 he seemed to be trying to weaken their bonds and distance himself from her. But there was no clear break before he went to England and he knew that she planned to follow him. She'd applied to graduate school at Oxford before she met Lowell, had taken a ten-hour entrance exam at Harvard and had to go to England for the interview. Her parents did not actively discourage her from following Lowell and allowed her to make her own decision. They said, "If this is important to you, then pursue it." But they also warned her, "You must realize that it will not end happily."

Ritter did not tell Lowell that she was coming to the University of Essex in Colchester, where he began to teach in the fall of 1970. In her youthful ardor, she thought it would be more romantic and exciting to surprise him by her sudden appearance:

I'd seen him in April, heard from him in June, and this was September. He didn't know I was coming. I appeared in his class. It was very dramatic.

It was very impulsive of me, but I'd been given every reason to feel that this was going to pick up where we'd left off. But there was a radical change. . . .

I found his classroom and walked in and sat in the back. He was droning on almost inaudibly. He was listless and foggy. The students were restless. He saw me and sent a smile through the shockwaves, but kept on droning. The whole scene was a slow-motion horror movie. He'd just had a breakdown. He bore little resemblance to the Robert I knew except that he was exquisitely fragile.

She was even more shocked and disillusioned to discover that he'd fallen in love with Caroline Blackwood. She learned that Lowell, torn between returning to Hardwick in New York or remaining in England with Blackwood, "was devastated not only in trying to sort out the Elizabeth / Caroline mess, but in facing the fact that the lithium had not saved him. He drank and smoked like a fiend and rattled on obsessively." She went to his classes and visited him at his Pont Street flat in London. She tried to minister to him and absorb some of his pain, and at the same time to quell her own.

Ritter was then forced to assume a sacrificial role. She "became a confidante, a person whom he knew loved him deeply and would do anything for him. And I had lunch with him every day and we talked about which woman [apart from her] he should choose. It was a bit masochistic perhaps, but he was in really bad shape" and had no one but his former lover to turn to. Lowell drew in his old loves to help him handle the new ones, yet was also adept at keeping parts of his life separate. Dudley Young, a junior colleague whom Lowell lodged with at midweek in Essex, never met or even heard of Ritter. She was surprised to hear from me about Lowell's brief affair at All Souls.

Lowell invited Ritter to spend a weekend at Milgate, Blackwood's messy country house near Maidstone in Kent. Not surprisingly, Ritter found the visit bizarre and distressing, and tried to explain her own conflicted feelings:

It is hard to imagine how I could have gone. I must have felt that exposure would help me get used to the fact that Robert had migrated to another planet. I watched them drink and spar. There was food all over the place and freezing drafts sending dust balls into the air. Why didn't I leave? Amazing that I stayed for more than five minutes. I think I was shell-shocked. I think I wanted to make sure that Robert was safe and comfortable.

Not at all her usual ebullient self, Ritter was shy and withdrawn at Milgate. Grey Gowrie, also there that weekend, remembered her "as anxious and mousy, and treated kindly by both Cal and Caroline."

Finally, the intolerable situation came to an end. Ritter said "We were both staying in London and we would journey separately to Essex for a couple of days, on a train, and I would stay in a hotel and he would stay at school, or with Caroline. . . . I was still this loving person, only no longer sleeping with him. But we were very close, and I think the guilt started to build up in him about what had happened to me. . . . It was horrible. He was aware of the pain that was being caused and he was in pain himself. I tried to be strong and kind, but I couldn't handle it and had to leave." Her Oxford oral exam was also a disaster. She was in a terrible emotional state and couldn't answer all the questions. As tears started to run down her cheeks, she wiped them with her hand and continued to talk. The three examiners suddenly looked alarmed. Her eye had hemorrhaged, blood was flowing down her face and she was rushed to the hospital.

Six years later, on February 19, 1976, Lowell wrote Ritter about their sad farewell, "I still see you leaving for the Maidstone-London train, with the story of the blood coming from your eyes and so much else." Two weeks later, referring to her poem "Upstaged" (about herself, not Lowell), he wrote Blair Clark, who had also become her friend: "I sent Martha Ritter a note care of you, which she doesn't seem to have gotten. I just said I had worried about her since we last saw her, and that I thought her poem remarkably perfectly natural, yet self-telling, and that it should be published. O ghosts of the past." (Her poem appeared in the *Radcliffe Quarterly* in December 1976.)

In retrospect, Ritter does not regret her affair with Lowell. But when the dust settled, she felt, "I could pull myself back from the edge and stay sane." The sudden dénouement with Lowell had made her wary and self-protective when she later contemplated marriage to other men. She knew a Lowell-like intensity would not lead to a stable relationship, but still yearned for the all-consuming passion that she'd had with him. But she felt that Lowell, in his lithium-levelheadedness, helped her develop and define herself.

Lowell published one poem about Ritter, "Dawn," an aubade. He later changed the title to "Morning" and, ironically, included it in his tribute to wife and daughter, *For Lizzie and Harriet*. In "Dawn" he emphasizes their difference in age (January was the old, eleventh month in the Roman calendar), and equates her with the beauty of the natural world—with the sun, flowers and anthropomorphic clouds. He's reluctant to relinquish her when she steals back to her residence after a night of love. He compares her to a sensual dolphin (before he awarded this sacred icon to Blackwood) and credits her with regenerating him:

> Chaucer's old January made hay with May.
> In this ever more enlightened bedroom,
> I wake under the early rising sun,
> sex indelible flowers on the air—
> shouldn't I ask to hold to you forever,
> body of dolphin, breast of cloud?
> You rival the renewal of the day.

The gifted Ritter was a perfect example of the fox who knows many things in contrast to the hedgehog who knows one big thing. Her varied talents as both actress-novelist and journalist–social activist pulled her in different directions and may have prevented her from achieving one great thing. She studied acting for five years with Uta Hagen, appeared in off-Broadway and television shows, and made popular television commercials. But in 1979 she turned down an offer to appear in her first Broadway play: Tom Stoppard's *Night and Day*, with Maggie Smith. Instead, she went with her mother to China and taught English language and literature at Beijing Normal University, just as the country was beginning to emerge from the devastating Cultural Revolution. Back in America a year later, she studied Chinese medicine. From 1984 to 1993 (with two years off) she was director of public affairs for the New York City Planning Department, and wrote speeches for two mayors, David Dinkins and Ed Koch.

Around the time she knew Lowell, Ritter suffered a series of medical problems: the pneumonia at Harvard and eye hemorrhage at Oxford as well as stomach pains in Russia and severe headaches in Israel. She had post-traumatic stress disorder in New York after her years of work and plans for train service from Manhattan to Kennedy airport suddenly collapsed and a coworker went on a murderous rampage. Worst of all, in 1983 a freak accident changed her life. During rush hour on Seventh Avenue in Manhattan, a piece of brick (a whole brick would have killed her) fell twenty-one stories and hit her on the head. Of all the people walking on that street at that time, she was the only person injured. Her spine was compressed and she couldn't hold up her head; she endured intense pain and needed two years of physical therapy to recover. She sued the bank that owned the building, but their lawyers claimed that the accident had been caused by erosion from pigeon droppings and was an act of God. The two sides settled in the middle of the trial, but she did not receive adequate financial compensation for her suffering and medical bills.

In retrospect Ritter, always the fox, seems to have missed significant opportunities in her life. She rejected promising suitors and chose to marry a man whom she eventually divorced. She studied acting for many years and then refused a rare chance of a Broadway part. She left her city planning job for two years to write a novel that was accepted by a major publisher, contracted and paid for. When it was suppressed without any explanation she gave up on it. She did, however, make significant contributions to social progress. She did research for the Ford Foundation and devised a successful plan to find jobs for the hard-core unemployed. But the organization, which owned the research material, gave it to the journalist Ken Auletta. He used it in his book *The Underclass* (1999), and got credit for popularizing the innovative work that she had done. She also analyzed the political, economic, environmental and legislative issues and wrote the main argument for the Alaska Lands Conservation Act. It was passed in Congress in 1980 and protected millions of acres of precious wilderness.[8]

W. H. Auden—thinking perhaps of Picasso's series of weeping women based on his lover Dora Maar—criticized Lowell by stating, "I do not like men who leave behind them a smoking trail of crying women."[9] Lowell himself confessed, "Sometimes I think I am the enemy of womankind." Lowell recognized that his love affairs could have devastating results, and always tried to keep in touch with his lovers—to check on their well-being, to acknowledge his gratitude and his guilt. At the height of their affairs these women had passionate and exhilarating lives, yet his abrupt departures and descents into madness were hurtful and shocking.

These young women's dreams were based more on illusion than on reality, more (to use Homer's terms in the *Odyssey*) on the gates of ivory than on the gates of horn. But each one could affirmatively answer Yeats' great question in "Leda and the Swan": "did she put on his knowledge with his power / Before the indifferent beak could let her drop?"[10] Lowell, who was entertaining and knowledgeable, and sometimes wrote poems about his lovers, had the power to change lives as well as to portray them. Few women wanted to leave, even when he damaged them. He also had a positive influence on many of his attractive, well educated and talented women, and most of them achieved considerable success in later life. Lowell made them suffer, but they all proved resilient and went on to develop their talents. Buckman, a magazine and book editor, contributed to the *Partisan Review*. Dawson helped found a cosmetics company and wrote successful children's books. Madonia, a talented musician, worked with some of the greatest opera singers. Adden wrote her doctoral dissertation on Heidegger. Hochman published poetry and fiction. Vetra was a world-famous dancer. Ritter helped create important social policy.

SEVEN

Women Friends, 1947–1970

I

Lowell was capable of forming deep and enduring friendships with women writers, untainted by the mania that encouraged him to fall violently in love. Two of his older women friends, Mary McCarthy and Elizabeth Bishop, were among the most distinguished writers of his time. He was a mentor to the younger poets, Adrienne Rich, Anne Sexton and Sylvia Plath—the last two his students at Boston University. His wide learning and acute insights about poetry held them entranced.

Mary McCarthy (1912–1979)—the daughter of a lawyer, heavy drinker and ne'er-do-well—was born in Seattle and moved with her family to Minneapolis in 1918. That year, when she was six years old, both her parents died suddenly in the influenza epidemic that followed the Great War. She was brought up by a great-aunt and -uncle, who treated her cruelly and beat her. In 1923 she returned to Seattle and attended a convent school. She lost her Catholic faith at twelve, her virginity at fourteen. After graduating from college in 1933, she married her first husband and divorced him in 1936. She then worked for a publisher and wrote scathing reviews for the *Nation* and *Partisan Review*. She married the brilliant and influential critic Edmund Wilson in 1938 and divorced him in 1946. McCarthy was an intelligent Latinate stylist, subversive satirist and sceptical observer of social nuance, a novelist, travel writer, literary and theater critic who was passionately interested in politics and ideas. When Lowell met her in 1947, she was already well established in the critical, reviewing and publishing *Partisan Review* crowd.

A close friend and literary rival of Hardwick, McCarthy was more beautiful and more sexually adventurous, in and out of marriage. She had gone to Vassar, Hardwick to the University of Kentucky. She had a wider range of interests than Hardwick, and was a better novelist and critic, more intellectual and successful, more politically committed in her protests against the war in Vietnam. McCarthy pilloried Rahv in her novel *The Oasis* (1949) and Wilson in *A Charmed Life* (1955). Jarrell satirized her in *Pictures from an Institution* (1954); and Hardwick, using a pseudonym, parodied and mocked McCarthy's *The Group* in "The Gang," published in the *New York Review of Books* in September 1963. Envious of McCarthy's sexual boldness and literary success, Hardwick couldn't resist wounding her even if it ruptured their friendship. A biographer wrote that Hardwick regretted her rashness and "later wrote McCarthy in Paris to apologize for the parody, which 'was meant simply as a little trick,' she insisted. She hoped Mary would forgive it, for she valued her friendship and 'utterly exceptional company,' and didn't know how to express the 'sense of desperation' she would feel if it couldn't be put aside."[1] Since McCarthy was unwilling to lose the friendship of Lowell, who took no part in the attack, she eventually forgave Hardwick.

In a lyrical letter to McCarthy, Lowell recalled her generous hospitality and refined taste when he visited her and her fourth husband, the diplomat James West, in Paris in 1963. She'd showed him all the sights, put him up in her luxurious flat, and took him and her well-bred dog on a picnic in the country: "I think of being twice met at Orly [airport] with waits, the Church at Senlis, St. Genevieve, the somehow huge Turkish bath bareness of the Panthéon, then your apartment with every inch shining with the dash and care of your selection, and finally the shadows deepening on the grass of Saint Cloud, the dachshund trotting off to safety, and the fruit still holding out and lasting with Flemish splendor."[2]

Though Lowell was certainly fond of McCarthy (his neighbor in Castine), he disliked her severity, which made her seem like a headmistress forever disappointed in her pupils. Hardwick spoke for both herself and Lowell in her comment on the self-confident and inflexible McCarthy: "There is something puritanical and perplexing in her lack of relaxation, her utter refusal to give an inch of the ground of her own opinion."[3]

Lowell was privately critical of his friend for setting impossible standards on his visit to Paris and told Adrienne Rich: "We've been rather frighteningly improved by Mary, who always does her homework—in everything, it might be said, cooking, dressing, responses in the local Episcopal service—and knows the [French] language."[4] He also wrote Bishop, McCarthy's rival for his interest and affection, that he was exhausted and irritated by McCarthy's striving for perfection and lack of spontaneity as she moved upward from bohemian austerity to haut-bourgeois splendor: "[She has] a lovely apartment, William Morris wall-paper, every item clean as a ship, and mostly brought over from England, meals planned and worked on for days, elevating, industrious trips to churches and museums, everything performed and executed to the last inch." McCarthy went all out to impress her guests and, like Hardwick, was extremely opinionated: "I find Mary a bit hard . . . to get at. The beautiful big house, the beautiful big meals, the beautiful big guests, the mind, as Hannah Arendt puts it, that wants to be ninety per cent right. . . . At times I think of Randall in his off-moods, though Mary is never discourteous."[5] It was particularly galling to discover that she was right most of the time.

McCarthy was too censorious and intimidating to inspire Lowell's real affection. He sometimes criticized her mixture of negativity and solemnity: "Mary can't open her mouth about anything without my wanting (or one's wanting) to put my foot in it and block her. . . . But then the glorious energy, mean at every point, the Irish pure disinterested joy in wrecking plus a Jewish seriousness, but really awfully glorious."[6] Later on, when his young stepdaughters refused to go to bed at the proper time, he would threaten to discipline them with a dread instrument, "Mary McCarthy's spanking machine."[7]

In the first of his three poems on McCarthy, Lowell contrasted her character to his own. She had the "loveliness of a duchess" and provided "enlightenment in our dark age though Irish, / our Diana, rash to awkwardness." He wrote—reducing her competitive accuracy by ten percent—that when they argued, "I hide my shyness in bluster; you align / words more fairly, eighty percent on target—/ we can only meet in the bare air"—like arrows shot by the huntress Diana into the bright sky. In his third poem he quoted her personal letter to him, contrasting her middle-aged visits to Manhattan to the more exciting trips of the past:

> "The real motive for my trip is dentistry,
> a descending scale: long ago, I used to drive
> to New York to see a lover, next the analyst,
> an editor, then a lawyer . . . time's dwindling choice."[8]

Lowell loved her clever, amusing and nostalgic self-analysis, which he felt was too good to waste in a letter. McCarthy, stung by his appropriation and with firsthand experience of private confidences sacrificed to Lowell's art, was entirely on Hardwick's side in the dispute about *The Dolphin*. She thought Hardwick was much better off without him.

II

Many of Lowell's close friends were orphaned and scarred in childhood. Jarrell's father disappeared when he was boy; the fathers of McCarthy and Plath died when they were small children; the fathers of Berryman and Kunitz committed suicide. Bishop (1911–1979), six years older than Lowell, was born in Worcester, Massachusetts, and had a traumatic childhood. Her father died when she was eight months old, her mother was permanently confined in an insane asylum when she was five. Raised by her grandparents in Nova Scotia and with her father's family in Worcester, she graduated from Vassar (a year after McCarthy) in 1934 and was strongly influenced by the poetry of her mentor, Marianne Moore.

While McCarthy was rather critical of Lowell, Bishop was heavily dependent on him. Unlike Lowell's three wives and the tough, sharp-tongued McCarthy, Bishop was sickly, shy and self-effacing. Like Lowell, she was also a heavy drinker, often perilously balanced on the borderline of madness, subject to severe depressions, mental breakdowns and suicidal urges. She was sensitive and delicate, her verse was cool and cautious, and she hated publicity and personal revelations. With the vulnerable and deferential Bishop, Lowell had deep sympathy and a true meeting of the minds.

Bishop recalled in a memoir that when they first met through Jarrell in 1947 she was, though a lesbian, physically attracted to Lowell: "Lowell arrived and I loved him at first sight. . . . He was very handsome and handsome in an almost old-fashioned poetic way." She later told him, "What I remember about that meeting is your dishevelment, your lovely curly hair . . . and how much I liked you, after having been almost too scared to go. . . . You were also rather dirty, which I rather liked, too." Though most women would find his dirtiness repulsive, she found it endearing. She'd had frequent conversations with Marianne Moore, but talked freely and naturally with Lowell, for the first time in her life, about how poets create their work. Later on, she paid tribute to his influence on her life and art:

"You have no idea, Cal, how really grateful to you I am and how fortunate I feel myself in knowing you, having you for a friend. When I think of how the world and my life would look to me if you weren't in either of them at all—they'd look very empty."[9] In a deft portrait of his character, she called him "wonderfully quick, intuitive, modest and generous."[10]

Though Lowell was well aware of Bishop's sexual inclination, he once revealed his own attraction to her by almost proposing marriage. She tactfully refused his proposal, and always maintained a decorous distance, though she once confessed that she would like to have a child with him. With all her physical and psychological problems, she would have been the worst possible wife for Lowell. Since sex neither complicated nor ended their relations, they were free to become close friends. While Bishop was residing far down on the map, remote and isolated in Brazil, she lived vicariously through Lowell's letters, and his literary news and sexual gossip were always welcome. Complaining to Anne Sexton about the primitive aspects of Brazil, she said, "after Italy, it is just one vast, ungarnished, unswept room, with so very little in it—and the distances are great."[11]

Hardwick, with Lowell's other Elizabeth in mind, observed that "Cal was encouraging. He liked women writers and I don't think he ever had a true interest in a woman who wasn't a writer."[12] Unlike Roethke, Berryman and Jarrell, Bishop was neither a rival nor a threat. Lowell helped create her reputation, did a great deal to advance her career with blurbs, reviews and grants. He got her jobs at the University of Washington and, sometimes as his replacement, at Harvard. Caroline Blackwood said that Bishop, insecure about her teaching position, "wrote hysterical letters about Cal going to Harvard. . . . She didn't want Cal as a figure in Harvard because he eclipsed her. . . . She was jealous of Cal and Bidart."[13] But Bidart explained that Lowell would never have come back to Harvard if it cost Bishop her job. When he returned, they both taught there.[14]

Bishop was the American Philip Larkin. Both lived far from the centers of literary power, had a slight output, published infrequently and died in their sixties. Each brought out four volumes of verse, spaced ten years apart, from the mid 1940s to the mid-1970s. Their poetry—precise and formal, sceptical and restrained—was marked by subtle wit, sharp light and clear detail. Both writers had miserable childhoods, and wrote about absence, disappointment, sadness, loss, wrong choices and the unlived life. Devoured by the wolves of memory, they leavened their mournful themes with intelligence, humor and technical skill.

Lowell, one of the first poets to perceive Bishop's technique and achievement, wrote an influential review of her first book, *North & South*. In the *Sewanee Review* (Summer 1947) he called her sharply observed poems—so different from his own—"moral, genteel, witty and withdrawn . . . unrhetorical, cool and beautifully thought-out." He praised "the splendor and minuteness of her descriptions," called her "one of the best craftsmen alive," and grandly concluded that "Roosters" and "The Fish" are among "the best poems that I know of written by a woman in this century."[15] His blurb for her third book, *Questions of Travel* (1965), praised her "grave tenderness and sorrowing amusement." Bishop gracefully reciprocated with her blurb for *Life Studies,* similarly placing Lowell with the best poets of his century: "In these poems, heart-breaking, shocking, grotesque and gentle, the unhesitant attack, the imagery and construction, are as brilliant as ever, but the mood is nostalgic and the meter is refined. . . . In the middle of our worst century so far, we have produced a magnificent poet."[16] "So far" was typical of her ironic wit.

Both lonely only children, Bishop and Lowell shared the trauma of having insane or deeply depressed mothers. Lowell's rhythm, tone and theme of loss in his autobiographical "Hospital II" (1973): "You left two houses and two thousand books, / a workbarn by the ocean, and two slaves,"[17] influenced Bishop's major poem, "One Art" (1976): "I lost my mother's watch. And look! my last, or / next-to-last, of three loved houses went."[18] As Lowell acknowledged, Bishop influenced his major poem, "Skunk Hour": "The dedication is to Elizabeth Bishop, because rereading her suggested a way of breaking through the shell of my old manner. Her rhythms, idiom, images, and stanza structure seem to belong to a later century. 'Skunk Hour' is modeled on Miss Bishop's 'The Armadillo.'"[19]

Lowell had involved Bishop in his affairs with Carley Dawson and Ann Adden, spent time with her on his disastrous trip to Brazil, been undressed by her when he was drunk and—when she emphasized moral values over the demands of art—was fiercely condemned by her for using Hardwick's letters in *The Dolphin*. Their friendship survived these troubles, and she could still both criticize and confide in him. Like her alligator in "Florida," Bishop had "five distinct calls: / friendliness, love, mating, war and a warning."[20] At the end of his life Lowell became rather irritated with her nagging and criticism, and in a letter to Hardwick said that Bishop complained of "so many things down to my not writing meter, making errors in description. Of course no one is more wonderful, but so fussy and hazardous now."[21]

In February 1970 Bishop wrote to Lowell about the psychological and sexual problems with her American lover in Brazil: "Well, you are right to worry about me, only please DON'T!—I am pretty worried about myself. I have somehow got into the worst situation I have ever had to cope with and I can't see the way out." Bishop, with her high regard for privacy, was angry and hurt when Lowell included her letter in "For Elizabeth Bishop 3" and gave him a sharp reprimand, her "war and a warning." After wounding her, Lowell tried to save their friendship by abjectly writing, "I fear I may owe you an apology for versing one of your letters into my poems on you in *Notebook*."[22] He not only had identified her and used her words without permission, but also had reproduced them verbatim instead of transforming them into art.

In his fourth poem on Bishop, Lowell contrasted his own furious method of composition—constantly writing and revising all day, every day—with Bishop's striving for perfection, long dry spells and painfully slow progress:

> [Do] you still hang your words in the air, ten years
> unfinished, glued to your notice board, with gaps
> or empties for the unimaginable phrase—
> unerring Muse who makes the casual perfect?[23]

Bishop's "North Haven: In memoriam: Robert Lowell" (1978), refers to an island in Penobscot Bay, Maine, and was one of her last poems. It connects the fifteen-year-old Lowell (still at St. Mark's school) to the titular island and concisely defines his tragic character:

> Years ago, you told me it was here
> (in 1932?) you first "discovered *girls*"
> and learned to sail, and learned to kiss.
> You had "such fun," you said, that classic summer.
> ("Fun"—it always seemed to leave you at a loss . . .).

The last stanza repeats (with two different meanings) "You left . . . you've left"—both the sea and islands, afloat and anchored, as well as life itself. "Derange" refers to both his mind and his poems, which after his death are finally and permanently fixed. She also describes his mode of composition as he'd described hers. Then, reversing Rilke's famous line in "Archaic Torso of Apollo"—"You must change your life"[24]—Bishop concludes that her sad friend, who vainly searched for fun, cannot change. In his first poem on Bishop, Lowell wished that "our two souls might return like gulls to the rock"[25] and she echoes this idea in her elegy:

> You left North Haven, anchored in its rock,
> afloat in mystic blue . . . And now—you've left
> for good. You can't derange, or re-arrange,
> your poems again. (But the Sparrows can their song.)
> The words won't change again. Sad friend, you cannot change.[26]

As in Ecclesiastes 1:4, the sea, islands, flowers and birds will always last: "One generation passeth away, and another generation cometh: but the earth abideth for ever." Bishop's tender mutability poem exalts the immortality of art over the transience of human life.

III

Lowell's intense friendship with the fiery Adrienne Rich (1929–2012) began in about 1957, when they both lived in Boston, and ended badly. She was born in Baltimore, her father a professor of pathology at Johns Hopkins medical school, her mother a musician. A precocious child, Rich had a dazzling career and a tragic personal life. She graduated from Radcliffe, won a Yale Younger Poets award and a Guggenheim fellowship to Oxford. She married Alfred Conrad, a Harvard economist and father of her three sons, the second one the same age as Harriet Lowell. Rich then became a radical feminist; the couple separated in 1970 and Conrad shot himself later that year.

Rich felt wary of Lowell, but he loved her sparkling conversation about poetry and poets, and recalled that in the late 1950s she "used to come out twice a week to see me at McLean and a couple of hours would whirl by in what seemed like a few minutes of talk."[27] Rich also formed a close friendship with Hardwick and said, "Elizabeth and I were having babies at about the same time. She lent me her maternity clothes after Harriet was born, they used to visit us on Sundays when their nurse was off duty." Hardwick (at least at first) liked Rich enormously and responded enthusiastically to her: "Adrienne was a witty, intelligent, charming, outgoing person when I knew her. We used to see each other all the time, even as much as every Sunday, when the two families would get together with the children at one or the other house or on a picnic and then shoo the children away so that we could all talk. Adrienne was so alert, so intelligent, so witty."[28] "She was a wonderful mother and wife, one of the most brilliant and beguiling women I've ever known."[29]

Rich acknowledged that Lowell's personal and poetic example influenced her poems. The poet Peter Davison, who knew them both, confirmed that "Lowell's interest in her work helped validate her as a poet, for, she says, he treated her as a poetic colleague. . . . Her relations with Lowell's poetry, especially after the first-person revelations in *Life Studies,* helped her 'recall herself to a sense of the language.'"[30] Lowell's poem "Child-Pastel of Adrienne Rich" deftly portrayed her brilliant childhood, her marriage, children and "playing bourgeois," and her infatuation with the influential radicals Frantz Fanon and Malcolm X. But her hothouse childhood had hurt her, and Lowell compared her father to James Mill, who nurtured the genius of his son John Stuart Mill, but made his life miserable and drove him to a nervous breakdown. Lowell suggested that by embracing what he considered humorless and sometimes rabid feminism Rich had gone against the grain of her natural talent and ruined her poetry. He asked the woman he called the disabled veteran of the political wars, "how long will you bay with the hounds / and beat time with crutches? Your groundnote is joy." Lowell's assertion in "They": "Lie with a woman and wake with Liberation, / her bondage is our lash, her labor our dismissal,"[31] echoed Friedrich Nietzsche's provocative maxim: "You are going to women? Do not forget the whip!,"[32] which would have infuriated Rich. Hardwick shared Lowell's antagonism to Rich's radical social and political ideas: "I don't know what happened. She got swept too far. She deliberately made herself ugly and wrote these extreme and ridiculous poems. . . . Rich transformed herself from long-suffering poet-wife to radical lesbian feminist."[33]

In June 1971, after Lowell had left Hardwick for Blackwood, Rich (by then militantly anti-men) expressed sympathy for Hardwick, whom she saw as a victim, and delivered a moral lecture to Lowell: "I feel we are losing touch with each other, which I don't want. . . . I feel a kind of romanticism in your recent decisions, a kind of sexual romanticism with which it is very hard for me to feel sympathy. . . . My affection and admiration for Elizabeth make it difficult to be debonair about something which—however good for her it may ultimately be—has made her suffer."[34]

Rich's criticism of Lowell's personal life was compounded by her caustic condemnation of *The Dolphin* in the *American Poetry Review,* which finally put paid to their friendship. She could not dissociate the moral from the artistic question, and argued that the quotations vitiated the poetry: "What does one say about a poet who, having left his wife and daughter for another marriage, then titles a book with their names [*For Lizzie and Harriet*], and goes on to appropriate his ex-wife's letters written under the stress and pain of desertion, into a book of poems nominally addressed to the new wife? . . . I think this bullshit eloquence a poor excuse for a cruel and shallow book. . . . The inclusion of the letter-poems stands as one of the most vindictive and mean-spirited acts in the history of poetry."[35]

In a letter of 1976 Lowell alluded to Wallace Stevens' "rage for order" and explained why his friendship with Rich had ended. Using a series of pejorative terms to describe her, he accused Rich of insincerity and opportunism. Betrayed and angry, he attributed her sudden transformation to a desire for reputation and fame that she'd failed to achieve when writing more modest and formal poetry: "Adrienne in her pre-prophetic days and for more than ten years was one of my closest friends. I could say she has become a famous person by becoming cheap and inflamed; but that isn't it. Her whole career had been a rage for disorder, a heroic desire to destroy her early precocity for form and modesty. And wasn't she right? And wasn't she unrecognized mostly when she first became a better poet and before the time of her fevers? And who knows how the thing will turn out—such a mixture of courage and the auctioneer now?"[36] He felt sad to lose a valued friend whose dogmatic views he could not accept.

IV

Anne Sexton and Sylvia Plath, older and more talented than the other students, audited Lowell's graduate poetry writing class in the spring of 1959 at Boston University. He disingenuously said, "Teaching is rather awful— boning up on what you can't use, then faking," but he was actually a learned, exciting, idiosyncratic and sometimes overwhelming instructor.[37] His teaching was also seductive. He attracted bright men and women, charmed and disarmed them, and turned them into eager disciples. Some even imitated his mannerisms: his drawling speech and the unusual way he waved his hands around when speaking. Richard Tillinghast recalled that "as he talked he deployed his hands in a style all his own, molding sentences, pushing outward with his palms, kneading ideas into place as though they were taking shape in the air just inches from his face."[38]

Many pupils were more impressed by Lowell's dynamic personality and exalted reputation than by his performance in the classroom, and thought he was better as a teacher of poetry than as a critic of students' poems. He taught them how to read as well as write poetry, and combined close analysis of great works with unstructured, wide-ranging lectures. Anne Hussey, in Lowell's Harvard class in 1973, noted that his passion for revision extended from his own poems to those of his pupils: "I had to watch out not to let Lowell take over because he could take anybody's work and turn it into his own work and make it a wonderful Lowell work, but it was no longer your work."[39]

Kathleen Spivack (whose memoir, greatly enhanced by the contributions of other writers, exaggerated her friendship with Lowell) was rather critical of his teaching: "Lowell himself was almost unintelligible. He muttered in a strange accent, looking down at a page. Occasionally, he asked rhetorical questions while sitting on the windowsill, his back turned to the class. . . . Toward students' work, Lowell's opinions had the randomness of a natural event. Praise or damnation fell equally upon our heads. Lowell's criticisms were erratic. Yet, if a poem inspired him to ramble, it was always inspired rambling." Though she claimed that Lowell was a poor teacher, she also stated that he "managed to train so many poets."[40] The answer to this apparent contradiction is that the brightest students were drawn to his charismatic person and poetry, and learned to extract the maximum benefit from his classes. His most prominent students at Boston University and Harvard included not only the future poets Sexton and Plath, but also George Starbuck, Robert Pinsky, Alan Williamson and Richard Tillinghast as well as the future publisher Jonathan Galassi and literary agent Andrew Wylie. At Iowa, Lowell taught Donald Justice, William Dickey, Philip Levine and W. D. Snodgrass.

Levine disliked Lowell's teaching, had unrealistic expectations and was angry when Lowell failed to praise his poems. Nevertheless, Levine expressed admiration for him and wrote: "To say I was disappointed in Lowell as a teacher is an understatement, although never having taken a poetry workshop I had no idea what to expect. But a teacher who is visibly bored by his students and their poems is hard to admire. . . . Still, he was Robert Lowell, master of the powerful and fierce voice that all of us respected; though many of us were disappointed, none of us turned against the man or his poetry."[41]

Snodgrass took exactly the opposite view. He was thrilled (not disappointed) and found Lowell concerned (not bored) with his students' work.

Snodgrass contrasted Lowell's wild reputation with his gentle demeanor and was stimulated by his teaching:

> A Lowell poem seemed like some massive generator, steel-jacketed in formal metrics against the throb of rhetoric and imagery. . . . Until his arrival he was the one topic of conversation: the time he'd done as a conscientious objector, his periods of madness, his past violence. We were surprised to find that, though tall and powerfully built, he seemed the gentlest of mortals, clumsily anxious to please. . . .
>
> However high our expectations, no one was disappointed by Lowell's teaching. . . . Week after week we came away staggered under the bombardment of ideas, ideas, ideas. None of those works would ever look the same again; neither would our estimation of our adequate responses to any work of art. . . . Who could be less than grateful for a mind so unpredictable, so massive, so concerned?[42]

Robert Pinsky (in his contribution to Spivack's book) gave the best description of Lowell's array of dedication, knowledge and passion. He taught "unpredictable, intense, rigorous sessions, unlike the tinkering of 'workshop' or the solemnity of 'seminar.' His spirit, which I admired greatly, made us all cheerful, eager, alive to our art. What impressed me was that he was so entirely devoted to poetry—he was a *man of poetry*, more than a 'great man' or 'famous writer.' . . . He liked absurdity and lore, and learning. Above all, the ardent chain of learning about poetry through the generations—criticism, gossip, technique, history, all the broad or miniscule study of the art."[43]

Lowell had a professional rather than personal relationship with Anne Sexton (1928–1974) and Sylvia Plath (1932–1963), his unusually attractive prize pupils, and rarely saw them outside the classroom. Sexton grew up in Wellesley (like Plath), had never been to college and had worked as a model. Married to a complaisant husband and with two daughters, she lived comfortably in the Boston suburbs and had many affairs. In 1959, when Sexton submitted her poems for his writing class, Lowell responded with praise that she valued: "Of course your poems qualify. They move with ease and are filled with experience, like good prose. . . . I have been reading them with a great deal of admiration and envy."[44]

But Sexton wrote Snodgrass that when the course started the students were intimidated and did not respond to his probing questions: "The class just sits there like little doggies waggling their heads at his every statement.

For instance, he will be dissecting some great poem and will say 'Why is this line so good? What makes it good?' and there is total silence. Everyone afraid to speak."[45] Lowell could be harsh, Sexton recalled, and "works with a cold chisel and with no more mercy than a dentist."[46] Then, contradicting herself, she said, "Lowell is really helping me as kindly as possible. . . . Lowell is very good for me; I mean his advice is good. A hard task master, but it is good for me." Helpful as always, Lowell showed her first book, *To Bedlam and Part Way Back* (1960), to Stanley Kunitz and William Alfred, and then passed it on to the poetry editor at Knopf. Grateful for all Lowell's assistance, Sexton told him, "You gave me the confidence I needed and as always your thinking was clear and definitive."[47]

Proud of Sexton's achievement, Lowell continued to praise her in interviews, letters and print. Citing two important influences, he called her "Edna Millay after Snodgrass. She has her bite. She is a popular poet, very first person, almost first on personality."[48] When *To Bedlam* was published, a year after *Life Studies,* Lowell provided a selling blurb that accurately predicted its success: "Mrs. Sexton writes with the now enviable swift lyrical openness of a Romantic Poet, yet in her content she is a realist and describes her very personal experience with an almost Russian accuracy and abundance. Her poems stick in my mind. I don't see how they can fail to make the great stir they deserve to make." In a letter to Bishop he confirmed his high regard for Sexton's memorable work, but was troubled by her depression and mania that were so close to his own and edged toward suicide: "In an odd way she is much more inspired than she knows how to be, and has done what scores of young poets, some of them more knowing than she is, will never do: written a book that can be remembered. I don't really like the tone underneath, or care much about the experience, or rather the experience's impact on Anne Sexton."[49]

In a letter to Sexton (who went to poetry conferences with a rhyming dictionary and falsies in her bra to support her, and wrote poems like "Ballad of a Lonely Masturbator" and "Menstruation at Forty") Lowell privately offered criticism of the faults she'd have to eliminate if she wanted to fulfill her potential as a poet: "There are loose edges, a certain monotony of tone, a way of writing that sometimes seems to let everything in too easily, bald spots, uninspired moments that roll off disguised by the same certainty of voice, poems that all one can say about them is that they are Sexton and therefore precious."[50]

Indulging in her favorite extracurricular activity, Sexton would repair after class to the bar of the Ritz Hotel near the Boston Common. She always parked illegally in the "Loading Only Zone," which she felt was okay since she was "only going to get loaded!" With George Starbuck and Plath she'd plunge into soul-searching and literary gossip, especially about the endlessly fascinating Lowell. She and Plath (who probably knew or guessed that Sexton was sleeping with Starbuck) would frequently discuss their suicide attempts as if they were comparing fashionable clothing and accessories. "Often, very often," Sexton recalled, "Sylvia and I would talk at length about our first suicides; at length, in detail and in depth. . . . We three were stimulated by it, even George, as if death made each of us a little more real at the moment." As they recounted in that posh place the pleasure of ending the pain and the triumph of precarious survival, the grim subject seemed even more exciting. Sexton called Plath "so bright, so precocious and determined to be special. . . . Intense, skilled, perceptive, strange, blonde, lovely." [51] Sexton won the Pulitzer Prize for *Live or Die* in 1967 and killed herself seven years later.

V

Despite Plath's beauty and brilliance, many people found her personally unappealing and were even repelled by her quest for perfection, egoism and ambition combined with the horrors and self-pity in her work. Like Lowell, she suffered cyclical mental breakdowns and was hospitalized in McLean. Hardwick's clinical, sympathetic description of Plath's mental illness was clearly based on her own experience with Lowell and revealed that the two manic poets had a great deal in common: "Persons suffering in this way simply do not have room in their heads for the anguish of others—and later may seem to survive their own torments only by an erasing detachment. . . . We think of these self-destructive actions as more or less sudden or as the culmination of an unbearable depression, one that brings with it a feeling of unworthiness and hopelessness, a despair that cannot imagine recovery." [52]

Plath had graduated from Smith College in 1955 and had won a Fulbright fellowship to Cambridge University. In June 1958, at the end of a year's teaching at Smith, Plath reported that she and her husband, the English poet Ted Hughes, "met the mad and very nice poet Robert Lowell (the only one, 40-ish, whom we both admire, who comes from the Boston Lowells and is periodically carted off as a manic depressive) when he came to give a reading at the University of Massachusetts. He is quiet, soft-spoken, and we liked him very much. I drove him around Northampton, looking for relics of his ancestors, and to the Historical Society and the graveyard."[53] For Plath, the salient aspects of Lowell's character were his impressive genealogy and Boston background, his appealing personality and his mania, which fascinated both her and Sexton.

Six months later, when invited to the Lowells' home on Marlborough Street, Plath had the impression that their marriage was ideal. She noted (as Snodgrass had) Hardwick's amusing imitations and Lowell's affectionate behavior (an implicit contrast to Hughes' surly self-absorption). Hardwick was "charming and highstrung, mimicking their subnormal Irish housegirl whom they have at last let go, he kissing her tenderly before leaving, calling her he would be late, and all the winsome fondnesses of a devoted husband."[54] Plath hoped, some day, to create a literary circle like Lowell's and preside over it herself.

When Lowell's class began in the spring of 1959 Plath had given up her teaching job at Smith, moved to Boston and was typing up psychiatric case histories at Massachusetts General Hospital. Lowell, once again a patient at McLean from April to June that year, was paroled to teach his courses at Boston University. Spivack, in the same class, noticed Plath's aloofness, her struggle for recognition and her formidable knowledge: "She seemed reserved and totally controlled as well as unapproachable to the younger writers. . . . She had a fierce competitive edge that made one rather afraid of her. . . . Lowell's obscure references were not obscure to Sylvia; she was the best educated of the group."[55]

Plath's own super-organized classes had been very different from Lowell's spontaneous meanderings. Like Sexton, Plath was at first underwhelmed by his class and felt the students' discussion of each other's poems was more valuable to her than Lowell's tuition—except when he focused on her own work: "Lowell's class yesterday a great disappointment: I said a few mealymouthed things, a few BU students yattered nothings I wouldn't let my Smith freshmen say without challenge. Lowell good in his mildly feminine ineffectual fashion. Felt a regression. The main thing is hearing other students' poems & his reaction to mine." Eager for Lowell to recognize her talent and resenting his comparison of her work to Sexton's, Plath recorded, "Criticism of 4 of my poems in Lowell's class: criticism of rhetoric. He sets me up with Anne Sexton, an honor, I suppose. Well, about time."[56]

Again like Sexton, Plath later felt that Lowell's personal and poetic example gave her freedom to describe her own mania and inspired her to reach new poetic heights. She experienced the same kind of artistic advance that Lowell himself had achieved after reading Bishop's poems: "I've been very excited by what I feel is the new breakthrough that came with, say, Robert Lowell's *Life Studies,* this intense breakthrough into very serious, very personal emotional experience which I feel has been partly taboo. Robert Lowell's poems about his experience in a mental hospital, for example, interested me very much."[57]

Lowell and Plath carefully studied each other's work, and Lowell predictably influenced the much younger Plath. In Lowell's "Thanksgiving's Over" (1946) the wife, having studied in Germany, exclaims, "You are a bastard, Michael, aren't you! *Nein.*" In Plath's most famous poem, "Daddy" (1966), the narrator screams at her German father, "daddy, you bastard, I'm through."[58] In "Memories of West Street and Lepke" (1959) Lowell connects his own electroshock treatments to the soon-to-be electrocuted Lepke. Though Lepke does not connect his murderous life with his mental life, the electric chair will make that fatal connection for him. In *The Bell Jar* (1963) Plath connects the electrocution of the convicted spies Julius and Ethel Rosenberg at the opening of the novel to her own electroshock treatments later on.[59]

It is surprising to find verbal echoes of Plath in Lowell's poetry. Plath's metaphor of the stifling bell jar influenced Lowell's line in "Fall 1961" (1964), "The state / is a diver under a glass bell."[60] In her suicide and resurrection poem "Lady Lazarus" (1961), the perfectionist Plath writes, "Dying / Is an art, like everything else. / I do it exceptionally well." In "Last Night" Lowell picks up her famous line and asks, "Is dying harder than being already dead?"[61]

Plath moved to England at the end of 1959 and Lowell never saw her again. After her suicide (on the third try) at the age of thirty, Lowell felt threatened by her death and repeatedly referred to her in his letters. In 1963 he told Al Alvarez, a close friend of both Plath and Hughes, that he was completely surprised by her shocking act: "She used to come to a few of my classes. I knew a little about her depressions but never saw anything, and thought the gods were smiling on her and Ted. I gather the death was suicide and that they had split up." The following year, in a letter to T. S. Eliot, Lowell raved about her poems in *The Colossus* (1962)—which Eliot's firm would publish in England—and compared her to one of the best American poets. He wrote that the last poems of Plath have a "dare-devil desperation. . . . I only thought of her as sensitive, accomplished and anonymous—now she seems as brilliant to me as Emily Dickinson, and with something of the same nervous compression."[62] Lowell repeated his comparison to Dickinson when writing to Bishop. Recognizing in Plath the same mental illness that inspired his own writing, he suggested that she had sacrificed her sanity to create her poems: "They seem as good to me as Emily Dickinson at the moment. Of course they are as extreme as one can bear, rather more so, but whatever wrecked her life somehow gave an edge, freedom and even control, to her poetry. . . . It's searingly extreme, a triumph by a hair, that one almost wished had never come about."[63]

In his enthusiastic foreword to Plath's posthumously published *Ariel* (1966), the cornerstone—partly due to Lowell's praise—of her tremendous reputation, he described her physical appearance and hidden talent, used the prevailing term "confessional" and noted another of their similarities: "father-hatred" both in "91 Revere Street" and in "Daddy." Lowell's father was a pathetic failure; Plath's father, a scientist, seemed to have willed his own death by refusing to recognize and treat his diabetes: "She was willowy, long-waisted, sharp-elbowed, nervous, giggly, gracious—a brilliant tense presence embarrassed by restraint. . . . I sensed her abashment and distinction, and never guessed her later appalling and triumphant fulfillment. . . . Everything in these poems is personal, confessional, felt, but the manner of feeling is controlled hallucination, autobiography of a fever. . . . Suicide, father-hatred, self-loathing—nothing is too much for the macabre gaiety of her control."[64]

Though Lowell said "it's hard to write now of her posthumous royal shadow, her honest cruelty, her insolent rightness," he continued to write about her.[65] Tacitly emphasizing their similarities, he described his own poetry as well as hers: "Somehow her death is part of the imaginative risk. In the best poems, one is torn by saying, 'This is so true and lived that most other poetry seems like an exercise,' and then one can back off and admire the dazzling technique and invention."[66] In 1971 he told Ian Hamilton, "I glory in her. . . . In an extreme Life-and-Death style, she is as good as Sir Walter Raleigh," the Jacobean adventurer and poet who was executed in 1618.[67] Writing to Hardwick that same year, Lowell was more critical of Plath's extremes and (as with Sexton) frightened by her raw emotion: "You feel strong attraction, strong disgust. 'Daddy' is too much for me, and I think it is weakened by being too much Sylvia—O stridently! Some of her new poems in . . . *Ariel* are terrific."[68]

Lowell's weak elegy, "Sylvia Plath," begins with three statements in the form of questions. The first quotes John Bayley's critical judgment of Plath—"A miniature mad talent"—which recognizes the real if limited scope of her manic poetry; the second—"rising in the saddle to slash at Auschwitz"—alludes to her horse Ariel and her poem "Daddy'; the third describes the conflict between her career and family. He also resents the distortion of her work by feminists who use her to justify their attacks on marriage and babies. He emphasizes Plath's fierce life "tearing this or that" and what he calls "the expanding torrent of your attack."[69] Lowell had encouraged Plath's searing poetry by his experience and his art, but was disturbed by his responsibility for its suicidal direction and cultish influence.

VI

Lowell's tortured connections with wives and lovers were complemented and balanced not only by his calmer relations with women friends, but also by his close friendships with men, which brought out the best side of his character. Except for his school buddies, Blair Clark and Frank Parker, all of Lowell's close friends (and all three wives) were writers.[70] Lowell claimed that he had more intellectual friends than anyone else and had never lost a friend, but also confessed—thinking of his rare disputes with Schwartz, Auden and Rich—that losing friends always made him feel terribly guilty.

Lowell was attractive to men as well as to women. He was lovable, social and hospitable, constantly urged friends to visit him and saw them whenever he traveled. William Meredith remarked that "nobody had any trouble staying friends with Cal. He was an extremely loyal and generous man."[71] Richard Wilbur recalled one occasion when he'd said goodbye and left Lowell's party in Boston, and Lowell followed him out to his car and jumped into the front seat. He felt he'd neglected Wilbur that evening and wanted "to talk it up."[72]

Though Lowell was well aware of the envenomed factions among poets, he was generous rather than cutthroat. Recalling William Blake's idealistic statement, "I cannot think that Real Poets have any competition,"[73] he told the ambitious Ted Roethke that some competition was inevitable, even stimulating, but that all poets smarted from the critical lash: "I remember [the Scottish poet] Edwin Muir arguing with me that there is no rivalry in poetry. Well, there is. No matter what one has done or hasn't done . . . one feels each blow, each turning of the wind, each up and down grading of the critics. We've both written enough and lived long enough perhaps to find this inescapable. Each week brings some pat on the back or some brisk, righteous slur, till one rather longs for the old oblivion."[74]

Most poets ask, in King Lear's modern-sounding words, "Who loses and who wins, who's in, who's out?" (5.3.15). When Algernon Swinburne died in 1909, the heir-presumptive Yeats set the contemporary tone by echoing *Romeo and Juliet* and declaring, "Now I am king of the cats."[75] When Frost died in 1963, Berryman nervously asked, "Who's number one? Who's number one? Cal is number one, isn't he?" Berryman also asked his fellow poet Howard Nemerov a rhetorical question that obsessed him: "If you ever really made it big, would you want to be the only one? Out there in front all by yourself?"[76] Though Lowell tried to remain loftily above the skirmish, he acknowledged that fame is the spur and that healthy rivalry gives a certain frisson to poetry: "A graver matter is the competition, the boxing match. Without it, I think we miss some of the pleasure of writing: part of it is rather like a tennis match. Who would play without scoring?"[77]

Lowell's relations with the talented, impressive but self-aggrandizing poet James Dickey provides a useful test case. Dickey constantly jockeyed for position in the endless king-of-the-cats race. He frequently attacked Lowell in letters to his own friends, but flattered Lowell when persuading him to appear on a television tribute to Dickey. After Lowell's death, he sent Hardwick a telegram saying how much he'd loved Lowell. In gossipy letters to Bishop, Lowell seemed amused by Dickey's competitive antics. He referred to Dickey's drunken violence and sexual escapades when Dickey was visiting college campuses, and commended his poem "Fire-Bombing," narrated by a bomber pilot who drops napalm on Okinawa at the end of World War II: "The optimistic James Dickey is one of the most desperate souls I know of, dreaded by the faculties where he has read. Rather good poet though, particularly on horrible things like fire-bombing."

Lowell also expressed, despite Dickey's faults, admiration for his absurd but stimulating declarations: "I had a day with Jim Dickey, assisting in an *Encyclopedia Britannica* (!) movie on him. Every so often (he began drinking at 9:30 AM) he would say loathsome things like 'The future of American poetry is in this room.' Or 'my problems are worse than yours.' They are; yet at times one felt his great energy to say something, so lacking in most writers."[78] During a 1967 lunch at Chez Dreyfus in Cambridge, Dickey recounted one of his favorite but improbable stories and claimed that he'd dispatched a ferocious bear with a bow and arrow. Lowell, who loved bear stories, imitated the bear and laughed in advance of his own jest: "But the bear wasn't dead, Jim. . . . When you got back to your office, the bear was sitting at your desk. It was Robert Bly," his old enemy, who'd recently published an attack called "The Collapse of James Dickey."[79]

In this atmosphere of intense competition Lowell, who had the greatest reputation, cultivated goodwill and advocated reciprocity of literary favors. Always generous in his praise of poets like Bishop, Sexton and Plath, he also remained loyal, in his lifelong patronage, to the mediocre art of Frank Parker and the tepid fiction of Peter Taylor. Lowell was instrumental in obtaining for his friends introductions to publishers and patrons, invitations to read their poems and offers to teach, as well as grants and prestigious prizes. He explained to the rather naïve Bishop the byzantine procedure for getting worthy pals into the American Academy of Arts and Letters: "I think we are each allowed one *nomination.* I am nominating Randall, if you'll nominate Flannery [O'Connor], I'll second. I am trying to get [Richard] Blackmur to nominate Mary [McCarthy]. Then we can all second each other's candidates."[80] A word from Lowell was usually sufficient to get whatever he wanted.

The poet Karl Shapiro had clashed with Lowell, who'd supported Pound for the Bollingen Prize in 1949, despite his anti-Semitism and wartime treason. Shapiro later said that "Lowell was a cold-blooded literary politician who created, controlled and sometimes crushed reputations," but gave no examples of the crushing.[81] Lowell may have neglected poets like Shapiro, but didn't try to cut down rivals. Two other poets gave more accurate accounts of Lowell's influence and generous spirit. Kunitz recalled that "Lowell sensed the smallest change of fashion, taste, reputation and shift of power. He played the literary dictator and insisted that everyone defer to him. But everyone truly admired him and willingly bent the knee."[82] The English poet Donald Davie observed, "He is himself the most modest and magnanimous of men: the generosity of his tributes to his masters, his peers, his juniors, is not merely good breeding, still less prudent diplomacy, but it is heartfelt."[83]

EIGHT

Caroline Blackwood, 1970–1977

I

In the spring of 1970 Lowell fell in love with the beautiful, aristocratic, wealthy, elegant, witty and talented writer Lady Caroline Blackwood (1931–1996), heiress to the Guinness brewery fortune. Fifteen years younger than Hardwick, the former model appeared in the early paintings of Lucian Freud as stunning and sensuous as Botticelli's Venus. The fine-boned, waiflike creature with large blue eyes had what Lowell described as "Alice-in-Wonderland straight gold hair" and was "fair-featured, curve and bone from crown to socks."[1] Lady Caroline Blackwood resembled her namesake Lady Caroline Lamb, another married aristocrat and novelist, who had an affair with the handsome poet Lord Byron in the early nineteenth century. Lamb made the memorable remark that Byron was "mad, bad and dangerous to know." Blackwood did not realize how madder and badder Lowell could be. As with Lamb and Byron, Blackwood and Lowell wrote about each other and when Lowell eventually left she hoped to recapture him.

Blackwood was very different from the inexperienced and undeveloped young women Lowell had fallen in love with during his manic episodes. She was closer to him in age, came from an illustrious family, had been married twice and had three children, owned houses in New York and (after 1970) in London. She had her own circle of famous friends, had started to publish satiric essays in the *London Magazine* and *Encounter,* and was not awed by Lowell's reputation as a poet. Wounded, reckless and unstable, she was just as dangerous to know.

Blackwood's maternal ancestor Arthur Guinness began to brew stout, the thick black beer with a head of foam, in the 1750s and became enormously rich. Her great-grandfather, the 1st Marquess of Dufferin and Ava, had a distinguished career, was Viceroy of India from 1884 to 1888 and during his reign annexed Burma to British India. Lowell, in his element, liked hobnobbing with aristocrats and learning the intricacies of the peerage. When his former student Richard Tillinghast was in his hippie phase and said he was going to India, Lowell quizzed him about his plans and proudly mentioned Blackwood's viceregal connections. Instead of impressing others, Lowell himself was impressed by the glamour of her ancestry. [2]

Caroline's father—Basil Blackwood, Lord Dufferin—was educated at Eton and Balliol College, Oxford, and had a dazzling political career. In the 1930s he was private secretary to the Secretary of State for War and the Lord Privy Seal, and he became Under-Secretary of State for Colonies. In 1940, as the Japanese troops steadily advanced in Burma, he refused a position in Winston Churchill's coalition government and became a captain in the Royal Horseguards. Blackwood belonged to Force 136, the Special Operations Executive in Southeast Asia, which created frontline propaganda against the Japanese. On March 25, 1945, on a covert mission with the Indian Field Broadcasting Unit about one hundred miles southwest of Mandalay, he was killed at the age of thirty-five in a Japanese ambush. His military personnel file at the National Archives in Kew, London, states: "At about 1500 hours, the section escorted by a platoon of a British Regt. went out to broadcast. Lord Dufferin and the Jemedar [Indian officer] and the Platoon were ahead of the section about 200 yards. The enemy opened fire and Lord Dufferin was hit in the chest. Capt. SONG [a Japanese-speaking Korean] says he saw him clutch his chest and stagger about with the platoon as it withdrew. Attempts to withdraw Lord Dufferin were frustrated due to enemy fire." His family was notified of his death through diplomatic channels by the Crown Princess of Sweden; his body was never recovered. In "Runaway," addressed to Caroline, Lowell wrote about "your father's betrayal of you, / rushing to his military death in Burma, / annexed for England / by his father's father, the Viceroy." [3] Blackwood's death in battle was a notable contrast to Bob Lowell's tame career.

Caroline Blackwood had bountiful gifts and a tragic family life. Like the mother in D. H. Lawrence's "The Rocking-Horse Winner," she "was a woman who was beautiful, who started with all the advantages, yet she had no luck. . . . Everybody said of her: 'She is such a good mother. She adores her children.' Only she herself, and her children themselves, knew it was not so."[4] Cared for by a series of irresponsible and often cruel nannies, Caroline grew up in a crumbling Georgian mansion on a five-thousand-acre estate outside Belfast and was forced to attend an all-boys school near her home, where she was bullied. Superior to Lowell in class and wealth, she was always bold, sexually adventurous and vulnerable—more like Stafford than Hardwick. She was traumatized by the loss of her father and the rejection of her mother, who spent most of her time in London. Neglected as a child, she became a depressed and alcoholic adult, mentally fragile and physically ill. When Lowell met her she had had (like him) two failed marriages, and after Lowell her life continued on its disastrous course. Her youngest daughter was badly burned in 1972; her oldest daughter Natalya, aged seventeen, who'd slept with Blackwood's first husband, killed herself with an overdose of heroin in 1978. Her brother Sheridan—"a roué who was rich, charming, clever, married and gay"—died of AIDS in 1988. Her son by Lowell became a troubled young man.

Like the famous beautiful muses Lou-Andreas Salomé and Alma Mahler, Blackwood attracted supremely talented men. Her first husband, from 1953 to 1959, was the brilliant English painter Lucian Freud (grandson of Sigmund). But "she felt he was too dark, controlling and incorrigibly unfaithful," left him and ran off to Spain.[5] They had no children, but in the course of his life he had as many as fourteen with his first wife and many mistresses. Blackwood's second husband, the musician Israel Citkowitz, was, like Lucian Freud, Jewish, handsome and much older than Blackwood. Born in Poland, he came to America at the age of three and grew up in Brooklyn. He studied composition with Aaron Copland and Roger Sessions and piano with Nadia Boulanger, and became a composer, pianist, music critic and teacher. But he never fulfilled his early promise and had stopped composing before his marriage to Blackwood in 1959. Instead, he became a kind of nanny and looked after their three daughters. (The youngest, Ivana, had actually been fathered by the English screenwriter Ivan Moffat.) Later on, when Blackwood returned to London, Citkowitz was separated from but still married to her. He remained financially dependent on her and lived rent-free in one of the three flats in her house at 80 Redcliffe Square in Chelsea. Like Kingsley Amis later in life, Citkowitz moved into the house of his former wife and her current husband, but made himself useful and posed no threat. Blackwood was no longer interested in him, Lowell liked him. When Citkowitz died he said, "It would take a book to tell about him, a book by a Russian—we were all as good friends as the chance allowed us to be, a friendly part of my life really."[6]

II

In the late 1960s Blackwood had lived with Citkowitz and their three daughters in a townhouse on West 12th Street in Greenwich Village. Robert Silvers, editor of the *New York Review of Books* and her lover from 1963 to 1970 while she was married to Citkowitz, used to take her to dinners at the Lowells' apartment, where they had their first awkward encounters. Lowell didn't try to be pleasant or even civil with Blackwood and bearishly waited for her to make the first move. She recalled, "I was always put next to him. And it used to be my dread. To break the silence once, I said I admired the soup. And he said, 'I think it's perfectly disgusting.' And then we had a silence." A few days after their first meeting, Blackwood spotted the heavily medicated Lowell carelessly weaving his way through dense city traffic while her taxi nearly ran him over. Despite his recent rudeness, she "felt very concerned for him—it was *so* dangerous. I remember thinking, he's not going to last very long, and feeling awfully sad."

In London in the spring of 1970, when Lowell was a fellow at All Souls in Oxford, he and Blackwood met again at his publisher's party. Lowell felt alone in London and, as he had done before with Vija Vetra, immediately attached himself to Blackwood and settled into her house in Chelsea. She recalled that "he moved into Redcliffe Square—I mean instantly, that night. He had this fantasy that Bob Silvers had given him my telephone number because he wanted Cal and me to get married. Of course, that was the last thing Bob wanted. But Cal persisted with that fantasy always—that this was fate—organized by Bob."[7] As the women in Lowell's circle wandered familiarly from man to man the sexual relations became quasi-incestuous. Schwartz and Lowell slept with Buckman; Rahv, Tate and Lowell slept with Hardwick; Silvers and Lowell slept with Blackwood; Citkowitz and Lowell slept with Hochman; Freud slept with Natalya.

Esther Brooks, who met Blackwood in England, recalled that she drank heavily and smoked pot. As Blackwood spun off in a merry-go-round of thought, Brooks couldn't follow her conversation and didn't know what she was talking about.[8] In June 1970 Mary McCarthy gave a shrewd analysis of Blackwood's character and predicted stormy weather for the couple: "[She's] a beautiful, odd girl, somewhat like a blonde Carmen, somewhat schizoid, history of psychiatric treatment, mysterious, childlike, innocent, candid. . . . My doubts aren't so much about Cal's seriousness as about Caroline's ability to bear the weight of his personality, which can be crushing, overbearing, and so on. I wouldn't have the strength to live with him twenty-four hours."[9] A few months later in November, McCarthy, the veteran of four husbands, warned Lowell, "As for Caroline, I'd already come to the conclusion that it couldn't work between you. I mean marriage."[10]

According to rumor, during his courtship of Blackwood Lowell had one brief, irresistible fling, a rare affair with a married woman, when he slept with the wife of a colleague at All Souls. Isaiah Berlin, another Oxford professor, was very cross about Lowell's "rotten behaviour." The story was that the woman—attractive, likable and mischievous—set out to seduce Lowell and he surrendered without a fight. To illustrate her cheeky and provocative character, Karl Miller remarked that she once approached the rather touchy Kingsley Amis at a party and said, "I've just read your latest novel." "Yes?," he curiously asked. "And I thought it was one of your worst." Furious, Amis went purple in the face and told her to "fuck off!" Her husband, a decent man and rather out of his depth when he became entangled with her, supposedly knew what was happening and waited for the affair to blow over.[11]

The truth, much stranger than the fiction, was one of the most bizarre episodes in Lowell's life. Catharine Mack Smith, the object of his attentions, was brought up in Cambridge, the daughter of a classics professor, James Stevenson. Small and slim, with dark hair, high cheekbones, large eyes and a pert nose, she was intelligent, charming, witty and flirtatious. She graduated from Bristol University and became a "child bride" in 1963 when she married the distinguished historian of Italy Denis Mack Smith. She saw Lowell, who spoke in a solemn monotone and was a terrible reader of his own poems, appear in a large hall packed with enthusiastic undergraduates. She'd read some of his poetry in *Life Studies,* but didn't know about his sudden infatuations with many women.

She first met Lowell at an All Souls' dinner on one of the rare nights when husbands could invite their wives. She was twenty-nine, Lowell was twenty-three years older. She was struck by his wild scowl and very long hair that hung down to his collar. He was very high that night and talked very rapidly in a nonstop, self-involved way. He spoke of "my Lizzie and my Harriet," but didn't mention Blackwood. He seemed to find All Souls very boring. He used it as "a lookout for pickups" and told her "you're the only pretty girl I've met since I came to England." She didn't know about his use of lithium or realize that he was going into his manic phase. He was terribly drunk and seemed instantly infatuated with her. After dinner they moved to the next room for coffee and sat on a long sofa. With other people present, he suddenly lunged across her and pushed her onto her back, but she managed to escape.

The Mack Smiths lived near Isaiah Berlin, their gardens extending back to back, and she was invited to a party at Berlin's house when her husband was in Italy for the weekend. Lowell, once again, was incredibly drunk. After the party he insisted on accompanying her home and they stumbled back to her house through the undergrowth. He sat down and, though he'd already consumed several bottles, said, "I want some more wine." When she went downstairs to fetch the wine she alerted the nanny, who was home with Catharine's two small children and would have rescued her if she'd screamed. Despite the alcohol and mania, Lowell was coherent and fascinating about himself. She was enthralled by his glamour and flattered by his attention, and had never experienced anything like his exciting behavior. He enigmatically said, "I don't want you to be twenty-nine, I want you to be thirty-two," and fantasized about all the beautiful women he'd seduced, including Jackie Kennedy, Marilyn Monroe and (truthfully) the Italian writer Gaia Servadio, which she found very off-putting.

Catharine said she was not attracted to him, but he tried to seduce her while she was alone and "behaved horribly." He took off his trousers and asked, "Do you like my prick?" She didn't quite know what to do, but was not frightened and didn't think he would try to rape her. Drunk and exhausted, he finally fell asleep in her bed and she slept in the spare room. The next morning she took him some coffee and saw him masturbating out the bedroom window. She recalled that when she "found him in flagrante with himself, I asked 'why are you doing that?,' and he growled through his appalling hangover, 'well, ya wouldn't let me ferk ya, honey.'" She would not have slept with a married man, as she "was not brought up that way." They did not have sex that night or at any other time and she would have said so if they had. But it was a great story and she could not resist telling all her friends. Since he'd spent the night in her house, everyone in gossipy Oxford mistakenly assumed they had slept together.

She and Lowell met at two other lunches two days running, when he was not drunk and behaved more politely. The first lunch was with the poet Elizabeth Jennings, who got very drunk and fell down. The second was with Lizzie Spender, Stephen's daughter and then a student at Oxford, who does not remember that occasion. Lowell vanished at the end of term and she never saw or heard from him again.[12]

Lowell's break with Hardwick, while he was in England, was agonizing. One letter to her in the summer of 1970 was nostalgic and apologetic: "You couldn't have been more loyal and witty. I can't give you anything of equal value. Still much happened that we both loved in the long marriage. I feel we had much joy and many other things we had to learn." In another letter he tried to defend himself: "I don't feel very boastful, but I don't think I am a bastard." A third letter, written in a crabbed style that reflected his inner torment, was grateful, dismissive and uncertain: "I don't think I can go back to you. Thought does no good. I cannot weigh the dear, troubled past, so many illnesses, which weren't due to you, in which you saved everything. . . . I can't compare this memory with the future, unseen and beyond recollection with Caroline. I love her very much, but I can't see that. I am sure many people have looked back on a less marvelous marriage than ours on the point of breaking, and felt this pain and indecision—at first insoluble, then when the decision has been made, incurable."[13]

In response to this terrible news Hardwick's letters from New York veered wildly from frantic affection to keep him to frantic abuse to punish him. He told Adrienne Rich that the worst thing about his marriage was their ceaseless nervous strife, as though (adopting his favorite role) "a bear had married a greyhound."[14] Frank Bidart confirmed that when he stayed with the Lowells in New York and Castine at the end of their marriage in 1970, "they had a big fight every night. They had so little understanding of how to talk to each other in a civilized manner and could not figure out how to do this. There was a great contrast between their book learning and their lack of knowledge about how to lead a companionable and harmonious life."[15]

Blackwood was more glamorous and exciting than Hardwick, to whom he'd been married for twenty long years, but she was also deeply troubled. Christopher Ricks, who met Lowell when the poet moved to England, observed that in Walker Evans' famous photograph of Blackwood, lying down in a boat with her head on the bow like a mermaid, she seemed serene but never was. He called her a ravaged beauty, intense, nervous, high-strung, on the edge and frightening.[16] Though Lowell had a manic episode in 1970 and was hospitalized in Greenways Nursing Home in London, he put the best face on it. He told Hardwick that his love for Caroline was the real thing, that he'd been just as manic when he courted and married her, and that Blackwood ("in an odd way") had a solid character: "Caroline isn't . . . one of my many manic crushes, rather . . . just as you were at Yaddo and after. She is airy and very steady and sturdy in an odd way."[17]

At this point Hardwick faced the truth and told friends, "This time it's serious. Caroline wants to get married. I've lost him." She bitterly added that in Blackwood he'd found his equal for unreality and carelessness, and at last had "met someone as crazy as he is." Peter Taylor thought that Blackwood was "even crazier than Cal."[18] Blackwood believed that Lowell was fond of Hardwick and felt guilty about leaving her, but that it would have been worse if he'd stayed with her.[19] Allen Tate remarked that when Lowell left Hardwick for Blackwood, he gave up another marriage (and child), his political commitment to the anti-war movement and his life at the center of American culture. Lowell didn't have the same stature in the British literary world, and lost a great deal of power and prestige when he moved to England.

Lowell's relations with Blackwood were also tense. At the same time that he was separating from Hardwick, he expressed his love, doubts and fears in letters to Blackwood and his friends. In July he pleaded with her, "I love you with all my heart and mind, what can I do if you give me nothing to go on? I can't crowd in on you. Let's for God's sake try again, cool and try. So much love should go on to something." In November he told Peter Taylor that his love for Blackwood—in contrast to his short-lived, manic affairs—had survived his madness and that his feelings for her were genuine: "I fell in love part manic, was sick in a hospital a good part of the summer, got well, stayed in love. There was great joy in it all, great harm to everyone."[20] He confided to the critical Mary McCarthy that he and Blackwood had very different ideas about commitment: "I think the jag that hit Caroline and me was whether to get married, she not wanting to and I not wanting to go on in perpetuum unmarried."[21] To John Berryman—who'd been through two failed marriages and was less than two years away from suicide—Lowell expressed fears about entering another shaky commitment with a strong possibility of failure: "A new life. One to be envied, but today it fills me with uncertainties that mount up terror."[22]Blackwood's youngest daughter, Ivana, did not believe that the "marriage was doomed from the start. Blackwood loved him and called him 'the love of her life.' During her pregnancy with Sheridan and just after he was born, she didn't drink, Lowell was mentally stable and they had good times together."[23] Blackwood agreed that Lowell, cruel only when he was manic, was usually cozy, affectionate, fun and easy to get on with. Their best time was their first four years together, in the early 1970s, when Lowell did not suffer any manic attacks.[24] Christopher Ricks had very positive memories: "I knew him only for seven years and only in one world, a world in which he was generous, fertile, considerate and gentle, relaxed at full-length on a couch or a bed, talking with but not for effect, mischievous, unthreatening and unthreatened."[25]

III

Blackwood and Lowell lived in her rambling eighteenth-century brick house, Milgate Park in Bearsted, a name that Lowell loved. It was near Maidstone in Kent, about thirty miles southeast of London. Though everything appeared to be grand, the huge house was actually falling apart and impossible to maintain. Lowell compared it to the squalid inn where Chichikov stops in Gogol's *Dead Souls*. The grandeur and decay of Milgate, and Blackwood's neglect of her children, repeated the set-ting and tragedy of her own childhood in Northern Ireland. There were, Ivana recalled, endless servants, nannies and au pairs—all of them useless. Instead of doing their jobs, they drank numerous cups of tea, grew crops of marijuana in the greenhouse and constantly smoked pot.[26] Jonathan Raban said that Lowell (a quintessential urban poet) managed to ignore the reality of the place and take pleasure in his role as grandee in a rural setting: "He missed the smartness of New York, but I think he found an almost compensatory thing in the dull squirearchy of England. He did love being the squire at Milgate . . . looking over a kind of Kent that Rob-ert Lowell, squire and poet, might well have actually owned, as far as the eye could see. There was a kind of terrific glamour in that for him."[27]

Blackwood could not tolerate alcohol and became a nasty drunk. Their conflicts intensified when she and Lowell drank too much and started to fight. As a small child Ivana had learned to avoid confrontations when Blackwood became argumentative after her second bottle of wine, but the more combative Lowell got into terrible arguments with her. Karl Miller recalled that they were always skating on thin ice and noted ominous signs even before they were married. She was always a bit disturbed and became even more so when drunk. She then (as Esther Brooks also noted) made no sense, and could play the snobbish and silly grande dame.[28] In "With Caroline at the Air-Terminal," Lowell (following his frequent practice) quoted a letter from Blackwood in which she tried to explain, "If I have had hysterical drunken seizures, / it's from loving you too much. It makes me wild, / I fear."[29]

In the midst of their chaotic life, Blackwood became pregnant with Sheridan. Like Hardwick's pregnancy with Harriet, it was unexpected. Lowell had kept in touch with Martha Ritter (whom he'd left for Blackwood) and in May 1971, announcing the impending birth, wrote her that his departure from Hardwick was final, and that she and Harriet were more content without him: "Rather mysteriously this event has brought a calm to both of us and somehow makes the separation and divorce more rational. Harriet and Lizzie even seem happier. Of course there's an inescapable sadness in the joy."[30]

Sheridan was born in September 1971, when Lowell was fifty-four, and he relished his son's antics as he'd once enjoyed Harriet's. He told Kunitz that the voracious and destructive infant reminded him of a colorful poet: "At seven months he was 'eating everything in sight: blanket, rug, small dog, our fingers,' and seemed 'a microcosm of James Dickey, but on the wagon.'"[31] Sheridan looked eerily like Lowell, and friends had never seen such a close resemblance between father and son. Karl Miller once saw Sheridan dressed in an Eton suit and collar, ensconced in a cubbyhole under the stairs and playing with dolls.[32] In Ireland in 1977, when Lowell told the six-year-old Sheridan that "his own father had thrown him into the water before he could swim," Sheridan said he would like to kill him— though Bob Lowell was long dead. Lowell at first seemed unaware that his son, growing up with irresponsible parents in their madcap household, might be damaged. But Blackwood said that at the end of their marriage Lowell knew that his mania "was destroying me. And he knew that in the end it would destroy Sheridan. It would have been terrible for a child to see his father like that. I don't think he'd have recovered."[33] The same, of course, was true of the equally vulnerable Harriet.

In March 1973 Lowell told Bishop that "Lizzie is sending her dearest lamb, mine too, into the tiger's den" when Harriet visited Milgate.[34] Ivana remembered that it was difficult for the sixteen-year-old Harriet to see her father with another wife and new family, and she may have felt that Lowell had replaced her with her new half-brother. Harriet was so quiet and withdrawn that it was hard to tell if her visit had been a success. As an adult, Harriet also visited the Blackwood family on Long Island, but she was still very shy and Ivana couldn't get close to her.[35]

Sheridan's birth strengthened Lowell's bond with Blackwood and propelled them into marriage. As they combined their romantic fantasies and tried to anchor them to reality, they joined, like Lowell and Hardwick, the number of brilliant (and sometimes troubled) literary couples in history: the Shelleys, Carlyles and Brownings in the nineteenth century, and in modern times Edmund Wilson and Mary McCarthy, Robert Penn Warren and Eleanor Clark, Iris Murdoch and John Bayley, Ted Hughes and Sylvia Plath. They also, on the third try for each, resembled their much married friends: Rahv, Wilson and McCarthy (four marriages each), Tate, Kunitz, Berryman and Stafford (three), Eliot, Jarrell, Dickey and Hecht (two). In their circle, artistic talent came with emotional instability.

Blackwood gave an amusing account of their dual divorce-and-marriage, a shoddy affair in the Dominican Republic in October 1972: "It's so laid on, like a package tour—a limousine meets the plane, takes you straight to the place where you get divorced—it was a double divorce, of course, because I was divorcing Israel. The limousine waits and then on to the marriage, which was just a shed with a lot of people typing. They typed all through our marriage. . . . Talk about lack of solemnity."[36] Four months later Lowell wrote J. F. Powers (who was also married with four children) a shrewd description of his recently transformed life: "I have a new wife, a new son, and three new step-daughters—a lonely existence changed to a herd. . . . [My wife] is 15 years younger than I am. I pretend, not plausibly, to be what I was ten years ago. . . . I am happier than I have ever been, though so much older. We've been together three years and have passed through the first months of illusion."[37] He was, however, still struggling to sustain that illusion.

Children are usually hostile to their mother's new husband, especially when their father (in this case, Israel Citkowitz) is still in residence. In *The Rainbow*, for example, D. H. Lawrence described, in tender scenes, how Will Brangwen slowly wins over the angry little Anna Lensky after he marries her widowed mother. Esther Brooks thought Lowell tended to be breezy, offhand and awkward with Blackwood's daughters. He didn't see very much of them and didn't develop strong ties with them. The children lived separately from their parents in a remote wing of the huge house. When old enough, they were sent off to boarding school.[38]

But Lowell did establish a special tenderness with his three stepdaughters. Blackwood said that though Lowell was not the kind of father who kicked a football around the garden, he got on well with the children. They were very content with Lowell, whom they considered a sweet teddy bear (a positive complement to the fierce bearlike Arms of the Law).[39] Ivana first saw him, just after he married her mother, when the couple returned from Holland and brought the girls wooden clogs and matching Dutch outfits. When asked, "Were you pleased with the gifts?," she replied, "Actually, they were quite hideous." Most at ease with Ivana, the youngest child, Lowell was interested in her and paid attention to her. He also liked her dog Lulu, who followed her around all day. She thought Lowell was weird and wonderful, funny and free, unconventional and playful, childish and childlike.[40] "I adored Robert," she wrote. "He came into my life when I was young, perhaps only four, and to me he was the gentlest, coziest man possible. A tall teddy-bearish presence."[41] When Lowell was in America, teaching at Harvard and visiting his other family, the girls wrote little poems and cards "To Robert" begging him to come home.

One of Lowell's dolphins featured in a photograph of him with Caroline and two of her pretty daughters at Milgate. The long-haired Lowell, in the middle and crouching in a pinewood corner to get into the photo, leans on a cane, stares at the camera and rests his hand on the tail of a three-foot dolphin statue. Ivana, barefoot and seated on a velvet-cushioned chair, holds up a pet black-and-white rabbit that partly covers her face. Caroline and Evgenia, sitting at the bottom of the carpeted staircase, wear identically patterned summer frocks. Caroline, with puffed sleeves and arms folded on her lap, seems at ease before the camera and smiles winningly. Evgenia, wearing sandals, her knees touching and legs akimbo, holds a small dachshund and looks open-mouthed and admiringly at Lowell.

But all was not well, and having Lowell for a stepfather could be dangerous. Esther Brooks, visiting Milgate, remembered the children rushing into the room and shouting that their friend "Melanie's stuck in the bog and can't get out! Please come help her, Robert!" Oblivious to the danger and absorbed in his own gloom, he responded by stating his tragic view of life: "We are all stuck in the bog. Nobody can help us. It's impossible to help someone out of their bog when we can't get out of our own bog." Mesmerized by Lowell's statement but jolted by the children's panic, Brooks shouted, "This is a real bog, damn it all!," ran into the soggy pasture and rescued the child who had been sucked knee-deep into the mud. [42]

Like Esther Brooks, Karl Miller thought that Blackwood's daughters had a terribly exacting childhood and adolescence, and were lucky to survive. [43] (The oldest child, Natalya, did not survive.) Lowell and Blackwood— drinking and arguing, absorbed by and obsessed with their own problems—were unaware that something terrible was happening to Ivana. She had no real father in childhood and was especially vulnerable. Citkowitz was her nominal father, Moffat her actual father and Lowell her stepfather. But Citkowitz died when she was eight, Lowell died when she was eleven, and she did not know that Moffat was her father until she was an adult.

When she was only six years old Ivana was frequently forced to have oral sex with a household servant, the husband of her nanny, who threatened to set his dogs on her if she told anyone. Ivana said that she actually liked this kind of perverse attention, which suggests (at the very least) that she got precious little attention from her parents, nannies and older sisters, and felt emotionally deprived. Later, Ivana sadly wrote that it felt "exhilarating to be able to exert such power over an adult man. . . . The attention felt good. . . . I would wait up for Mike's visits with a mixture of dread and excitement. . . . On the nights when he didn't visit I was disappointed." [44]

The sexual abuse continued until something even more horrible happened to her. Ivana wrote that in the kitchen, "there was a stool next to one of the counter tops, and I jumped on it. . . . Somehow my foot got tangled in the cord that was dangling from the counter. A kettle of boiling water crashed down on top of me. . . . I had third degree burns over seventy percent of my body." The guilt-ridden Lowell then made a rare and admirable personal sacrifice. In the burns unit of the hospital, "the nurse insisted there was no place for [her parents] to stay, but Robert found a small towel and spread it out on the cold hospital corridor floor outside my door. He and my mother lay down on it to spend the night near me." [45] In February 1972 Lowell wrote Hardwick that Ivana had been close to death for a month: "This week was hell, just ending. Ivana's case was and is very grave; doctors reports conflicted; no point was reached when we could feel she was out of danger." In March he told Kunitz, "In January my six year old stepdaughter tipped an electric kettle on herself (not knowing it was there) it fell in her lap and the top came off. It's hard to remember when she was not in the hospital"—and she remained there for three months. [46]

Blackwood's moving essay "Burns Unit," the best thing she ever wrote, described Ivana's ordeal with dramatic skill and cinematic realism. This ghastly event, with her own daughter as victim, gave Blackwood the fullest opportunity to display her obsession with horrific and pitiful details. Watched by their anguished parents,

> the burned would be there so very still inside their isolated and tropically-heated glass cubicles. . . . The main activity of this Unit was waiting—waiting to be better—waiting to be dead. . . . All the patients in this hospital were laid out on display like exhibits, they could all be viewed from an outer "polluted" corridor. . . . There they all lay like Francis Bacon figures framed in their dehumanised postures with black charred legs strapped apart and their genitals pierced by their catheters. . . . Inside the suffocating highly-heated cubicle the child whose body was the colour of blackened bacon would be screaming for water with the terrible delirious thirst of the newly burned.

In this unforgettable essay Blackwood equaled the descriptions of the charred pilots in Richard Hillary's *The Last Enemy* (1942), which influenced a similar account in Michael Ondaatje's *The English Patient* (1992). [47]

Lowell's poem about Ivana, in which her childish tantrums and mania are stilled by the burns that no child should ever have to suffer, was a tender contrast to Blackwood's clinical objectivity:

> Small-soul-pleasing, loved with condescension,
> even through the cro-magnon tirades of six,
> the last madness of child-gaiety
> before the trouble of the world shall hit. . . .
> Though burned, you are hopeful, accident cannot tell you
> experience is what you do not want to experience. [48]

Christopher Ricks saw Blackwood and Lowell soon after Ivana was burned and noticed a "frightening air of uneasy peace." [49]

IV

Lowell's exhaustion, medication and heart disease precluded any love affairs during his manic episodes with Blackwood. He'd had serious mental breakdowns when he began his liaisons with both Hardwick in 1949 and with Blackwood in 1970. In 1967 he started taking lithium which worked, despite the danger of overdose, for his first four years with Blackwood. But he burst out in manic episodes in January and November 1975, and again in January and September 1976. Hardwick had always hoped that Lowell would return to sanity; Blackwood hoped he would remain sane, and gave vivid accounts of his symptoms when he became ill. "I couldn't believe it was going to happen when he was normal," she said. "That sounds stupid, because really you know it's going to."[50] All the attacks occurred quite suddenly. Lowell knew they were coming, felt a deadly tingle crawling up his spine and pleaded with her to "stop me from going mad!"[51]

Blackwood always knew Lowell was ill when he wanted to pray in Westminster Abbey or when he insisted that *Mein Kampf* was as good as *Moby-Dick*. She told an interviewer that Lowell, making futile attempts to escape from his manic self, would try to merge his personality with hers. His illness often manifested itself in trailing her everywhere: "Part of his madness was that he put part of his identity into me. It was so claustrophobic—if I went down to the harbour, he would follow me. He would take my books and sign them Robert Lowell. He'd say, 'Cal and Caroline are the same, we are the same.'"[52] Ivana confirmed that his behavior could be quite terrifying. One evening, in what might have been an irrational attempt to take on the pain of her burns, "he smothered himself with Harpic toilet cleaner, and the strong chemicals severely burned his skin."[53] Lowell was not exaggerating when he wrote in "Last Night," "[I] found myself / covered with quicklime, my face deliquescent" as his skin shriveled and blistered.[54] Blackwood also found him teetering on the edge of the narrow balcony outside the fourth floor of Milgate, "imagining himself to be Mussolini addressing his troops."[55] When powerless, he identified with figures of power.

Like Stafford and Hardwick, Carley Dawson and Sandra Hochman, Blackwood also became the victim of Lowell's manic violence. He gave her a black eye and she feared for her children. She thought they were safe when Citkowitz was there, but said that in July 1970 in the Redcliffe Square house, which was divided into three separate flats, "he locked me in the flat upstairs and he wouldn't let me telephone—and I had the children downstairs. But I didn't dare go down to see them, because I knew that he'd come too. And I simply didn't want him in the same flat as the children in the state that he was in. Neither did I want to be locked in with him. It was the longest three days of my life."[56]

Frightened by Lowell's illness, Blackwood began to drink heavily and veered toward her own mental breakdown. In January 1976 he was sent back to Greenways and she remembered that his last two days at home were sheer horror. She was afraid (like Mary Hemingway with Ernest) that he'd be released before he was well and confessed that she was too fragile to take care of him: "I'm no use to him in these attacks. They destroy me. I'm really better if I'm away when he has one. It's like some-one becoming an animal, or someone possessed by the devil. And that's what tears you apart. You think, I love this person, but I hate him. So where are you?"[57] Bidart agreed that Blackwood couldn't handle Lowell, who made her own precarious condition much worse: "Blackwood was ill-equipped to deal with Lowell's inevitable hospitalizations. 'She would get tremendously upset, she would not want him to be released. The doctors would say he was fine, she wouldn't believe them. Once she actually left England so she would not be there for the doctors to release him to her care. And this increased her own drinking, and it got to be mayhem.'"[58] Blackwood could not bear the emotional burden and her inability to help Lowell during his crises was a decisive factor in the breakup of their marriage.

When Ian Hamilton asked her, "Did he think you'd abandoned him?," Blackwood confessed: "Yes, I'm afraid he did. He'd say, 'Supposing I go mad—you won't be able to bear it, will you?' And I'd say, 'Perhaps you won't go mad.'"[59] When they were living apart toward the end of his time with her, Lowell expressed fear that his mania would (as with Stafford) actually drive her mad and seemed unwilling to subject her to his madness: "I really feel too weak and battered by it all. I fear I do you more harm than good. I think your blackness would pass if you didn't live in fear of manic attacks. And they don't seem curable—almost thirty years. How's that for persistence? I miss you sorely."[60]

Blackwood's undated and unpublished letters, sent when she'd escaped to friends in Europe and they were separated during his crises in the mid-1970s, reveal how they vacillated between estrangement and union. She plaintively wrote: "If I see you when you are so sick I know everything between us will become distorted and destroyed. Your sickness is so dis-tressing to me and I am so bound up with you that I can't help you and will break down again myself. . . . Please get better Cal. I love you so much." She also felt responsible for and even part of his mania, and feared that he was pulling her into his own abyss: "I think about you every minute of the day and I love you every minute of the day. . . . You are right to object to me calling it 'your' sickness. It is mine. Or ours. . . . Without you everything seems hollow, boring, unbearable. . . . At the moment I feel really sub-humanly low." Lowell appropriated the first sentence of this letter, verbatim, into his poem "Caroline: Marriage?"

Blackwood also wrote, in this trying time, that she felt part of Lowell just as he'd felt part of her and—unlike Hardwick in her angry mood— insisted that she was never bored by him: "I am quite bored—I think that is because you are not here. I had forgotten what it is like to be bored, because even when we tangle I have never been bored for a second with you. . . . I long to be back with you revising and feel like an amputee without you." Finally, she echoed Mary Keelan's letter when Lowell had flown back to America without her: "I miss you so much already and your plane probably hasn't even taken off yet." She also recalled Hardwick's belief by bravely insisting, despite all their difficulties, that she was glad she'd married him: "I don't know if you will really ever come back. I just know that I have been happier with you than I have ever been—ever. So even if the whole thing ends up for me with sadness, I will always think that it was worth it." [61]

Lowell tried to assure his friends that Blackwood—though sick from overdrinking, suffering from nervous depression and filled with "panics, moments of excitement, fear, grandiosity, inertia" [62] —was actually marvelous, "lively, oxlike and functioning," and that nothing was wrong with her reason. [63] But few people would describe that ethereal creature as "oxlike," and her condition was actually quite serious. Jonathan Raban, who'd lived in the basement flat in Redcliffe Square, noted that Blackwood (like Stafford and Hardwick) was suicidal, and both she and Lowell were destroying each other. It now seemed, in their dance of death, that Blackwood, rather than Lowell, posed the greater threat to her children:

Cal held himself back because he saw the panic in Caroline, and Caroline in a way held herself back from her thing, from her fear of Cal. They treated each other with an almost drunken delicacy, and you could feel a massive amount of self-restraint on both sides, and terror—terror that if one of them flipped, the whole thing would crash. . . .

He was in a state of anguish and misery for the last period that they were in London and immediately before leaving Milgate. Caroline

seemed to be in a state of perpetual threat to commit suicide. . . .
Caroline was in a considerably worse state than Cal. . . .

Caroline's mania—the alcoholism, the two suicide attempts—
[there was] the one in Kent, the one in Ireland. . . . One time she
took some pills and a lot of alcohol and had to be stomach-pumped
in Maidstone Hospital. According to Cal, she was constantly threatening to kill herself and Sheridan and Ivana. . . .

They were playing a totally dangerous game—each accusing the
other of being mad, with a certain amount of truth on both sides,
and *literally* driving each other into madness.[64]

V

Lowell had left the center of the New York literary world and now, living
outside of London and commuting to teach at Essex, was on the periphery
of English cultural life. But he continued, whenever possible, to maintain
congenial contact with poets—a welcome respite from his hothouse existence with Blackwood. In a rather condescending dismissal of the personal
revelations in *Life Studies,* Philip Larkin had called the poems "curious,
hurried, off-hand vignettes, seeming too personal to be practised, yet none
the less accurate and original."[65] Seven years later, mocking the title of
Lord Weary's Castle, Larkin was even more critical in a letter: "Old R. L.
who's never looked like being a single iota of good in all his born days.
Lord Hairy's Arsehole. Gibber, gibber."[66] Nevertheless, Lowell admired
him more than any contemporary English poet. Though Larkin could
rarely be persuaded to leave his bolt-hole in Hull, he accepted Lowell's
invitation to spend a weekend at Milgate. "He looked older than T. S.
Eliot," Lowell wrote, though Larkin was thirty-four years younger than
Eliot, "six foot one, low-spoken, bald, deaf, deathbrooding, a sculptured
statue of his poems. He made me feel almost an undergraduate in health,
and somehow old as the hills."[67] Ivana thought Larkin was weird looking
and scary, and couldn't understand why he was famous.[68]

Joseph Brodsky, just after being exiled from Russia, remembered Lowell's characteristic generosity and kindness in London. Brodsky recalled:
"He and I met in 1972 at that same Poetry International Auden brought
me to. Lowell volunteered to read my poems in English, which was an
extraordinarily noble gesture on his part. Then he invited me to visit him
in Kent, where he was vacationing [i.e., living with Blackwood] that sum-

mer. A certain intuitive understanding arose between us instantaneously. . . . Whenever I think about Lowell, I remember his enormous attention. The expression on his face was extremely good-natured."[69]

Brodsky's "Elegy: For Robert Lowell" (1977) was written in English in superbly rhymed three-to-seven-line stanzas. Like Auden's elegy for Yeats, the different sections have different verse forms and Brodsky transforms Auden's "he became his admirers" into "Now you become a part/of the inanimate" world. The first and longest section uses religious imagery ironically—like the pun on grammar and heaven in "future perfect"— since Brodsky was Jewish and Lowell no longer religious. He evokes Lowell through the altar and choir, the Cross, Salvation and the Almighty Lord, and cunningly compares the white pointed steeples of New England churches to spooky hoods. Despite the promises of religion, the poet merely dies and his friends must contemplate the emptiness he's left behind.[70]

Frank Bidart was to Lowell's writing life as Blair Clark was to his personal life. He was always ready to put his own work aside, respond immediately and even fly across the Atlantic when summoned to help. Kathleen Spivack's description suggests that Bidart might have inhabited Lord Weary's Castle: "He had a high forehead and exhausted eye sockets. He was tall and round-shouldered, and stooped as if staying upright was too tiring."[71] Lowell's canny remark that Bidart knew Lowell's poetry better than he himself did and liked it better recalls his statement that Hardwick understood his mania better than he himself did. Bidart always got on well with both Hardwick and Blackwood, though Hardwick, thinking that he'd encouraged Lowell to publish *The Dolphin,* later became angry with him.

Lowell treated his poems like toys and liked to toy with them. Unlike Blake, Lawrence and Ginsberg, he did not value the moment of original inspiration and rapture of the immediate present. Instead—like Henry James with the New York Edition of his work—Lowell was a compulsive reviser, especially when he couldn't write new poems and disastrously when he was manic. (No one has ever analyzed the variants in hundreds of his poems; and scholars, in what may finally be a matter of taste, may never agree about which versions are superior.) Though Bidart tried to temper Lowell's endless revisions, he also caught the bug and confessed that with his own poems, "I punctuated the lines differently for months, to the point where my friends winced when I pulled out a new version."[72]

Stimulated by their visitors and in the midst of all their personal chaos, both Blackwood and Lowell continued to write and publish their books. He encouraged her to write essays and novels, just as Edmund Wilson had encouraged the young Mary McCarthy, and Blackwood gradually changed from perpetual muse to artist in her own right. Like Lowell's previous wives, Blackwood had enormous spirit and cutting wit, was clever and caustic, and rebelled against social conventions. A critic wrote that the sensational material, including "Burns Unit," in *For All That I Found There* described "anguish, dementia, despair—injuries of all kinds, insanity, rape, murder, internecine marriages, a disastrous face-lift, suicidal isolation. Her destructive power is to direct an unflinching gaze at the intolerable."[73]

The main character in Blackwood's novella *The Stepdaughter* (1976) was based on her own eldest daughter, Natalya Citkowitz, who died two years later. Lowell appears in the book as Arnold, who dumps his physically repulsive and psychologically damaged thirteen-year-old daughter, Renata, on to his third wife. He then announces that he is leaving his wife, but refuses to take responsibility for the unwanted child. The wife explains that her ex-husband is manipulative and possessive: "Arnold had always chosen to remove himself from all painful human situations in order to pretend they do not exist. . . . He himself wants to re-marry, and he prefers to make me remain single so that he can always feel that I am alone and still waiting for him, if ever at some future date he might need me available."[74] In the most disturbing, guilt-ridden, real-life incident in the novella, the mother pays no attention to her own little daughter, who is badly burned when she touches a red hot stove.

Like parts of Hardwick's *Sleepless Nights, The Stepdaughter* is a one-sided, first-person epistolary novel. Like the hero of Saul Bellow's *Herzog* (1964), the narrator writes letters in her head and to herself. As in Hardwick's novel, the Lowell character never actually appears and is seen only through the eyes of his former wife. But Blackwood's book was published while Lowell was still alive, and was dedicated to him, Sheridan and her three daughters.

The novella is really about the stepmother, not the stepdaughter. A version of Dostoyevsky's *Notes from Underground* set in modern Manhattan, it's narrated by a desperate woman—trapped, depressed and verging on a mental breakdown. She's emotionally and geographically stranded between Arnold's first wife, confined in a mental institution in Los Angeles, and his French fiancée in Paris. The novella describes the effect on the narrator of Arnold, who has not only left her, but also left her with his estranged daughter. Like Lowell, Arnold has immense social assurance and is generous with money. But he has also been twice divorced, is clever and cruel, destroys her confidence (like the husband in Stafford's "A Country Love Story"), tells her she's become a drag, and has himself become a mechanical and tiring sexual partner. Finally, she condemns him as "fiercely unprotective and uncaring . . . utterly corrupt and despicable . . . [and] a heartless son of a bitch." Nevertheless, she'd be delighted if he came back to her. The novella expressed Blackwood's anxiety about being abandoned by Lowell, who'd been extremely unstable, and might well be planning to return to Hardwick. The therapeutic book explored her fears about her husband, her children and her sanity.[75]

Two poems in Lowell's *Day by Day,* published in August 1977, reveal his creative technique and his attitude toward his wives. "Epilogue," on Jan Vermeer, takes a line right out of Kenneth Clark's chapter on the Dutch artist in *Looking at Pictures* (1960). Clark observed that in Vermeer's painting "daylight . . . passes over the map . . . like an oncoming tide over the sand."[76] Lowell adapted this and wrote of "the sun's illumination / stealing like the tide across a map."[77] In his prophetic "Ulysses and Circe" Lowell portrays his own life through a classical model. He is the wily Ulysses, Blackwood the temptress Circe, Hardwick the faithful wife Penelope, to whom he can always return. In the poem the erotic wanderer is heroic, the wife patient and passive. Hardwick waits for Lowell to free himself from his current entanglement and come back at last to the longed-for security of his home.

When Lowell's appointment at Essex ended in 1973 and he took up his old position at Harvard, Blackwood and the children reluctantly followed him to Brookline and Cambridge for three semesters in the mid-1970s. Ivana recalled that her parents got along well on Blackwood's first visit, though her mother was restless and not interested in Harvard, didn't make much effort to socialize and had very few friends. Ivana herself found Boston provincial and cold. She had been taken out of her English school and didn't fit into the Friends School in Cambridge, where she was teased about her accent, her weird house and her strange parents.[78]

Robert Pinsky said the Lowells saw the Harvard writers William Alfred and Monroe Engel, but that the other professors never invited them socially and did not treat Lowell well.[79] (Auden was also rudely ignored when he returned to Christ Church, his old Oxford college, as Professor of Poetry in 1956.) At the end of 1976, as their domestic life deteriorated, Blackwood was glad to escape what she called their intolerable atmosphere of "turmoil, anger, drama, tension."[80] Jonathan Raban explained that Blackwood, who'd had a patchy education, developed an irrational horror of the university: "She had a hatred of academics that exceeded all normal bounds. She really despised and loathed and was frightened by those Harvard people."[81] She thought Lowell's years of sanity in the early 1970s were not due to lithium but to staying away from America.[82] Boston, she felt, revived his disturbing and frightening memories of his mother.

In 1977, when Blackwood could no longer afford to maintain Milgate, she made another unfortunate move and for tax purposes rented a flat in a Poe-like House of Usher. Castletown House in Celbridge, Ireland, a huge Georgian stately home, was fourteen miles west of Dublin. Lowell, who visited there in May and September 1977, called it "a slightly reduced version of Versailles."[83] Blackwood said it had an "eerie and menacing atmosphere. It is certainly not a place where any sensitive person would choose to spend the night."[84] On his last, solitary night in Castletown, Lowell, hopelessly impractical and sensitive to confinement, became locked in the vast mansion. Ian Hamilton wrote, "First the telephone failed, then the electricity. He tried to leave the house to make calls from the nearby village of Celbridge but, in the dark, was unable to locate a latch on the one door . . . that could be opened from inside without a key." He struggled back to the top-floor flat in the dark and was released by the cleaning lady the next morning.[85]

In his lifetime Lowell had thirty-nine different addresses, not counting his considerable time in prisons and mental hospitals. He'd spent long periods in Italy, Holland and England, and ranged as far as Brazil and Argentina, Spain and Norway, Poland and Russia, Israel, Egypt and Turkey. In the 1970s he rambled through five handsome residences: the New York apartment and the Castine house in America; Redcliffe Square in London, Milgate in Kent and Castletown in Ireland. Constantly on the move during the last four years of his life, he frantically traveled back and forth to sixteen different places: Boston, Mexico, Spoleto, Boston, London, New York, Boston, London, Boston, Dublin, Boston, Knoxville, Moscow, Dublin, London and New York. Just as D. H. Lawrence had desperately tried to escape from disease and regain his health by frequent moves around the world, so Lowell seemed to feel that by constant flight he could escape from—though he often exacerbated—his madness and maintain his sanity.

VI

By 1977 Lowell's marriage had reached breaking point. But he now became prey to the tormenting indecision about whether to remain with Black-wood or return to Hardwick (if she'd have him), a reprise of his torment and indecision in 1970 about whether to remain with Hardwick or commit himself to Blackwood. Jonathan Raban described the apparently insoluble dilemma of two people, deeply in love, who couldn't exist together: "He was one of those people who are incapable ultimately of living properly outside marriage—and Caroline is one of those people who is incapable of living properly inside marriage. . . . She couldn't enter into the dull normality of a Lizzie/Cal marriage that would just be a marriage." [86]

Grey Gowrie believed that Lowell's marriage to Blackwood was doomed from the start. She was a lover and muse, but not a wife, and both were too impossibly high strung to live together. But Lowell, who thought he would die at sixty (and did), felt he had to have Blackwood in the little time that remained. [87] He also told another friend that it was quite impossible to live with Blackwood—who needed someone to take care of *her*—and that *her* madness was even more destructive than his own. He was still in love with her, but "couldn't take it" any longer. [88] In an anguished letter of May 1977 to Blackwood, he compared their marriage to cataclysmic events, feared that he might lose control and hurt her, and stated that their life together was finished: "The last two years have been terrifying for us both—and neither of us has made it any better for the other. It hasn't been a quarrel, but two eruptions, two earthquakes crashing. . . . I feel you ended things during my Irish visit, ended them wisely and we can't go back. I have had so much dread—the worst in my life—that I would do something, by my mere presence I would do something to hurt you, to drive you to despair." Two months later, in another heart-mind struggle, he held out a faint hope of reconciliation yet predicted disaster if he returned: "I feel broken by all conversation, and a voice inside me says all might be well if I could be with you. And another voice says all would be ruin, and that I would be drowned in the confusion I made worse." [89]

Ivana said they had a nice family life in Ireland in the spring of 1977 and that Lowell went fishing with Sheridan in the nearby River Liffey. In

September Lowell did not pack all his things as if he were leaving forever, did not give the impression that he was returning to Hardwick and did not suggest that he would never come back. He left a sweet farewell note for Blackwood; and Ivana said her last goodbye on the steps of Castletown when she was returning to Dartington school and Lowell was going to New York. They made plans for the future and he promised, "See you at Christmas, it's only till Christmas." After he died the girls asked, "What about Christmas?"[90] Lowell might have said he was coming back because he really intended to return or was still undecided or wanted to gently ease the pain of separation and make his departure less traumatic for himself and everyone else.

Emphasizing Lowell's premonition of death—"he knew he would die and kept saying he would die"—Blackwood believed that he wanted to make amends and finally say farewell to Hardwick, but that he didn't leave his Irish family and faithfully promised to come back.[91] When asked what would have happened if he'd lived, she less optimistically confessed: "It would have gone on in the same way. I would have kept running away, and then it would have been all right, and then it wouldn't. It would have been a mess." She then quoted Lowell's depressing statement, "I have absolutely no future, because I'll just wreck the people I love."[92]

Lowell saw a striking parallel between Randall Jarrell's marital conflict and his own dilemma. Jarrell, in love with a younger woman, quarreled with his wife, Mary, but felt he needed her care to survive. As Lowell wrote Bishop: "There was also a girl (late thirties) that Hannah [Arendt] met at Goucher College in Baltimore. (No one else knows this.) He finally wrote to her that he couldn't cope with life unless he went home to Mary. . . . There was a bang up quarrel with Mary just before he went to the hospital for the last time. . . . I think it was suicide, and so does every one else who knew him well. Hannah said to me, 'What is so awful was that it was so fitting.'. . . He seems to have been begging [Mary] for a divorce, *before* he was sick last fall."[93] After his death Mary persuaded her academic courtiers to claim that Jarrell, walking on the highway on a dark night, had been accidentally hit by a car, but none of his friends believed her false and self-serving story. Lowell, sometimes tempted by suicide, felt personally threatened when Jarrell resolved his own dilemma by killing himself.

Blackwood was more beautiful, youthful and exciting than Hardwick, but she now had four children and another huge decaying house. She was just as chaotic and emotionally unstable as he was, and was terrified that his mania would cause her own breakdown. Hardwick, instead of running away from Lowell, stood by him. She managed the practical side of his life and knew how to take care of him, could handle his mania and provide a secure existence. He thought she'd been "awfully good to [him] through all these difficult seven years" and believed she'd always be waiting for him whenever he needed her.[94] In June 1977, when the spring term ended at Harvard, Lowell, unable to cope on his own, tested the turbulent waters with Hardwick and prepared the way for his return. He first moved into the New York apartment with her, then spent the summer fighting bitterly with her in Castine. Hardwick thought Lowell was returning to her; Blackwood thought he would be coming back to Ireland. Though still tormented by indecision, the familiar situation also pleased Lowell. Once again, two attractive, intelligent and talented women were hotly competing for his love.

Girding herself for more tedium and torture, Hardwick told Mary McCarthy that her role was now therapeutic. There was "no great renewed romance, but a kind of friendship, and listening to his grief."[95] But Mary Gordon, visiting the Lowells in the 1970s, was "embarrassed to see this icon of female accomplishment scurrying around to do her betraying husband's bidding. 'Lizzie, get me a handkerchief,' he said. . . . She literally ran around the apartment looking for a handkerchief. 'Cal, I think we only have Kleenex,' she said, abashed. 'Oh, Lord, Lizzie, what have you come to?'"[96]

Hardwick also had to ask herself, as she'd once asked Lowell, whether his decision to return was sane or mad. Darryl Pinckney wrote (in a contorted sentence), "Hardwick felt guilty that her first thought was of the independence she'd be giving up when in 1976 at Harvard, Lowell, exhausted by his stormy life with Blackwood, whom he still loved—she represented Aphrodite and ruin, he said—asked Hardwick if she'd consider taking him back."[97] It seems strange that Hardwick was more concerned with surrendering her life as an independent woman than she was with resuming responsibility for Lowell's attacks of madness.

In his poem "Artist's Model" Lowell quotes Macbeth's soliloquy, "If it were done . . . then 'twere well / It were done quickly" (1.7.1–2). But, torn between his Circe and Penelope, the one he loved and the one he needed, he couldn't make up his mind, quickly or slowly. Most friends thought that Lowell would repeat his lifelong pattern and return as he always did to Hardwick. Seamus Heaney, who saw Lowell in Ireland, wrote in an uncollected poem that when they were pissing together at the side of the road, "He intimated he'd probably not be / Returning to Caroline."[98] Grey Gowrie noted that his marriage to Blackwood "was in trouble, effectively at an end now, for Lowell had spent the summer with Elizabeth in Maine. . . . He knew he needed to go home and he went."[99] Esther Brooks, who was close to Hardwick, was even more emphatic. Brooks thought it was "totally clear, absolutely given and finally resolved" that Lowell was coming back to Hardwick, who remarked, "I hope it will go well." When Lowell told a friend that he was planning to return to Hardwick, she incredulously asked, "Does she really *want* that?" To which he gravely replied, "Why, yes!"[100] Hardwick also had the considerable pleasure of triumphing over her rival in their seven-year struggle for the mad genius. Like the faithful lover in John Donne's "A Valediction: Forbidding Mourning," Lowell could say, "Thy firmness makes my circle just, / And makes me end, where I begun."[101]

Frank Bidart, a close observer, was more sceptical about Lowell's final decision. He stayed with Lowell and Hardwick in New York just before Lowell left to see Blackwood in May 1977 and lived with them during the summer in Castine before Lowell's last visit to Ireland in September. They were often calm and congenial on the surface, but their unhappiness terrified Bidart, who'd never seen Lowell when he was not in love with someone. Lowell told Bidart that he couldn't let Hardwick down again after all his broken promises; he couldn't leave her a second time, have any more love affairs nor continue his old way of life. He carried around Blackwood's letters as if they were sacred totems but, with two possible choices, lamented that he "had no place on earth to go to."

Lowell loved and wanted Blackwood, but made her sick and couldn't live with her. He liked and was grateful to Hardwick, but didn't love her. He didn't know which woman to choose, couldn't see what would happen to him and had no answer to the dilemma—which was finally decided by fate. If he had, in fact, returned to Hardwick, he would have joined the surprisingly long list—including Allen Tate—of authors, artists and actresses who married (and often divorced) the same person twice.[102]

VII

When Lowell flew from Dublin to New York on September 12, 1977, he carried his most valuable possession: Lucian Freud's magnificent portrait

of the twenty-one-year-old Blackwood, *Girl in Bed* (1952).[103] Grey Gowrie
had helped him buy the painting from Colin Tennant (Lord Glenconnor)
for £28,000 (about $70,000). (It's now in a private collection and worth
$15 million.) In the painting Blackwood, lying under a white quilt, rests
her head on her hand and leans on a pillow. She has long delicate fingers,
flowing blond hair, huge blue eyes, ruddy cheeks and a winsome expression. Unable to decide which woman he wanted to live with and unwilling
to let go of Blackwood, Lowell carried her precious image with him just as
he'd carried around her letters. He seemed to need Blackwood's symbolic
support, and kept her portrait so he could have, literally and figuratively,
both his past and present wives.

Though Lowell was mentally stable during the last year of his life, he
suffered from coronary disease and had entered McLean in February 1977
with congestive heart failure. That month, calmly contemplating what
Henry James called "the distinguished thing," he wrote Blackwood that
his stay in the hospital "was painless, eventless; perhaps what death might
be at best. . . . If that's all life is, it's a coldly smiling anticlimax—gone the
great apocalypse of departure. . . . It seemed to me that death would be
nothing. What gentler thing could one ask for?"[104] But when Gail Mazur
saw him at Harvard in May he seemed gaunt and drained, exhausted and
sick.[105] He also, like all mortals, wanted a quick, painless death and hoped
to go at "the moment when insects die / instantly as one would ask of a
friend."[106]

Lowell's life ended dramatically, like the best concluding lines of his
poems, and his final decision about which wife to choose remained uncertain. After visiting Blackwood in September, he flew to New York and, at
the age of sixty, had a heart attack in the taxi that took him into Manhattan from Kennedy airport. Clutching Blackwood's portrait, he reached
the apartment dead on arrival. The taxi driver, who couldn't rouse Lowell,
at first thought he was drunk and had passed out. The doorman called
Hardwick, and as she opened the door of the taxi Lowell fell over on the
seat. David Heymann wrote that "the cab raced on to Roosevelt Hospital,
half a mile away. 'His body was still warm,' testified an attending para-
medic; but his heart and breathing had stopped."[107] After the hospital had
declared him dead, Hardwick went back to her apartment, unwrapped the
brown paper parcel and found the portrait of Blackwood—Lowell's last
legacy in both senses.

The older generation of American poets—Frost, Stevens, Pound,

Eliot, Ransom and Tate—had survived into old age, and both Kunitz and Eberhart lived to be over one hundred. But many in Lowell's generation—Roethke, Schwartz, Plath, Jarrell, Berryman and Sexton—all died when young or middle aged, the last four by suicide. Though Lowell died when he was only sixty, he outlived these contemporaries and wrote elegies about five of them. After his own tumultuous life, the modern Ulysses finally found a safe haven, sleep after toil, port after stormy seas.

Lowell's wives fought over him to the very end. Stafford "had threatened to sweep up [to Boston] in style, in a rented black Cadillac . . . and was at the last minute persuaded not to attend the Beacon Hill Service."[108] The ever-tolerant Hardwick invited Blackwood—distraught and at her worst—to stay with her in New York and managed to calm her down before the service. But Blackwood gave Hardwick a dramatic exhibition of what it was like for Lowell to live with her. As Hardwick wrote to Mary McCarthy, "Caroline somehow moved in with me for 8 days and nights to prepare the Memorial Service. I don't think any single night I slept more than two hours. Her poor drunken theatricality hour after hour, day after day, night after night, was unrelieved torture for me and I am sure for herself much more."[109]

A woman friend noted that Blackwood, who liked to wear heavy mascara, "was quite something at the funeral. Every child had black smudges like Indians put under their eyes."[110] Afterward, another friend took the children to see *Star Wars* to distract them and get them away from Blackwood. Seamus Heaney quoted Blackwood's witty remark about all the literary celebrities who turned up in the church: "My dear, you could tour it."[111] Heaney also quoted McCarthy's caustic comment on the service, "the biggest cover-up since Watergate."[112] But she could hardly have expected Lowell's friends to discuss his harsh treatment of Hardwick on that solemn occasion.

All three wives were muses who inspired Lowell. Though well aware of what they would suffer if they married him, they were fatally attracted. They were driven by the snobbish appeal of his great name, by the formidable connections that would advance their careers, and by a fatal love of risk-taking: drinking, dealing with madness and living to extremes. They also admired his generosity and courage, his knowledge and art. Stafford was a physical victim, sucked dry and then abandoned. Blackwood, though still in love with him, agreed to separate in order to survive. Hardwick remained devoted and loyal through all her suffering, and kept returning for more intellectual fireworks and psychological damage. She was always willing to absolve his guilt, take him back and encourage him to resume his rightful place in the center of American culture. Lowell's obsessive revision of his life—his colleges and religions, politics and attitude to war, mental hospitals, residences and countries, lovers and wives—resembled the endless revision of his poems. Though his life was unstable and the cost was high, his dedication to art was absolute.

APPENDIX ONE
The Search for Lowell's Lovers

Though the computer now makes it easier to locate people through Google, AnyWho and White Pages, it was still quite difficult to find Lowell's nine identifiable lovers, five of whom were still alive. I wanted to bring these women out of the shadows and into the limelight, to find out about their lives before and after they met Lowell, and to describe their characters and achievements. I was fortunate to receive help from several of their relatives.

Through an obituary of Anne Dick's sister, I contacted her niece Anne Newman. She phoned me and put me in touch with Anne's only child, May Eliot Paddock. Though guarded and reserved, she agreed to an interview. I got more information from Richard Eberhart's *The Mad Magician,* Sarah Stuart's *My First Cousin Once Removed,* Patricia Bosworth's biography of Anne's friend, the photographer Diane Arbus, Ian Hamilton's interview with Frank Parker and my interview with Frank's widow Judith Parker.

While writing *Manic Power: Robert Lowell and His Circle,* I interviewed Gertrude Buckman in London in August 1985. I got more material about her from the *Partisan Review,* the *Letters* and biography of Delmore Schwartz, Jean Stafford's "A Country Love Story," Stafford's two biographies and David Laskin's *Partisans.*

Carley Dawson, who lived until 2005, was not mentioned in the journals and letters of her lover Saint-John Perse, in the many French works about him or in books on the leading figures in Washington social life. But I got some material from the biographies of Dawson's friends Joyce

Grenfell and Caresse Crosby. There were letters from Lowell in her archive
at the University of Oregon, where I came across the address of her only
child, Stephen Hawkins. He didn't answer my letters and his phone was
disconnected, so it was impossible to know whether or not he was willing
to talk, whether he was still there or had moved away, whether he was alive
or dead. I wrote to the postmaster of his small town in western New York,
who forwarded my letter to Hawkins' ex-wife. She wrote saying he was in
a nursing home and that she would answer my questions. Then, inexplica-
bly, a lawyer intervened who advised her not to talk to me.

Giovanna Madonia's first husband was the Milanese poet Luciano Erba.
I wrote to Erba's English translator, Peter Robinson, who gave me the
address of Erba's second wife and widow, who failed to respond. I returned
to Robinson, who wrote on my behalf to the widow, who said Madonia
was living in France. I located her in Igny, a suburb of Paris, but (like
Hawkins) she didn't answer my letters and her phone was disconnected.
So I'd gone a full circle and was back where I'd started. Then I remembered that Madonia came from Forlì, near Ravenna and the Adriatic coast
of Italy, and thought she might have returned there to live with her family
in old age. I was pleased to find a Giovanna Madonia in her hometown
and wrote to her in Italian, but she turned out to be Madonia's namesake
and niece. She explained that the real Madonia had died a few years ago,
aged eighty-one, and gave me the name and address of Madonia's son in
Paris. Madonia's second husband was the distinguished painter Leonardo
Cremonini and her son Pietro was an architect. I wrote to him in Italian
and, in several letters, he answered my questions in French. I sent him the
French translation of my life of Hemingway and, after many letters, he
sent me his mother's photograph.

I found Ann Adden through the Bennington College alumni association. She was extremely reluctant, at first, to reveal her personal life and
I had to convince her (as I did Martha Ritter) that I was writing a serious
book. Adden (like Vija Vetra) couldn't find Lowell's letters to her, which
were lost when she lived on a sailboat for five years. But she sent me, by
way of an introduction, her long essay on oriental mysticism, many letters
that supplemented our long interview and her youthful photo for use in
my book.

Sandra Hochman's address and phone number were (like Vija Vetra's)
in AnyWho, but she didn't answer several letters and phone calls. Finally,
she called me to say she wouldn't help. But I convinced her to let me read

her unpublished 300-page memoir about Lowell by putting her in touch with my literary agent and paying $75 (slashed from her original demand of $3,000) for Xeroxing and postage. After I'd sent her a letter with additional questions about her memoir, she was surprisingly aggressive, hostile and rude on the phone. But when she unexpectedly called a week later (forcing me to cancel another scheduled interview), she was lively and enthusiastic, and filled in all the missing details. Hochman's poems *Earthworks* and the Bishop-Lowell letters were also illuminating. Carried away by our long talks, Hochman fantasized about dedicating her next book to me and flying me to New York for the premiere of her play.

I was lucky to catch the dancer Vija Vetra, still chirpy in accented English at the age of ninety, between trips to her native Latvia and to Greece. Though still angry at Lowell's cruel treatment, she had a clear memory, answered all my questions, sent me a file on her dance career and gave me permission to use her exotic photo. Edmund Wilson's *The Sixties* has a revealing entry about Vetra.

At first I tracked down the wrong Martha Ritter, at Franklin Pierce College in Rindge, New Hampshire, and then (the same woman who'd changed jobs) at Mount St. Mary's College in Emmitsburg, Maryland. I eventually found the Martha Ritter I'd been seeking through the Harvard University alumni association. (There were two Giovanna Madonias and two Martha Ritters.) It took a long conversation to convince Ritter that I was a reputable biographer and that my book was serious. I sent her my questions in advance; she sent me Lowell's letters from All Souls, Oxford, several of her articles about social issues and Jo Bruns' *Take Two* with a chapter about Ritter. Most unusually, she read thirty single-spaced pages of her autobiography to me in three marathon conversations while I took notes, and she then sent the typescripts so I could complete the picture. After my extensive involvement I formed sympathetic friendships with Adden and Ritter, and we planned a reunion on Lowell's 100th anniversary in March 2017.

The most frustrating search was for Mary Keelan, whom I found twice. She'd been described as Irish, rather than Irish American, so I tried to find her through the Irish Embassy in Washington, and through my Irish friends, Valerie Hemingway, Denis Donoghue and his colleague W. J. McCormack. I searched for information about Ivan Illich and his Center for Intercultural Documentation in Cuernavaca, Mexico, where Lowell had met Keelan. I also wrote to Jonathan Kozol and interviewed Shepherd

Bliss, who'd been there with her. I then discovered that Keelan had become a librarian and wrote to the American Library Association for which she'd edited a tape recording, *Tongues Tied and Untied: Censorship in the Media* (1992). They told me she'd worked for the Mid-Hudson Library System in Poughkeepsie, New York. The director forwarded my letters to her, but she never answered.

Thinking she might have done graduate work, I found that the Modern Language Association Directory of 1976–77 listed her in the Riverdale district of northern New York City, and guessed that she might have studied at Columbia University. Their alumni association forwarded my letters to her, but she again failed to respond. She preferred to remain in the shadows; I'd spent a lot of time and got no results. Keelan, anonymous in Ian Hamilton's biography, was identified by Paul Mariani. I was therefore able to get copies of her letters to Lowell at Harvard. I discovered more about her from Hamilton's interviews with Frank Parker and Sidney Nolan, and found that she was the subject of Lowell's twelve "Mexico" sonnets.

APPENDIX TWO

Annotations to
Lowell's Poems

Though the editorial notes by Frank Bidart and David Gewanter for Lowell's *Collected Poems* (2003) are excellent, they inevitably missed many significant literary references and allusions, and did not clarify some difficult passages. The following page numbers refer to this edition. Lowell had a vast knowledge of poetry, and the sound and sense of thousands of lines echoed in his head. For him, reading was raiding. An awareness of his sources reveals the technique and enhances the meaning of his poetry.

14 – "The Quaker Graveyard in Nantucket" – echoes Henry Wadsworth Longfellow's "The Jewish Cemetery at Newport," in Rhode Island (1854).

18 – "The Lord survives the rainbow of His will" – Man is bound by the covenant but God, who is not, may passively stand by and allow evil mankind to destroy itself.

37 – "Napoleon Crosses the Berezina" – river and tributary of the Dneiper, near Minsk in modern Belarus.

55 – "In the Cage" – comes from the title of Henry James' story (1898).

94–95 – "Her Dead Brother" – describes Jean Stafford's relations with her beloved brother, killed in a jeep accident in France in 1944, and hints at their incest.

96 – "when her trophies hung" – John Keats, "Ode to Melancholy" (1820): "And be among her cloudy trophies hung."

107 – "You are a bastard, Michael, aren't you! *Nein*" (1946) – influenced Sylvia Plath's "Daddy" (1960): "daddy, you bastard, I'm through."

114 – "Now Paris, our black classic, breaking up / like killer kings in an

Etruscan cup" – Lowell conflates the black Etruscan vases, Charles Baudelaire's use of black to describe the city in "Parisian Dream," *Les Fleurs du Mal* (1857), and Ovid's exile on the Black Sea.

118 – "I chartered an aluminum canoe, / I had her six times in the English Garden" – T. S. Eliot, *The Waste Land* (1922): "By Richmond I raised my knees / Supine on the floor of a narrow canoe."

153 – "(a birdie Fordie!") . . . . Lloyd George was holding up / the flag" – in chapter 4 of Ford Madox Ford's novel *Some Do Not* (1924) suffragists interrupt the prime minister's golf game.

167 – "Bayard, our riding horse" – legendary magic horse from the medieval French epic poems, the *Chansons de geste.*

168 – " 'pumped ship' together" – uses a nautical term for getting water out of a boat to mean "pissing together."

169 – "Edward Winslow / once sheriff for George the Second, / the sire of bankrupt Tories" – Lowell's maternal ancestors supported the English monarchy in the American Revolution.

170 – "Have me, hold me cherish me!" – paraphrase of the traditional marriage vows in the *Book of Common Prayer* (1549).

173 – "smiling on all" and "he smiled his oval Lowell smile" – Robert Browning, "My Last Duchess" (1842): "all and each / Would draw . . . / Much the same smile."

180 – "*Lowell* had been misspelled LOVEL" – there is no letter W in the Italian alphabet.

180 – "wrapped like *panetone* in Italian tinfoil" – Lowell means *panforte,* a flat, chewy, spicy fruitcake.

187 – " 'hardly passionate Marlborough Street' " – Henry James, quoted in Mark de Wolfe Howe, *A Venture in Remembrance* (1941): "Do you feel that Marlborough Street—is precisely—*passionate?*"

188 – "jarred his concentration on the electric chair—/ hanging like an oasis" – James Boswell, *Life of Johnson,* September 19, 1777 (1791): "when a man knows he is to be hanged . . . it concentrates his mind wonderfully."

189 – "Tamed by *Miltown,* we lie in Mother's bed; / the rising sun in war paint dyes us red" – W. H. Auden, "A Summer Night" (1933): "Out on the lawn I lie in bed, / Vega conspicuous overhead."

189 – "its hackneyed speech, its homicidal eye" – Samuel Coleridge. "Kubla Khan" (1819): "His flashing eyes, his floating hair."

189 – "breaks like the Atlantic Ocean on my head" – Jonathan Swift, Letter of August 19, 1727, "I have a hundred oceans rolling in my ears."

190 – "the razor's edge" – *Katha Upanishad,* third *valli:* "the sharp edge of a razor is difficult to pass over" and Somerset Maugham, *The Razor's Edge* (1944).

191 – "my mind's not right" – James Boswell, *Boswell in Extremes, 1776–1778* (1970): "My mind was not right."

229 – "Yesterday the Grand Army, today its dregs!" – Victor Hugo, "L'Expiation" (1853): "Yesterday the Grand Army, today a herd" and "Auden, "Spain" (1937): "Yesterday all the past . . . to-day the struggle."

323 – "your ghostly / imaginary lover" – Elizabeth Hardwick's novel *The Ghostly Lover* (1945).

326 – "like Nebuchadnezzar / on his knees eating grass" – inspired by William Blake's color print (1805).

330 – "How vulnerable the horseshoe crabs / dredging the bottom" – Eliot, "The Love Song of J. Alfred Prufrock" (1914): "I should have been a pair of ragged claws / Scuttling across the floors of silent seas.'

360 – "*Item:* your body hairy, badly made . . . . *Item:* eyes hollow, hollow temples . . . . nose thin, thin neck" – William Shakespeare, *Twelfth Night* (1601), 1.5.265–8: "item, two lips, indifferent red; item, two grey eyes with lids to them; item, one neck, one chin."

362 – "The Severed Head" – alludes to famous decapitations: Perseus and Medusa, Judith and Holofernes, Salomé and John the Baptist, Bertrand de Born in Dante's *Inferno, Sir Gawain and the Green Knight,* Ichabod Crane in Washington Irving's "The Legend of Sleepy Hollow," Marie Antoinette and all the victims of the guillotine.

362 – "I heard him pour / mortar to seal the outlets" – Edgar Allan Poe, "The Cask of Amontillado" (1846), in which Montresor buries Fortunato alive.

365 – "the Number of the Beast" – Satan in Revelation 15:2: "victory over the beast . . . and over the number of his name."

375 – "Sweet salt embalms me" and 654 – "From the salt age" – refer to lithium, his salt-based medication used to treat mania and depression.

377 – " 'Rock of Ages' " – Christian hymn by Augustus Toplady (1763).

385 – "elephant and phalanx moving" – Hannibal crossing the Alps.

385 – "a million foreskins stacked like trash" – John Milton, *Samson Agonistes* (1671): "A thousand foreskins fell."

385 – "swimming nude, unbuttoned, sick / of his ghost-written rhetoric!" – Swift, "On His Own Deafness" (1734): "Deaf, giddy, helpless, left alone / To all my friends a burthen grown."

395 – "land's end" – in Cornwall, at the southwestern tip of England.

424 – "King David Old" – Ezra Pound, "Piere Vidal Old" (1909).

476 – "Why should shark be eaten when bait swim free?" – Shakespeare, *King Lear* (1605), 5.3.308–9: "Why should a dog, a horse, a rat, have life, / And thou no breath at all?"

512 – "now more than before fearing everything I do" – John Keats, "Ode to a Nightingale" (1819): "Now more than ever seems it rich to die."

523 – "black-gloved, black coated, you plod out stubbornly / as if in lockstep to grasp your blank not-I" and 819: "I see a late, suicidal headlight / burn on the highway." – descriptions of Randall Jarrell's suicide in 1965, when he threw himself in front of a car on the highway in North Carolina.

532 – "rising in the saddle to slash at Auschwitz" – alludes to Plath riding her horse *Ariel* and writing about Auschwitz in "Daddy."

535 – "if I forget you, Ann, may my right hand . . ." – "Psalms 137:5: "If I forget thee, O Jerusalem, let my right hand forget her cunning." See also 959 for this quote.

535 – "I love Lenin, he was so feudal. *When I listen to Beethoven,* / he said, *I think of stroking people's hair; / what we need are people to chop the head off.*" – Maxim Gorki, *Reminiscences* (1920), on how Beethoven's "Appassionata Sonata" inspired Lenin's murderous thoughts.

555 – "Seven Ages of Man" – Shakespeare, *As You Like It* (1599), 2.7.142–3: "one man in his time plays many parts, / His acts being Seven Ages."

585 – "Loser" – According to Lowell's friend Grey Gowrie, this poem is based on Gowrie's first wife, Xandra, talking about her father.

601 – "Is dying harder than already being dead?" (1973) – influenced by Plath's "Lady Lazarus" (1963): "Dying / Is an art like everything else. / I do it exceptionally well."

611 – "scarlet general" – Siegfried Sassoon, "Base Details" (1918): "I'd live with scarlet majors at the Base."

615 – "green sack of books" – Harvard students carried green cloth book bags.

626 – "This stream will not flow back" – Heraclitus: "other waters are ever flowing on to you."

626 – "this city of the plain" – Genesis 13:12: "Lot dwelled in the cities of the plain."

628 – "with bluebells in your hair" – Henrik Ibsen, *Hedda Gabler* (1890): "with vine leaves in his hair."

637 – "talking for a victory" – Boswell, *Life of Johnson,* October 26, 1759 (1791): "talking for victory."

653 – "You left two houses and two thousand books, / a workbarn by the ocean, and two slaves" (1973) – influenced Elizabeth Bishop, "One Art" (1976): "I lost my mother's watch. And look! my last, or / next-to-last, of three loved houses went."

665 – "float like a butterfly and sting like a bee" – poem by Mohammed Ali.

669 – "Lie with a woman . . . her bondage is our lash" – Friedrich Nietzsche, *Thus Spoke Zarathustra,* 1.18 (1883): "You are going to women? Do not forget the whip!"

693 – "*the new life*" – Dante, *La Vita Nuova* (1295).

697 – "*and for an hour, / I've walked and prayed*" – W. B. Yeats, "A Prayer for My Daughter"(1919): "I have walked and prayed for this young child an hour."

708 – "my eyes have seen what my hand did" – Julia Ward Howe, "The Battle Hymn of the Republic" (1862): "Mine eyes have seen the glory" and Eliot, "Gerontion" (1920): "After such knowledge, what forgiveness?"

731 – "That year killed / Pound, Wilson, Auden . . . / promise has lost its bloom." – John Berryman, "Dream Song 153" (1969): "I'm cross with god who has wrecked this generation. / First he seized Ted, then Richard, Randall, and now Delmore."

760 – "the immortal / is scraped unconsenting from the mortal" – carved on Lowell's gravestone.

814 – "your father's betrayal of you, / rushing to his military death in Burma, / annexed for England / by his father's father, the Viceroy" – Blackwood's father died in a Japanese ambush near Mandalay, Burma, in March 1945. Her great-grandfather, the 1st Marquess of Dufferin and Ava, was Viceroy of India.

832 – "anyone is unwanted in a medical sense— / lust our only father" – T. E. Lawrence, Letter of May 27, 1923: "I believe it's we who led our parents to bear us, and it's our unborn children who make our flesh itch"; and Robert Graves, "Children of Darkness" (1923): "We spurred our parents to the kiss, / Though doubtfully they shrank from this."

834 – "Is getting well ever an art, / or art a way to get well?" (1977) – influenced by Bishop, "One Art" (1976): "the art of living's not too hard to master / though it may look like (*Write* it!) like disaster."

838 – "the sun's illumination / stealing like the tide across a map" –

Kenneth Clark, *Looking at Pictures* (1960): "daylight . . . passes over the map . . . like an incoming tide over the sand."

852 – "A stonesthrow off, / seven eider ducks / float and dive in this watery commune" – Yeats, "The Wild Swans at Coole" (1917): "Upon a brimming water among the stones / Are nine-and-fifty swans."

867 – "Over the seas and far away" – John Gay, *The Beggar's Opera* (1728): "Over the hills and far away.'

868 – "Here Concord's shot that rang" – Ralph Waldo Emerson, "Concord Hymn" (1836): "Fired the shot heard round the world."

872 – "Angels will fear to tread" – Alexander Pope, "An Essay in Criticism" (1711): "Fools rush in where angels fear to tread."

873 – "In Salem seasick spindrift drifts or skips" – Hart Crane, "Voyages, II" (1926): "The seal's wide spindrift gaze toward paradise."

883 – "The laurels are cut down" – Théodore de Banville, "We'll to the Woods No More" (1846): "The laurels are all cut."

889 – "hypnotic yawp" – Walt Whitman, *Leaves of Grass* (1855): "I sound my barbaric yawp."

894 – "To bury man and yet to praise him" – Shakespeare, *Julius Caesar* (1599), 3.2.76: "I come to bury Caesar, not to praise him."

894 – "roll onward, roll" – Negro spiritual: "Roll Jordan, roll."

962 – "God is my shepherd" – Psalms 23:1: "The Lord is my shepherd."

981 – "Solomon / in all his beauty was arrayed like thee" – Matthew 6:29: "Solomon in all his glory was not arrayed like one of these."

983 – "a pillar of fire to show our path" – Exodus 13:21: "A pillar of fire, to give them light."

Hamilton, *Lowell,* 244 – "steel plates of a press / needling, draining my heart – Franz Kafka, "In the Penal Colony" (1919): "The long needle does the writing, and the short needle sprays a jet of water to wash away the blood."

Robert Lowell
vs. Lyndon Johnson

Lowell Agonistes, always prone to physical violence, also engaged in many intellectual combats. He went to jail as a conscientious objector to protest the mass bombing of German cities in World War II; he supported Ezra Pound in the Bollingen Prize controversy in 1948; he led an anti-Communist crusade at the Yaddo writers' colony in 1949; he publicly baited Dmitri Shostakovich in 1949 and Andrei Voznesensky in 1967 about oppression in the Soviet Union; he disputed with critics of his *Imitations* in 1961 and of *The Dolphin* in 1973; he competed for the Oxford Chair in Poetry in 1966; he manned the barricades at the Pentagon in 1967 and he joined Senator Eugene McCarthy's presidential campaign in 1968. His most significant controversy, his public refusal to attend the White House Festival of the Arts, has not yet been covered in Robert Caro's massive, still unfinished biography of Lyndon Johnson. The dispute has usually been seen from the viewpoint of Lowell, who portrayed Johnson in a poem and a play. But new material from the Lyndon Johnson Presidential Library in Austin, Texas, reveals how Lowell upset and frightened the White House.

On June 14, 1965, as America became more deeply enmeshed in the disastrous war in Vietnam, President Lyndon Johnson tried to court the literati, improve his image and diminish opposition to the war with an ill-conceived White House Festival of the Arts. In contrast to John and Jackie Kennedy's spectacularly successful dinners for André Malraux and other artistic luminaries when the White House became a kind of café for intellectuals, Johnson's imitation was an embarrassing failure.

With Mark Van Doren as master of ceremonies, the cultural representatives were to include Edmund Wilson, Saul Bellow, John Hersey, E. B. White and, to represent the ladies, Phyllis McGinley and Catherine Drinker Bowen. Johnson's advisers were shocked, and he was quite furious, when Wilson rudely refused the invitation on the telephone. The Princeton historian Eric Goldman—special consultant to Johnson and organizer of the festival—wrote that Wilson replied "with a brusqueness that I have never experienced before or after in the case of an invitation in the name of the President and First Lady."[1]

Lowell's tactics were more subtle and effective. He first accepted the invitation, then changed his mind. On May 30, 1965 Lowell, who always dealt directly with American presidents, sent a letter to Johnson—as he had once written to Franklin Roosevelt about his opposition to the war—and planned to send a copy to the *New York Times*. Eric Goldman at first condemned Lowell and attributed his letter to his mental instability: "My first reaction to the letter was fury. This, I told myself, was arrant troublemaking and publicity seeking—the acceptance of a White House invitation, then turning it down, the injection of irrelevant grand issues in high-sounding language, the play to the newspapers. Then, studying the actual contents of the letter and reflecting on what I knew of Lowell . . . I decided that my initial reaction was off base and that the letter had been written by a sincere and troubled man."[2]

Hoping to cool the crisis and diminish Johnson's wrath, directed against him for inviting the troublesome poet, Goldman phoned Lowell but failed to control the damage. On June 2 Goldman told George Reedy, the White House press secretary, "I talked to Lowell on the phone and tried to get him to reconsider. I did not try to persuade him to read at the Festival. I did argue that he should reconsider his letter to the President and releasing it to the press. He was adamant and told me he was giving his letter to the *New York Times*."[3] But Goldman was deeply impressed by Lowell's well-reasoned refusal and later wrote that "throughout the conversation the poet was gracious, free of self-righteousness about the position he was taking, and thoroughly understanding of the complications he was causing. I hung up the telephone with the impression of a fine human being. I also hung up with the feeling that all hell was about to break loose."[4]

The *Times* considered Lowell's letter important enough to be published on the front page on June 3, 1965. Enunciating one of his major ideas, and fears, Lowell wrote, "Every serious artist knows that he cannot enjoy public celebrations without making subtle public commitments. . . . I can only follow our present foreign policy with the greatest dismay and distrust. . . . We are in danger of imperceptibly becoming an explosive and suddenly chauvinistic nation, and may even be drifting on our way to the last nuclear ruin." Lowell concluded by echoing the Latin epigraph to his poem "For the Union Dead"—"They gave up everything to serve the state," and declared, "I feel I am serving you and our country best by not taking part in the White House Festival."[5] Twenty writers and artists, including some of Lowell's close friends—Hannah Arendt, John Berryman, Stanley Kunitz, Mary McCarthy, Peter Taylor and Robert Penn Warren—who were more distinguished than the actual participants, sent a telegram to Johnson, "supporting Robert Lowell in his decision not to participate in the White House Festival."[6]

Johnson's furious roar echoed through the corridors of the White House, and after the festival he exclaimed, "They insult me by comin', they insult me by stayin' away."[7] He screamed "they were not only 'sons-ofbitches' but they were 'fools,' and they were close to traitors." Goldman added that because of Lowell, "a minor event, a mere ceremonial festival of the arts, was blowing up into a situation which could have anything but minor significance."[8] On June 8, a week before the event, Jack Valenti, special assistant to Johnson, tried to reassure the president and make the best of a bad situation by denigrating Lowell. He maintained, "We should not let one erratic, unstable poet, plus a dozen headline-seekers damage a truly high-quality enterprise, which follows through with this administration's fruitful favoring of the arts."[9] Lady Bird Johnson took a patriotic but more realistic view of the damage Lowell had caused. She and her staff "discussed the one-by-one hammer blows of the front-page stories. . . . All of them seemed to delight in faulting their country and their President. They accented Robert Lowell's not coming."[10]

A White House aide compounded the disaster and again roused Johnson's formidable wrath by attributing a clearly identified excerpt from Matthew Arnold's "Dover Beach" to Lowell, who'd used it as an epigraph to *The Mills of the Kavanaughs,* and by putting it into a speech Johnson gave on August 4 to thousands of students on the White House lawn. Nine months later, on May 11, 1966, Barbaralee Diamonstein, who'd helped Goldman organize the festival, repeated the error—incredibly enough—by once again attributing the Arnold quote to Lowell and putting it on a White House program. As she lamely explained to Goldman, "These [lines] are the best I could find. Lowell becomes increasingly lugubrious, pessimistic, odd-pacifist, ancestor-guilty as things progress. Don't know if it is so wise to bring him up again." It wasn't, and heads began to roll.

In the same letter, Diamonstein retrospectively conceded that Lowell, in absentia, had a powerful political impact, gravely undermined the festival and worried the White House: "It was an artistic and creative event rather than a political one and Mr. Lowell was made to understand that from the very start. However, he subsequently chose not to participate. . . . To underestimate the meaning of the event as a catalyst in the foreign policy question that the American people were faced with would be an error."[11]

Lowell's friend Blair Clark, a professional political consultant, agreed with Goldman's judgment of Lowell's character and motives, and gave a shrewd estimate of Lowell's achievement: "That was a very successful operation of high-level cultural publicism. Cal the public figure—he knew what he was doing. I'm sure there were people who were terribly envious of his ability to manipulate himself as a public figure. He did it without any pomposity—but he definitely believed that he *was* a public figure. . . . Largely thanks to Lowell, the event was an unmitigated disaster."[12]

But Lowell was not quite finished with Lyndon Johnson. In "Waking Early Sunday Morning" he referred to the warmongering president, about to be defeated by a Vietnamese David, as "Hammering military splendor, / top-heavy Goliath in full armor."[13] In 1967 the Yale Repertory Theater won a $25,000 grant from the National Endowment for the Arts to produce Lowell's translation of Aeschylus' *Prometheus Bound*. The director, Robert Brustein, wrote that "President Johnson, enraged to discover that a government agency had awarded money to someone he believed had insulted him, demanded that the award be withdrawn. To the credit of the endowment—then under the chairmanship of Roger Stevens—Johnson's efforts were resisted."[14]

The political theme provided the main interest of Lowell's translation of *Prometheus Bound*. In his Author's Note to the play he stated that "no contemporary statesman is parodied," but admitted that "my own concerns and worries and those of the times seep in." He also suggested that he was using Aeschylus to make a political statement by saying that "Zeus has the character of a hard dictator."[15] Zeus is clearly based on Johnson; Prometheus represents Lowell's idealistic and influential opposition to the war in Vietnam, which began when he torpedoed the ill-fated White House Festival of the Arts.

NOTES

Introduction

1. Monroe Spears, "Life and Art in Robert Lowell," *American Ambitions: Selected Essays* (Baltimore: Johns Hopkins University Press, 1987), p. 46.

2. John Dryden, "Absalom and Achitophel," *John Dryden* (Oxford Authors), ed. Keith Walker (Oxford: Oxford University Press, 1987), p. 182.

3. Plato, *Ion, Four Dialogues,* trans. Percy Bysshe Shelley (London: Dent, 1924), pp. 6–7.

4. Plato, *Phaedrus,* trans. Walter Hamilton (London: Penguin, 1973), p. 46.

5. Søren Kierkegaard, *Either/Or,* trans. David Swenson (Princeton: Princeton University Press, 1959), 1.19.

6. Fyodor Dostoyevsky, *Notes from Underground,* trans. Andrew MacAndrew (NY: Signet, 1961), p. 93.

7. Friedrich Nietzsche, *"Twilight of the Idols," The Portable Nietzsche,* trans. and ed. Walter Kaufmann (NY: Viking, 1954), p. 549.

8. Friedrich Nietzsche, *The Will to Power,* trans. and ed. Walter Kaufmann (NY: Vintage, 1968), pp. 30–31.

9. Arthur Rimbaud, Letter of May 15, 1871, *Complete Works,* trans. Paul Schmidt (NY: Harper & Row, 1975), pp. 102–103.

10. Jean-Paul Sartre, *The War Diaries,* trans. Quinton Hoare (NY: Pantheon, 1985), p. 29.

One. Charlotte's Web

1. Ian Hamilton, *Robert Lowell: A Biography* (NY: Random House, 1980), p. 6.

2. Blaise Pascal, *The Pensées,* trans. J. M. Cohen (London: Penguin, 1961), p. 109.

3. Richard Tillinghast, *Robert Lowell's Life and Work: Damaged Grandeur* (Ann Arbor: University of Michigan Press, 1995), p. 47.

4. Randall Jarrell, *Letters,* ed. Mary Jarrell (Boston: Houghton Mifflin, 1985), p. 498.

5. Robert Lowell, "Antebellum Boston," *Collected Prose,* ed. and intro. Robert Giroux (NY: Farrar, Straus and Giroux, 1987), p. 291.

6. Elizabeth Bishop, *One Art: Letters,* ed. Robert Giroux (NY: Farrar, Straus and Giroux, 1994), pp. 351–352.

7. Jeffrey Meyers, ed., *Robert Lowell: Interviews and Memoirs* (Ann Arbor: University of Michigan Press, 1988), p. 161.

8. Robert Lowell, "91 Revere Street," *Life Studies and For the Union Dead* (NY: Farrar, Straus and Giroux, 1967), p. 38.

9. C. David Heymann, *American Aristocracy: The Lives and Times of James Russell, Amy and Robert Lowell* (NY: Dodd, Mead, 1980), p. 34.

10. Robert Lowell, "T. S. Eliot," *Collected Poems,* ed. Frank Bidart and David Gewanter (NY: Farrar, Straus and Giroux, 2003), p. 537.

11. Heymann, *American Aristocracy,* p. 301.

12. Lowell, "91 Revere Street," pp. 11–12, 44.

13. Raymond Sokolov, *Wayward Reporter: The Life of A. J. Liebling* (NY: Harper & Row, 1980), p. 277.

14. Jeffrey Meyers, *Remembering Iris Murdoch: Letters and Interviews* (NY: Palgrave Macmillan, 2013), p. 5.

15. Heymann, *American Aristocracy,* pp. 289–290.

16. Arthur Miller, *Death of a Salesman* (1949; NY: Penguin, 1986), pp. 44, 48.

17. Lowell, "Grandparents," *Life Studies,* p. 69.

18. Jeffrey Meyers, *A Reader's Guide to George Orwell* (London: Thames & Hudson, 1975), p. 20.

19. John Dos Passos, *The Best Times* (NY: New American Library, 1966), p. 210.

Hemingway portrayed his mother's humiliation of his cowardly father in "Now I Lay Me" (1927), where she burns his precious collection of stone axes and Indian arrowheads.

20. Letter from Jennifer Bryan to Jeffrey Meyers, May 13, 2013.

21. *The Lucky Bag* (Annapolis: Naval Academy Yearbook), 14 (1907), p. 82.

22. Lowell, "Antebellum Boston," p. 296.

23. Lowell, "Commander Lowell," *Life Studies,* p. 72.

24. Lowell, "91 Revere Street" and "Commander Lowell," pp. 35, 72.

25. Lowell, *Poems,* p. 432.

26. Paul Mariani, *Lost Puritan: A Life of Robert Lowell* (NY: Norton, 1994), pp. 27–28.

27. Hamilton, *Lowell,* pp. 386, 4–5.

28. Lowell, "During Fever," *Life Studies,* p. 80.

29. Lowell, "91 Revere Street," pp. 18, 32, 45–46.

30. National Personnel Records Center, St. Louis.

31. Edward Gibbon, *Autobiography,* ed. Dero Saunders (NY: Meridian, 1961), p. 109.

32. Terri Witek, *Robert Lowell and "Life Studies"* (Columbia: University of Missouri Press, 1993), pp. 58–59.

33. Lowell, "91 Revere Street," pp. 24, 43.

34. Letter from Christopher Davis to Jeffrey Meyers, April 18, 2013.

35. Lowell, "Antebellum Boston," pp. 296, 304.

36. Lowell, "Near the Unbalanced Aquarium," *Prose,* p. 357.

37. James Joyce, *A Portrait of the Artist as a Young Man* (1916; NY: Viking, 1956), p. 241.

38. National Personnel Records Center.

39. Lowell, *Poems,* pp. 74–75.

40. Lowell, "Commander Lowell," p. 71.

41. Parker quoted in Patricia Bosworth, *Diane Arbus: A Biography* (1984; NY: Avon, 1985), p. 56 (twice).

42. Richard Eberhart, "*The Mad Magician,*" *Collected Verse Plays* (Chapel Hill: University of North Carolina Press, 1963), p. 141.

43. Ian Hamilton, Interview with Anne Dick, British Library, and Hamilton, *Lowell,* pp. 32–33.

44. Lowell, *Letters,* ed. Saskia Hamilton (NY: Farrar, Straus and Giroux, 2005), pp. 7, 15.

45. Gustave Flaubert, *Madame Bovary,* trans Eleanor Marx Aveling (NY: Holt, Rinehart & Winston, 1966), p. 167.

46. Hamilton, *Lowell,* p. 32.

47. Hamilton, *Lowell,* pp. 33, 31, 38 (twice).

48. Sarah Payne Stuart, *My First Cousin Once Removed: Money, Madness and the Family of Robert Lowell* (NY: HarperCollins, 1998), p. 84.

49. Hamilton, *Lowell,* pp. 39, 41–42.

50. Lowell, *Poems,* p. 32.

51. Hamilton, *Lowell,* p. 41.

52. Lowell, *Letters,* pp. 13, 19.

53. Hamilton, *Lowell,* p. 50.

54. Bosworth, *Diane Arbus,* pp. 56–57, 111.

55. Hamilton, Interview with Frank Parker, British Library.

56. Stuart, *My First Cousin,* p. 123.

57. Lowell, *Letters,* p. 159.

58. Lowell, "Sailing Home from Rapallo," *Life Studies,* p. 78.

59. Lowell, "Unwanted," *Poems,* pp. 833, 832.

60. Hamilton, Interview with Christina Brazelton, British Library.

61. T. E. Lawrence, *Letters,* ed. David Garnett (1938; London: Spring Books, 1964), p. 414.

62. Robert Graves, "Children of Darkness," *Collected Poems* (Garden City, N.Y.: Doubleday, 1961), p. 67.

63. Lowell, *Poems,* p. 648.

64. Lowell, "Antebellum Boston," p. 298.

65. Hamilton, *Robert Lowell,* p. 229.
My friend's grandmother, a Boston Bigelow, had a similarly refined attitude toward anything unpleasant. When I expressed surprise that she was reading *The Comedians,* Graham Greene's horrific novel about Duvalier's Haiti, she said, "I quite enjoy the book as long as I skip all the *lurid* parts."

66. Hamilton, *Lowell,* pp. 28–29.

67. Lowell, *Letters,* pp. 10, 26.

68. Hamilton, *Robert Lowell,* p. 13.

69. Lowell, "Unbalanced Aquarium," p. 355.

70. Heymann, *American Aristocracy,* p. 409.

71. Elizabeth Hardwick, *Sleepless Nights* (NY: Vintage, 1980), p. 108.

72. John Crick, *Robert Lowell* (Edinburgh: Oliver & Boyd, 1974), p. 6.

73. Lowell, *Poems,* p. 371.

74. Jeffrey Meyers, *Robert Frost: A Biography* (Boston: Houghton Mifflin, 1996), p. 298 (twice).

75. Henry Wells, *Poet and Psychiatrist: Merrill Moore, M.D.* (NY: Twayne, 1955), pp. 109, 115.

76. Lowell, "Allen Tate 1. 1937," *Poems,* p. 517.

77. Yvor Winters, Review of Moore's *The Noise That Time Makes, Poetry,* 36 (May 1930), 104–105.

78. Dudley Fitts, Review of Moore's sonnets, *Sewanee Review,* 47 (April 1939), 268–269, 272.

79. Lowell, *Poems,* p. 832.

80. John Crowe Ransom, *Selected Letters,* ed. Thomas Daniel Young and George Core (Baton Rouge: Louisiana State University Press, 1985), p. 270.

81. Meyers, *Interviews and Memoirs,* p. 254.

82. Hamilton, Interview with Blair Clark, British Library.

83. Meyers, *Interviews and Memoirs,* p. 236.

84. Mariani, *Lost Puritan,* p. 111.

85. Hardwick, *Sleepless Nights,* p. 107.

86. Lowell, *Letters,* pp. 179, 219.

87. Lowell, *Letters,* pp. 209–210.

88. Witek, *Robert Lowell,* p. 72.

89. Meyers, *Robert Frost,* p. 300.

90. Lowell, "Unbalanced Aquarium," p. 361.

91. Lowell, "Sailing Home from Rapallo," pp. 77–78.

92. Hamilton, *Lowell,* p. 205.

93. Charlotte was amazingly like my own mother, who did not (unfortunately) produce a great poet.

94. Lowell, "Unbalanced Aquarium," p. 350.

95. Robert Frost, "The Figure a Poem Makes," *Poetry and Prose,* ed. Edward Connery Lathem and Lawrance Thompson (NY: Holt, 1972), p. 394.

Two. Southern Comfort

1. Scott Fitzgerald, *This Side of Paradise* (NY: Scribner, 1920), p. 23.

2. Lowell, *Letters,* p. 431.

3. Hamilton, *Lowell,* p. 19.

4. Diantha Parker, "Robert Lowell's Lightness," Poetry Foundation essay, November 25, 2010, available at www.poetryfoundation.org/article/240792.

5. Lowell, *Poems,* pp. 810, 800.

6. Lowell, *Poems,* pp. 505, 801.

7. Letter from Nick Noble, Archivist of St. Mark's, to Jeffrey Meyers, May 30, 2013.

8. Lowell, *Letters,* p. 3.

9. Hamilton, *Lowell,* pp. 14, 21.

10. Meyers, *Interviews and Memoirs,* p. 51.

11. Joel Roache, *Richard Eberhart* (NY: Oxford University Press, 1971), pp. 102–103.

12. Robert Lowell, "Current Poetry," *Sewanee Review,* 54 (Winter 1946), 340–341.

13. Hamilton, Interview with Frank Parker, British Library.

14. Lowell, "Ford Madox Ford," *Prose,* pp. 3–4.

15. Lowell, *Letters,* p. 17.

16. Elizabeth Hardwick, *Melville* (NY: Viking, 2000), p. 148.

17. Lowell, "Ford Madox Ford," *Prose,* p. 4.

18. Lowell, "Ford Madox Ford," *Life Studies,* p. 50.

19. Lowell, "Visiting the Tates," *Prose,* pp. 58, 60, 59.

20. Lowell, *Letters,* p. 17.

21. Thomas Underwood, *Allen Tate: Orphan of the South* (Princeton: Princeton University Press, 2000), p. 272.

22. Nancylee Jonza, *The Underground Stream: The Life and Art of Caroline Gordon* (Athens: University of Georgia Press, 1995), p. 182.

23. *The [Andrew] Lytle-[Allen] Tate Letters,* ed. Thomas Daniel (Jackson: University Press of Mississippi, 1987), p. 108.

24. Roache, *Eberhart,* p. 103.

25. Letter from Morten Dauwen Zabel to Edmund Wilson, July 17, 1937, Yale University Library.

26. Allen Tate, "Robert Lowell," *Poetry Reviews, 1924–1944,* ed. Ashley Brown and Frances Cheney (Baton Rouge: Louisiana State University Press, 1983), pp. 210–211.

27. William Doreski, *The Years of Our Friendship: Robert Lowell and Allen Tate* (Jackson: University Press of Mississippi, 1980), pp. 150, 138.

28. Hamilton, *Lowell,* p. 237.

29. Lowell, *Letters,* p. 394.

30. *Lytle-Tate Letters,* p. 274.

31. Elizabeth Bishop and Robert Lowell, *Words in the Air: The Complete Correspondence,* ed. Thomas Travisano and Saskia Hamilton (NY: Farrar, Straus and Giroux, 2008), pp. 321, 405.

32. *Lytle-Tate Letters,* p. 376.

33. Peter Taylor, *Conversations,* ed. Hubert McAlexander (Jackson: University Press of Mississippi, 1987), p. 125.

34. Lowell, "John Crowe Ransom," *Prose,* p. 20.

35. Taylor, *Conversations,* pp. 37, 35.

36. Hubert McAlexander, *Peter Taylor: A Writer's Life* (Baton Rouge: Louisiana State University Press, 2001), pp. 47–48.

37. Daniel Hoffman, "Afternoons with Robert Lowell," *Gettysburg Review,* 6 (Summer 1993), 488.

38. John Crowe Ransom, "A Look Backwards and a Note of Hope," *Harvard Advocate,* Special Supplement, 145 (November 1961), 22.

39. Ransom, *Letters,* pp. 226, 232, 237.

40. Mariani, *Lost Puritan,* p. 70.

41. Meyers, Interview with Stanley Kunitz, New York, December 22, 1982.

42. Hamilton, *Lowell,* p. 57.

43. Lowell, "Randall Jarrell," *Prose,* p. 90.

44. Lowell, *Letters,* p. 96.

45. Bishop and Lowell, *Words in the Air,* p. 25.

46. Hamilton, Interview with John Thompson, British Library.

47. Lowell, *Letters,* p. 30.

48. Lowell, *Poems,* p. 735.

49. Thomas Cutrer, *Parnassus on the Mississippi: The Southern Review and the Baton Rouge Literary Community* (Baton Rouge: Louisiana State University Press, 1984), pp. 196, 199.

50. Robert Fitzgerald, "The Things of the Eye," *Poetry,* 132 (May 1978), 108.

51. Esther Brooks in Meyers, *Interviews and Memoirs,* pp. 284, 283.

52. Meyers, Interview with Grey Gowrie, August 7, 2013.

53. Derek Walcott, "Robert Lowell," *The Company They Kept: Writers on Unforgettable Friendships,* ed. Robert Silvers and Barbara Epstein (NY: New York Review Books, 2006), p. 122.

54. William Meredith, "Remembering Robert Lowell," *Poems Are Hard to Read* (Ann Arbor: University of Michigan Press, 1991), p. 35.

55. Hoffman, "Afternoons with Robert Lowell," p. 486.

56. Edmund Wilson, *The Sixties,* ed. Lewis Dabney (NY: Farrar, Straus and Giroux, 1993), p. 428.

57. Flannery O'Connor, *The Habit of Being: Letters,* ed. Sally Fitzgerald (NY: Vintage, 1979), p. 188.

58. Mariani, *Lost Puritan,* p. 82.

59. Meyers, Interview with Caroline Blackwood, London, March 26, 1986.

Three. Jean Stafford

1. Hamilton, Interview with John Thompson, British Library.

2. Eileen Simpson, *Poets in Their Youth* (NY: Random House, 1982), p. 121.

3. Howard Moss, "Jean Stafford: Some Fragments," *Minor Monuments* (NY: Ecco, 1986), p. 281.

4. David Roberts, *Jean Stafford: A Biography* (Boston: Little, Brown, 1988), pp. 167, 159.

5. Mariani, *Lost Puritan,* p. 76.

6. Meyers, Interviews with Gail Mazur, September 22, 2013, and Fanny Howe, October 14, 2013.

7. Meyers, *Interviews and Memoirs,* pp. 182, 184.

8. Mariani, *Lost Puritan,* p. 77.

9. Simpson, *Poets in Their Youth,* p. 120.

10. David Laskin, *Partisans: Marriage, Politics and Betrayal among the New York Intellectuals* (NY: Simon & Schuster, 2000), p. 102.

11. Hamilton, Interview with Blair Clark, British Library.

12. Jean Stafford, "The Interior Castle," *Collected Stories* (NY: Farrar, Straus and Giroux, 1969), p. 192.

13. Roberts, *Stafford,* p.160.

14. Eberhart, "*Mad Magician,*" pp. 138–140.

15. Hamilton, *Lowell,* p. 109.

16. Ann Hulbert, *The Interior Castle: The Life and Art of Jean Stafford* (NY: Knopf, 1992), p. 184.

17. Brad Gooch, *Flannery: A Life of Flannery O'Connor* (Boston: Little, Brown, 2009), p. 173.

18. Simpson, *Poets in Their Youth,* p. 144.

19. A. Alvarez, "Robert Lowell," *Beyond All This Fiddle: Essays, 1955–1967* (London: Allen Lane, 1968), p. 73.

20. Robert Fitzgerald, "The Things of the Eye," p. 108.

21. *The Verse in English of Richard Crashaw* (NY: Grove, 1949), pp. 210–211.

22. Lowell, *Letters,* p. 30.

23. FBI file on Lowell, October 18, 1943 and October 17, 1962.

24. Max Egremont, *Siegfried Sassoon: A Biography* (London: Picador, 2005), pp. 143–144.

25. Ring Lardner, Jr., *I'd Hate Myself in the Morning: A Memoir* (NY: Thunder's Mouth Press, 2000), pp. 129–131.

26. Hamilton, *Lowell,* p. 93.

27. Meyers, *Interviews and Memoirs,* p. 163.

28. James Peck, *Underdogs vs. Upperdogs* [Workers vs. Capitalists] (Canterbury, N.H.: Greenleaf, 1969), p. 36.

29. Meyers, *Interviews and Memoirs,* p. 25.

30. Hamilton, *Lowell,* p. 96.

31. See Mark de Wolfe Howe, *A Venture in Remembrance* (Boston: Little, Brown, 1941), p. 225, quoting Henry James: "Do you feel that Marlborough Street—is precisely—*passionate?*"

32. Hamilton, *Lowell,* p. 91.

33. Lowell Naeve, *A Field of Broken Stones,* preface by Paul Goodman (1950; Denver: Alan Swallow, 1959), p. 29. Philip Metres clarified this issue in "Confusing a Name: Robert Lowell and Lowell Naeve: 'Lost Connections' in the 1940s War Resistance at West Street Jail and Danbury Prison," *Contemporary Literature,* 41 (Winter 2000), 661–692. But, *si non è vero, è ben trovato.*

34. Lowell, *Letters,* pp. 47, 53.

35. Roberts, *Stafford,* p. 166.

36. Mariani, *Lost Puritan,* pp. 130, 132.

37. W. D. Snodgrass, "A Liberal Education: Mentors, Fomentors and Tormentors," *Southern Review,* 28 (Summer 1992), 452.

38. Hamilton, *Lowell,* p. 120.

39. Roberts, *Stafford,* p. 270.

40. Roberts, *Stafford,* p. 251.

41. Jean Stafford, "An Influx of Poets," *New Yorker,* 54 (November 6, 1978), 46.

42. James Atlas, *Delmore Schwartz: The Life of an American Poet* (1977; NY: Avon, 1978), pp. 59–60.

43. Delmore Schwartz, *Letters,* ed. Robert Phillips (Princeton: Ontario Review Press, 1984), p. 168.

44. Stafford, "Influx of Poets," pp. 43, 56.

45. Hamilton, *Lowell,* p. 118.

46. Roberts, *Stafford,* pp. 246, 249.

47. Hamilton, *Lowell,* pp. 118, 120.

48. Roberts, *Stafford,* p. 258.

49. Hamilton, *Lowell,* p. 131.

50. Lowell, *Letters,* pp. 84–85.

51. Lowell, *Letters,* pp. 100–101.

52. Lowell, *Letters,* p. 94.

53. Meyers, Interview with Gertrude Buckman, London, August 15, 1985.

54. Hamilton, Interview with Elizabeth Hardwick, British Library.

55. Frank Bidart, "Celebration of Lowell," *Kenyon Review,* 22 (Winter 2000), 239.

56. Jean Stafford, "A Country Love Story," *Collected Stories,* pp. 138–145.

57. Stafford, "Influx of Poets," pp. 43–44, 51–52, 47, 56.

58. Fyodor Dostoevsky, *The Idiot,* trans. David Magarshack (1868; London: Penguin, 1955), p. 448.

59. Fyodor Dostoevsky, *Crime and Punishment,* trans. Jessie Coulson, ed. George Gibian (1866; NY: Norton, 1964), p. 277.

60. Hamilton, *Lowell,* pp. 101, 266.

61. Lowell, *Poems,* p. 329.
In "Jonathan Edwards in Western Massachusetts" doomed spiders swim to their watery death. In "Night Sweat" as Lowell struggles with madness, his wife saves him by tearing the surrounding "black web from the spider's sack." In "Stalin" (*History,* 1973), Lowell compares the bloodthirsty dictator to the black widow spider who devours her mate. Stalin killed most of his closest associates and his intimates were "dying like the spider-bridegroom." In "Redcliffe Square: Living in London" (*The Dolphin,* 1973) Lowell contrasts creeping spiders with the swimming dolphin. In "Fetus," in his last book *Day by Day* (1977), spiders represent his fading vision of the bleak landscape: "the focus is spidered / with black winter branches / and blackened concrete stores." Finally, applying the image to a dead and deadly friend, Lowell said sharing a flat with Delmore Schwartz, after the breakup of his marriage to Buckman, "was like living with a sluggish, sometimes angry spider" (Bishop and Lowell, *Words in the Air,* p. 603).

62. Lowell, *Poems,* pp. 525, 739, 324, 105, 83.

63. Hamilton, *Lowell,* p. 183.

64. Lowell, *Poems,* pp. 94–95.

65. Doreski, *Lowell and Tate,* p. 82.

66. Lowell, *Poems,* p. 18.

67. Simpson, *Poets in Their Youth,* p. 148.

68. Ross Labrie, *The Catholic Imagination in American Literature* (Columbia: University of Missouri Press, 1997), p. 160.

69. Hamilton, *Lowell,* p. 81.

70. Simpson, *Poets in Their Youth,* p. 134.

71. Hamilton, *Lowell,* pp. 141, 121, 122.

72. Lowell, *Letters,* p. 59.

73. Roberts, *Stafford,* p. 254.

74. Hamilton, *Lowell,* pp. 125, 184, 307–308.

75. Lowell, *Letters,* pp. 131, 117 (none of the numerous biographical and critical books on Léger mentions that Dawson was his lover).

76. Anne Conover, *Caresse Crosby* (Santa Barbara, Calif.: Capra, 1989), p. 135.

77. Hamilton, *Lowell,* pp. 131, 132.

78. Mariani, *Lost Puritan,* p. 162.

79. Letters from Lowell to Carley Dawson, March 29 and 26, 1948, University of Oregon Library.

80. Lowell, *Letters,* p. 88.

81. David Kalstone, *Becoming a Poet: Elizabeth Bishop with Marianne Moore and Robert Lowell* (NY: Farrar, Straus and Giroux, 1989), p. 140.

82. Mariani, *Lost Puritan,* p. 163.

83. Hamilton, *Lowell,* p. 13 (twice).

84. Mariani, *Lost Puritan,* p. 167.

85. Hamilton, *Lowell,* p. 133.

86. Gary Fountain and Peter Brazeau, eds., *Elizabeth Bishop: An Oral Biography* (Amherst: University of Massachusetts Press, 1994), p. 110.

87. Hamilton, *Lowell,* p. 134.

88. Bishop and Lowell, *Words in the Air,* p. 41.

89. Lowell, *Poems,* p. 116.

90. David Laskin, *A Common Life: Four Generations of American Literary Friendship and Influence* (NY: Simon & Schuster, 1994), p. 313.

91. Hamilton, *Lowell,* pp. 134–135.

Four. Mania

1. Letter from Grey Gowrie to Jeffrey Meyers, August 20, 2013.

2. Lowell, *Letters,* p. 321.

3. Anthony Hecht, "The Art of Poetry," *Paris Review,* 30 (Fall 1988), 182.

4. Hamilton, Interviews with John Thompson and Jonathan Raban, British Library.

5. Meyers, Interviews with Esther Brooks, October 2, 2013, and Frank Bidart, September 15, 2013.

6. Seamus Heaney, *Stepping Stones: Interviews with Seamus Heaney,* ed. Dennis O'Driscoll (NY: Farrar, Straus and Giroux, 2008), pp. 215–216.

7. Anthony Hecht, *Selected Letters,* ed. Jonathan Post (Baltimore: Johns Hopkins University Press, 2013), p. 218.

8. Vincent van Gogh, *Complete Letters* (Greenwich, Conn.: New York Graphic Society, 1958), 3:223.

9. Lowell, *Poems,* p. 741.

10. Meyers, *Interviews and Memoirs,* p. 77.

11. Walcott, "Robert Lowell," p. 124.

12. Wilson, *The Sixties,* p. 427.

13. Meyers, Interview with Karl Miller, September 2, 2013.

14. Edmund Wilson, *The Fifties,* ed. Leon Edel (NY: Farrar, Straus and Giroux, 1986), pp. 452–453.

15. Hamilton, Interview with Sidney Nolan, British Library.

16. O'Connor, *Letters,* p. 74.

17. Hamilton, Interview with Sidney Nolan.

18. Lowell, *Letters,* p. 304.

19. Hamilton, Interview with Frank Parker, British Library.

20. Meyers, Interview with Martha Ritter, October 3, 2013.

21. Hamilton, *Lowell,* p. 251.

22. Meyers, Interview with Grey Gowrie.

23. Diantha Parker, "Robert Lowell's Lightness."

24. Ann Fleming, *Letters,* ed. Mark Amory (London: Collins Harvill, 1985), p. 416.

25. Lowell, *Letters,* pp. 145, 722n.

26. Walcott, "Robert Lowell," p. 116.

27. Lowell, *Poems,* p. 824.

28. Hamilton, Interview with Sidney Nolan.

29. Hamilton, *Lowell,* p. 250.

30. Lowell, *Poems,* p. 988.

31. Meyers, Interview with Keith Botsford, August 20, 2013, and Hamilton, *Lowell,* p. 303.

32. Lowell was in Baldpate, Georgetown, Mass., north of Boston; Payne Whitney, East 68 Street, New York; the U.S. military hospital, Munich; a Swiss hospital in Kreuzlingen, on the Bodensee near Konstanz; Jewish Hospital, Cincinnati; Massachusetts Mental Hospital, Boston; McLean, Belmont, Mass., a suburb of Boston; Bellevue, First Avenue, New York; Columbia Presbyterian, West 168 Street, New York; Clínica Bethlehem, Buenos Aires; Institute of Living, Hartford, Conn.; Greenways, Primrose Hill, North London; The Priory, Roehampton, a South London suburb; St. Andrews, Northampton, sixty miles north of London; and Massachusetts General, Boston.

33. Paul Mariani, *William Carlos Williams: A New World Naked* (NY: Norton, 1981), p. 660.

34. Bishop and Lowell, *Words in the Air,* p. 257.

35. Hamilton, Interview with William Meredith, British Library.

36. Al Alvarez, *Where Did It All Go Right?* (NY: Morrow, 1999), p. 193.

37. Sandra Hochman, "Loving Robert Lowell: A Memoir of Lust, Genius and Madness," typescript, 2013, p. 213, courtesy of the author.

38. Hamilton, Interview with John Thompson, British Library.

39. Bishop and Lowell, *Words in the Air*, p. 639.

40. Hamilton, Interview with Caroline Blackwood, British Library.

41. Jeffrey Meyers, *Hemingway: A Biography* (NY: Harper & Row, 1985), pp. 548–549.

42. Ronald Hayman, *Artaud and After* (Oxford: Oxford University Press, 1977), p. 128.

43. Simpson, *Poets in Their Youth*, p. 193.

44. Hannah Arendt and Mary McCarthy, *Between Friends: Correspondence, 1949–1975*, ed. Carol Brightman (NY: Harcourt Brace, 1995), p. 204.

45. Lowell, *Poems*, p. 185.

46. Lowell, *Letters*, p. 458.

47. Laskin, *Common Life*, p. 320.

Five. Elizabeth Hardwick

1. Meyers, Interview with Esther Brooks.

2. Elizabeth Hardwick, "Going Home in America: Lexington, Kentucky," *Harper's*, 239 (July 1969), 78.

3. Hilton Als, "A Singular Woman," *New Yorker*, 74 (July 13, 1998), 66.

4. Bishop and Lowell, *Words in the Air*, p. 166.

5. Laskin, *Partisans*, p. 190.

6. Richard Locke, "Conversation on a Book" (interview with Hardwick), *New York Times*, April 29, 1979, p. 4 online.

7. Mary McCarthy, *Intellectual Memoirs* (NY: Harcourt Brace Jovanovich, 1992), p. 65.

8. Bishop and Lowell, *Words in the Air*, p. 239.

9. Lowell, *Poems*, p. 189.

10. Hardwick, Foreword to McCarthy, *Intellectual Memoirs*, pp. xvii–xviii.

11. Laskin, *Partisans*, p. 36.

12. Meyers, Interview with Gertrude Buckman.

13. Locke, "Conversation," p. 4 online.

14. Lowell, *Letters*, p. 402.

15. Locke, "Conversation," p. 4 online.

16. McAlexander, *Peter Taylor*, p. 103.

17. Laskin, *Partisans*, p. 211.

18. Iain Hamilton, *Arthur Koestler: A Biography* (NY: Macmillan, 1982), p. 134.

19. Meyers, Interview with Esther Brooks.

20. Laskin, *Partisans*, p. 190.

21. William Phillips, *A Partisan View: Five Decades of the Literary Life* (NY: Stein & Day, 1983), p. 113.

22. Laskin, *Partisans*, p. 189.

23. Jeffrey Meyers, "J. F. Powers," *Privileged Moments: Encounters with Writers* (Madison: University of Wisconsin Press, 2000), p. 131.

24. Mariani, *Lost Puritan,* p. 269.

25. Randall Jarrell, *The Complete Poems* (NY: Farrar, Straus and Giroux, 1969), p. 295.

26. Mariani, *Lost Puritan,* p. 172.

27. Bishop and Lowell, *Words in the Air,* p. 71.

28. Hamilton, *Lowell,* p. 149.

29. Meyers, Interview with Gertrude Buckman.

30. Lowell, *Letters,* pp. 128, 151.

31. Alfred Kazin, *New York Jew* (NY: Knopf, 1978), p. 204.

32. Lowell, *Letters,* p. 129.

33. Als, "Singular Woman," p. 70.

34. Lowell, *Letters,* pp. 705–706.

35. Lowell, *Letters,* pp. 141, 147.

36. Franz Kafka, *Letters to Felice,* trans. James Stern and Elisabeth Duckworth (London: Secker & Warburg, 1974), pp. 210–211.

37. Hamilton, Interview with Elizabeth Hardwick, British Library.

38. Hamilton, *Lowell,* p. 162.

39. Meyers, *Interviews and Memoirs,* p. 258.

40. Hamilton, *Lowell,* p. 198.

41. Meyers, Interview with Donald Hall, May 24, 2013.

42. Meyers, Interview with Richard Wilbur, August 13, 2013.

43. Elizabeth Hardwick, "The Art of Fiction," *Paris Review,* 96 (Summer 1985), p. 18 online.

44. Lowell, *Letters,* p. 510.

45. Hamilton, Interview with William Meredith, British Library.

46. Michael Wreszin, *A Rebel in Defense of Tradition: The Life and Politics of Dwight Macdonald* (NY: Basic Books, 1994), p. 481.

47. Mariani, *Lost Puritan,* p. 220.

48. Barry Miles, *Ginsberg: A Biography* (NY: Harper, 1990), pp. 281–282.

49. Lowell, *Letters,* p. 489.

50. Hamilton, *Lowell,* p. 192.

51. Meyers, Interview with Alan Williamson, September 5, 2013.

52. Mariani, *Lost Puritan,* p. 254.

53. Nancy Schoenberger, *Dangerous Muse: The Life of Caroline Blackwood* (NY: Doubleday, 2001), p. 207.

54. Wilson, *The Fifties,* pp. 452–453.

55. Meyers, Interview with Esther Brooks.

56. Elizabeth Hardwick, "Zelda," *Seduction and Betrayal* (NY: Vintage, 1975), pp. 106–107.

57. W. B. Yeats, "Easter 1916," *Collected Poems* (NY: Macmillan 1959), p. 179.

58. McAlexander, *Peter Taylor,* p. 111.

59. Meyers, Interview with Stanley Kunitz. Hardwick resembled Mary

Welch, who said "I guess my pride is expendable" and was willing to endure almost anything to remain Mrs. Ernest Hemingway forever.

60. Letter from Hardwick to Lowell, no date. Hardwick's letters to Lowell are in the Houghton Library, Harvard University, and the Harry Ransom Humanities Center, University of Texas, Austin.

61. Locke, "Conversation," p. 5 online.

62. Lowell, *Letters,* pp. 173–175.

63. Hamilton, Interview with Elizabeth Hardwick, British Library.

64. Letter from Judith Herzberg to Jeffrey Meyers, June 15, 2013.

65. Hamilton, *Lowell,* pp. 177–178.

66. Mariani, *Lost Puritan,* p. 210.

67. Charles Shields, *And So It Goes: Kurt Vonnegut: A Life* (NY: St. Martin's, 2011), p. 191.

68. Hamilton, *Lowell,* p. 167.

69. Snodgrass, "A Liberal Education," p. 452.

70. Lowell, *Letters,* pp. 249–250.

71. Meyers, Interview with Martha Ritter.

72. Meyers, Interview with Frank Bidart.

73. Lowell, *Letters,* p. 271.

74. Mariani, *Lost Puritan,* p. 338.

75. Stuart, *My First Cousin,* p. 145.

76. Lowell, *Letters,* p. 305.

77. Meyers, Interview with Keith Botsford.

78. Meyers, Interview with Antonia Kern Mills, August 22, 2013.

79. Meyers, Interview with Gertrude Buckman.

80. Meyers, Interview with Karl Miller.

81. Meyers, Interview with Ann Adden, June 29, 2013.

82. Meyers, Interview with Frank Bidart (on pain and jokes).

83. Meyers, Interview with Esther Brooks.

Harriet was well educated at the Dalton School in Manhattan and at Barnard College, where Hardwick taught, but changed schools and graduated from Hunter College. Afterwards, she worked at fund-raising for Barnard and other nonprofit organizations. She is happily married to a chemical engineer, but has no children.

84. Hardwick, *Sleepless Nights,* pp. 16, 70, 107, 108, 58, 12.

85. Hardwick, *Sleepless Nights,* pp. 7, 20, 98, 103 (twice), 121–122.

86. Hamilton, *Lowell,* p. 258.

87. Lowell wrote about this event in "Pacification of Columbia." When Columbia students climbed through the window of professor Gilbert Highet's office when he was conducting a dissertation defense and announced, "Diss bill-ding iss oggu-pyed," Highet replied in his plummiest English voice, "This rrooom is uccupied."

88. Letter from Lowell to J. F. Powers, November 29, 1953, courtesy of the late J. F. Powers.

89. Hardwick, "The Art of Fiction."

90. Bishop and Lowell, *Words in the Air,* p. 502.

91. Lowell, *Letters,* p. 325 (twice).

92. Foster, quoted in Thomas Flanagan, *There You Are* (NY: New York Review Books, 2004), p. 193.

93. T. S. Eliot, *Letters. Volume 2, 1923–1925,* ed. Valerie Eliot and Hugh Haughton (London: Faber and Faber, 2009), p. 124.

94. Lowell, *Prose,* pp. 210, 50.

95. Alvarez, *Where Did It All Go Right?,* p. 195.

96. Lowell, *Poems,* pp. 114, 365.

97. Charles Baudelaire, *Flowers of Evil and Other Works,* trans. and ed. Wallace Fowlie (NY: Bantam, 1964), pp. 81, 205.

98. Hamilton, *Lowell,* p. 349.

99. James Boswell, *Boswell in Extremes, 1776–1778,* ed. Charles Weis and Frederick Pottle (NY: McGraw-Hill, 1970), p. 27.

100. Lowell may have known Scott Fitzgerald's aperçu, "In a real dark night of the soul it is always three o'clock in the morning" (*The Crack-Up,* ed. Edmund Wilson [1945; NY: New Directions, 1959], p. 75).

101. Lowell, *Poems,* p. 189.

102. Meyers, *Interviews and Memoirs,* p. 63.

103. *The Poems of Catullus,* trans. and intro. Horace Gregory (NY: Grove, 1956), pp. 151, 19.

104. Lowell, *Poems,* p. 190.

105. I. A. Richards, *Selected Letters,* ed. John Constable (NY: Oxford University Press, 1990), pp. 179–181.

106. Edmund Wilson, *The Bit Between My Teeth* (NY: Farrar, Straus and Giroux, 1965), p. 547.

107. Lowell," Poets and the Theater," *Prose,* p. 133.

108. Meyers, *Interviews and Memoirs,* p. 88.

109. Marjorie Perloff, "The Blank Now," *New Republic,* 169 (July 7, 1973), 25.

110. William Weaver, *Duse* (London: Thames & Hudson, 1984), p. 221.

111. Henry James, "The Lesson of the Master," *Stories of Artists and Writers,* ed. F. O. Matthiessen (NY: New Directions, 1965), p. 138.

112. Bishop and Lowell, *Words in the Air,* p. 102.

113. Doreski, *Years of Our Friendship,* pp. 179–180.

114. Lowell, *Poems,* p. 518.

115. Laskin, *Partisans,* p. 266.

116. Hamilton, Interview with Jonathan Raban, British Library.

117. Hamilton, *Lowell,* pp. 425, 421.

118. Bishop and Lowell, *Words in the Air,* p. 708 and note.

119. Thom Gunn, "Out of the Box: Elizabeth Bishop," *Shelf Life* (Ann Arbor: University of Michigan Press, 1993), p. 83.

120. Grey Gowrie, "Robert Lowell: A Memoir," *News from the Royal Society of Literature* (London: Royal Society of Literature, 2003), p. 37.

121. Hamilton, *Lowell,* p. 422.

122. Robert Lowell, *The Dolphin* (NY: Farrar, Straus and Giroux, 1973), pp. 40, 56, 47.

123. Lowell, *Dolphin,* pp. 58, 69, 77.

124. Lowell, *Dolphin,* pp. 47, 42, 48, 58, 41.

125. Lowell, *Letters,* p. 570.

126. Lowell, *Dolphin,* p. 78.

127. Lowell, *Poems,* pp. 84, 511, 658.

128. Lowell, *Letters,* p. 546.

129. Lowell, *Letters,* p. 538.

130. Hamilton, *Lowell,* p. 434.

131. Mariani, *Lost Puritan,* p. 392.

132. Hamilton, *Lowell,* p. 399 (twice).

133. Hardwick, "Zelda," pp. 104, 102.

134. Elizabeth Hardwick, "America and Dylan Thomas," *A View of My Own* (1962; NY: Ecco, 1982), pp. 111, 103.

135. Hardwick, "America and Dylan Thomas," 104 (twice), 110.

136. Lowell, *Letters,* p. 577.

137. Lowell, *Letters,* pp. 590, 592.

138. Lowell, *Letters,* p. 594.

139. Simpson, *Poets in Their Youth,* p. 254.

140. Lowell, *Letters,* pp. 612 (twice), 652.

141. Arendt and McCarthy, *Between Friends,* p. 294.

142. John Milton, "Lycidas," *Poetical Works,* ed. Helen Darbishire (London: Oxford University Press, 1958), p. 451.

143. Arendt and McCarthy, *Between Friends,* pp. 257–258.

144. Hardwick, Telegram to Lowell, June 12, 1973 and Letter to Lowell, May 6, 1974, University of Texas.

145. Christopher Lehmann-Haupt, "Elizabeth Hardwick, Writer, Dies at 91," *New York Times,* December 4, 2007, p. 6 online.

146. Mariani, *Lost Puritan,* p. 376.

147. Arthur Schlesinger, *Journals, 1952–2000* (NY: Penguin, 2007), p. 407.

148. Tillinghast, *Robert Lowell,* p. 51.

149. William Styron, *Selected Letters,* ed. Rose Styron and Blakeslee Gilpin (NY: Random House, 2012), p. 392.

150. Katherine Anne Porter, *Conversations,* ed. Joan Givner (Jackson: University Press of Mississippi, 1987), p. 147.

151. Meyers, Interview with Fanny Howe.

152. Lehmann-Haupt, "Hardwick," p. 3 online.

153. Elizabeth Benedict, "Remembering Miss Hardwick," *Mentors, Muses & Monsters,* ed. Elizabeth Benedict (NY: Free Press, 2009), p. 14.

154. Mary Gordon, "Elizabeth Hardwick," *Mentors, Muses & Monsters,* pp. 94, 96.

155. Hardwick, *Melville,* pp. 17, 66, 67.

156. Hardwick, *Melville,* pp. 154, 103, 112, 51–52.

157. Lehmann-Haupt, "Hardwick," p. 5 online.

Six. The Heedless Heart

1. Stafford, "Influx of Poets," p. 60; Lowell, *Poems,* pp. 385, 753, 542, 835.

2. Heymann, *American Aristocracy,* p. 471; Hamilton, *Lowell,* p. 374; Hamilton, Interview with Frank Parker, British Library.

3. Letters from Pietro Cremonini (Madonia's son) to Meyers, October 3, 5, 16 and 30, 2013; Letter from Lowell to J. F. Powers, March 15, 1954; Letters from Madonia to Lowell, March 5 to June 26, 1954, Houghton Library, Harvard University (the Italian letters are translated by Valerie Meyers); Lowell, *Letters,* pp. 211, 214–215, 228–230, 237–239, 627; T. S. Eliot, "The Metaphysical Poets," *Selected Essays, 1917–1932* (NY: Harcourt, Brace, 1932), p. 250; Hamilton, Interview with Blair Clark, British Library; Hamilton, *Robert Lowell,* pp. 207–208, 213–215; Jarrell, *Letters,* p. 414; Lowell, *Poems,* pp. 118, 454.

4. Meyers, Interview with Ann Adden, June 29, 2013; Letters from Ann Adden to Meyers, June 20, July 13 and July 29, September 12, 2013; Lowell, *Poems,* pp. 397, 535–536; Letters from Ann Adden to Lowell, January 1958 and October 30, 1968, Harvard University; Hamilton, *Lowell,* pp. 243–245, 249, 241.

5. Letter from Sandra Hochman to Meyers, September 22, 2013; Hochman, "Loving Robert Lowell: A Memoir of Lust, Genius and Madness," typescript, 2013; Sandra Hochman, *Earthworks: Poems, 1960–1970* (NY: Viking, 1970), pp. 159, 143, 144; James Atlas, *Bellow: A Biography* (NY: Random House, 2000), pp. 308, 297; Hamilton, *Lowell,* pp. 285–286; Bishop and Lowell, *Words in the Air,* pp. 366, 384, 389, 385, 382; Lowell, *Letters,* p. 384.

6. Meyers, Interview with Vija Vetra, August 12, 2013; Hamilton, Interview with Vija Vetra, British Library; Hamilton, *Lowell,* pp. 316–320, 331; Wilson, *The Sixties,* pp. 450–451; Hamilton, Interview with Frank Parker, British Library.

7. Meyers, Interview with Shepherd Bliss, June 21, 2013; Letter from Jonathan Kozol to Meyers, September 4, 2013; Bishop and Lowell, *Words in the Air,* p. 638; Hamilton, *Lowell,* pp. 372–373; Letters from Mary Keelan to Lowell, January 9, 1968 and July 5, 1969, Harvard University; Andrew Marvell, *Poems,* ed. Hugh Macdonald (London: Routledge & Kegan Paul, 1952), p. 34; Lowell, *Poems,* pp. 515, 624–629; Hamilton, Interviews with Frank Parker and Sidney Nolan, British Library.

8 Meyers, three unusually long interviews with Martha Ritter, eight letters from Ritter to Meyers, September 3–November 19, 2013; Jo Brans, "A Patchwork Life," *Take Two* (NY: Doubleday, 1989), pp. 225–238; file of Ritter's articles sent to Meyers; Meyers, Interviews with Frank Bidart and Grey Gowrie; Hamilton, Interview with Martha Ritter, British Library; Hamilton, *Robert Lowell,* pp. 393–394, 417–418; Letters from Lowell to Ritter, May 5, 1971 and February 19, 1976; Lowell, *Letters,* p. 646; Lowell, *Poems,* p. 615; Mariani, *Lost Puritan,* p. 444.

9. Ludmilla Shtern, *Brodsky: A Personal Memoir* (Fort Worth: Baskerville, 2004), p. 212.

10. Yeats, *Collected Poems,* p. 212.

Seven. Women Friends

1. Carol Brightman, *Writing Dangerously: Mary McCarthy and Her World* (NY: Potter, 1992), p. 489.

2. Mariani, *Lost Puritan,* p. 316.

3. Hardwick, "Mary McCarthy," *View of My Own,* p. 33.

4. Lowell, *Letters,* p. 489.

5. Bishop and Lowell, *Words in the Air,* pp. 488, 643–644.

6. Bishop and Lowell, *Words in the Air,* p. 199.

7. Ivana Lowell, *Why Not Say What Happened?* (NY: Knopf, 2010), p. 29.

8. Lowell, *Poems,* pp. 554–555.

9. Bishop and Lowell, *Words in the Air,* pp. 809, 778, 388–389.

10. Kalstone, *Becoming a Poet,* p. 131.

11. Diane Middlebrook, *Anne Sexton: A Biography* (NY: Vintage, 1992), p. 255.

12. Hardwick, "The Art of Fiction," p. 6 online.

13. Hamilton, Interview with Caroline Blackwood, British Library.

14. Meyers, Interview with Frank Bidart.

15. Lowell, "Elizabeth Bishop," *Prose,* pp. 76, 78.

16. Bishop and Lowell, *Words in the Air,* pp. 580, 289–290.

17. Lowell, *Poems,* p. 653.

18. Elizabeth Bishop, *Complete Poems, 1927–1979* (NY: Farrar, Straus and Giroux, 1983), p. 178.

19. Lowell, "On Skunk Hour," *Prose,* p. 227.

20. Bishop, *Complete Poems,* p. 33.

21. Lowell, *Letters,* p. 651.

22. Bishop and Lowell, *Words in the Air,* pp. 664, 687.

23. Lowell, *Poems,* p. 595.

24. Rainer Maria Rilke, "Archaic Torso of Apollo," *Selected Poems,* trans. Robert Bly (NY: Harper & Row, 1981), p. 147.

25. Lowell, *Poems,* p. 593.

26. Bishop, *Complete Poems,* pp. 188–189.

27. Mariani, *Lost Puritan,* p. 342.

28. Peter Davison, *The Fading Smile: Poets in Boston, 1955–1960* (NY: Knopf, 1994), pp. 205, 203.

29. Laskin, *Partisans,* p. 262.

30. Davison, *Fading Smile,* pp. 194, 206.

31. Lowell, *Poems,* pp. 551, 669.

32. Friedrich Nietzsche, "*Thus Spoke Zarathustra,*" *Portable Nietzsche,* p. 179.

33. Laskin, *Partisans,* p. 262.

34. Hamilton, *Lowell,* p. 433.

35. Adrienne Rich, Review of *The Dolphin, American Poetry Review,* 2 (September–October 1973), 42–43.

36. Lowell, *Letters,* p. 647.

37. Lowell, *Letters,* p. 156.

38. Richard Tillinghast, "Celebration of Robert Lowell," *Kenyon Review,* 22 (2000), 277.

39. Fountain and Brazeau, *Bishop: Oral Biography,* p. 312.

40. Kathleen Spivack, *With Robert Lowell and His Circle* (Boston: Northeastern University Press, 2012), pp. 24, 25, 48.

41. Philip Levine, "Mine Own John Berryman," *Gettysburg Review,* 4 (Autumn 1991), 535.

42. Snodgrass, "Liberal Education," pp. 450, 451.

43. Pinsky, quoted in Spivack, *Lowell and His Circle,* p. 134.

44. Middlebrook, *Anne Sexton,* p. 91.

45. Anne Sexton, *A Self-Portrait in Letters,* ed. Linda Gray Sexton and Lois Ames (Boston: Houghton Mifflin, 1977), p. 49.

46. Meyers, *Interviews and Memoirs,* p. 179.

47. Sexton, *Letters,* pp. 51, 57, 134.

48. Meyers, *Interviews and Memoirs,* p. 169.

49. Bishop and Lowell, *Words in the Air,* pp. 327n, 331.

50. Lowell, *Letters,* p. 393.

51. Anne Sexton, "The Barfly Ought to Sing," *The Art of Sylvia Plath,* ed. Charles Newman (Bloomington: Indiana University Press, 1970), pp. 174, 175, 174, 177.

52. Hardwick, *Seduction and Betrayal,* pp. 112, 115.

53. Sylvia Plath, *Letters Home,* ed. Aurelia Plath (1975; NY: Bantam, 1977), p. 396.

54. Sylvia Plath, *Unabridged Journals,* ed. Karen Kukil (NY: Anchor, 2000), p. 463.

55. Spivack, *Lowell and His Circle,* pp. 27, 32.

56. Plath, *Journals,* pp. 471, 475.

57. "Sylvia Plath," *The Poet Speaks,* ed. Peter Orr (London: Routledge & Kegan Paul, 1966), pp. 167–168.

58. Lowell, *Poems,* p. 107, and Sylvia Plath, *Ariel* (NY: Harper & Row, 1966), p. 51.

59. Lowell, *Poems,* p. 188, and Sylvia Plath, *The Bell Jar* (1963; NY: Bantam, 1971), pp. 1, 117–118.

60. Lowell, *Poems,* p. 329.

61. Plath, *Ariel,* p. 7, and Lowell, *Poems,* p. 601.

62. Lowell, *Letters,* pp. 424, 445.

63. Bishop and Lowell, *Words in the Air,* p. 513.

64. Lowell, Foreword to *Ariel,* pp. vii–ix.

65. Lowell, *Letters,* p. 631.

66. Lowell, Letter on Plath, quoted by M. L. Rosenthal, *Salmagundi,* 1 (1966–67), 70.

67. Meyers, *Interviews and Memoirs,* p. 170.

68. Lowell, *Letters,* p. 576.

69. Lowell, *Poems,* p. 532.

70. Lowell's close writer friends included Tate, Ransom and Warren; Frost,

Pound, Eliot and Williams; Jarrell, Berryman, Roethke, Schwartz and Kunitz; Taylor, Powers and Bidart; Spender and Heaney; McCarthy, Bishop, Rich, Hannah Arendt and Flannery O'Connor.

71. Meredith, "Remembering Robert Lowell," p. 224.

72. Meyers, Interview with Richard Wilbur.

73. S. Foster Damon, *A Blake Dictionary* (Boulder, Colo.: Shambala, 1979), p. 451.

74. Lowell, *Letters*, p. 427.

75. R. F. Foster, *W. B. Yeats: A Life* (Oxford: Oxford University Press, 1997), 1:616 n. 69.

76. John Haffenden, *The Life of John Berryman* (London: Routledge & Kegan Paul, 1982), pp. 319, 328.

77. Lowell, *Letters*, p. 516.

78. Bishop and Lowell, *Words in the Air*, pp. 623, 656.

79. Henry Hart, *James Dickey: The World as a Lie* (NY: Picador, 2000), p. 377.

80. Bishop and Lowell, *Words in the Air*, pp. 298–299.

81. Meyers, Interview with Karl Shapiro, Davis, Calif., March 23, 1981.

In his novel *Edsel* (NY: Geiss, 1971), p. 118, Shapiro satirized Lowell and unfairly attributed his political beliefs to opportunism rather than to idealism: "I had no particular feeling about Wigg, as poets called him, except envy. Not envy for his poetry, which I thought wooden and fake . . . but envy for his genius for publicity. Whenever there was a Cause, Wigg could be seen on the platform, rolling his eyes and dealing out volumes of righteous indignation. . . . He was [also] handy with conversions."

82. Meyers, Interview with Stanley Kunitz.

83. Donald Davie, "Lowell's *Selected Poems*," *Trying to Explain* (Ann Arbor: University of Michigan Press, 1979), p. 76.

Eight. Caroline Blackwood

1. Lowell, *Poems*, p. 665.

2. Meyers, Interview with Richard Tillinghast, September 6, 2013.

3. Lowell, *Poems*, p. 814. See Jeffrey Meyers, "The Tragic Destiny of Basil Blackwood," *Standpoint*, 61 (April 2014), 46–49.

4. D. H. Lawrence, "The Rocking-Horse Winner," *The Complete Short Stories* (NY: Viking, 1961), 3.790.

5. Geordie Greig, *Breakfast with Lucian* (NY: Farrar, Straus and Giroux, 2013), pp. 191, 115.

6. Lowell, *Letters*, p. 629.

7. Hamilton, *Lowell*, p. 398 (thrice).

8. Meyers, Interview with Esther Brooks.

9. Arendt and McCarthy, *Between Friends*, pp. 257–258.

10. Schoenberger, *Dangerous Muse*, p. 227.

11. Hamilton, Interview with Natasha Spender, British Library; Meyers, Interview with Karl Miller.

12. Meyers, Interview with and letter from Catharine Mack Smith, October 26 and 27, 2014.

13. Lowell, *Letters,* pp. 542, 543, 551.

14. Lowell, *Letters,* p. 574.

15. Meyers, Interview with Frank Bidart.

16. Meyers, Interview with Christopher Ricks, September 10, 2013.

17. Lowell, *Letters,* p. 552.

18. Meyers, Interviews with Esther Brooks and Richard Tillinghast, quoting Peter Taylor.

19. Meyers, Interview with Caroline Blackwood.

20. Lowell, *Letters,* pp. 541, 555.

21. Lowell, *Letters,* p. 557.

22. Lowell, *Letters,* p. 563.

23. Meyers, Interview with Ivana Lowell.

24. Meyers, Interview with Caroline Blackwood.

25. Christopher Ricks, "For Robert Lowell," *Harvard Advocate* (special issue on Lowell), 113 (November 1979), 17.

26. Meyers, Interview with Ivana Lowell.

27. Hamilton, Interview with Jonathan Raban, British Library.

28. Meyers, Interview with Karl Miller.

29. Lowell, *Poems,* p. 702.

30. Hamilton, Interview with Martha Ritter, quoting Lowell's letter, British Library.

31. Mariani, *Lost Puritan,* p. 412.

32. Meyers, Interview with Karl Miller.

33. Hamilton, Interview with Caroline Blackwood, British Library.
Sheridan went to the progressive Bedales School in Petersfield, Hampshire, and graduated from London University. He then moved to America, where Blackwood and her daughters also lived, and hasn't done much since then. Reacting even more violently than Lowell against his privileged background, he became a card-carrying member of the Communist Party. Withdrawn, hermetic, hard to get hold of and hard to get on with, he has enough money to live on without working and "does his own thing." He doesn't live in the real world and doesn't have to. He hates being Lowell's son, feels it's a lot to take on and won't talk about his father. Sheridan never married, neither he nor Harriet had children and the Lowell line, like Blackwood's title, has come to an end.

34. Bishop and Lowell, *Words in the Air,* p. 740.

35. Meyers, Interview with Ivana Lowell.

36. Hamilton, *Lowell,* p. 430.

37. Lowell, Letter to J. F. Powers, February 18, 1973, courtesy of the late J. F. Powers.

38. Meyers, Interview with Esther Brooks.

39. Meyers, Interview with Caroline Blackwood.

40. Meyers, Interview with Ivana Lowell.

41. Ivana Lowell, *Why Not Say,* p. 27.

42. Meyers, *Interviews and Memoirs*, p. 283.

43. Meyers, Interview with Karl Miller.

44. Ivana Lowell, *Why Not Say*, p. 33.

45. Ivana Lowell, *Why Not Say*, pp. 34–36.

46. Lowell, *Letters*, pp. 582, 585.

47. Caroline Blackwood, "Burns Unit," *For All That I Found There* (London: Duckworth, 1973), pp. 108–111.

The only comparable descriptions of excruciating pain from surgery are Fanny Burney's account of the excision of her cancerous breast, without anesthesia, in her *Journals and Letters, Volume 6, France, 1803–1812*, ed. Joyce Hemlow (Oxford: Oxford University Press, 1975), pp. 610–614, and A. E. Ellis' portrayal of the pneumothorax operation on his tubercular lung in *The Rack* (1958).

48. Lowell, *Poems*, p. 694.

49. Meyers, Interview with Christopher Ricks.

50. Hamilton, Interview with Caroline Blackwood, British Library.

51. Meyers, Interview with Caroline Blackwood.

52. Rafaella Barker, "Once, Twice, Three Times a Muse," *Harpers and Queen*, September 1993, p. 206.

53. Ivana Lowell, *Why Not Say*, p. 30.

54. Lowell, *Poems*, p. 601.

55. Ivana Lowell, *Why Not Say*, p. 30.

56. Hamilton, *Lowell*, p. 400.

57. Hamilton, *Lowell*, p. 456.

58. Als, "Singular Woman," p. 73.

59. Hamilton, Interview with Caroline Blackwood, British Library.

60. Lowell, *Letters*, p. 667.

61. Letters from Blackwood to Lowell, no dates, University of Texas.

62. Bishop and Lowell, *Words in the Air*, p. 768.

63. Lowell, *Letters*, p. 635.

64. Hamilton, Interview with Jonathan Raban, British Library.

65. Philip Larkin, Review of *Life Studies*, *Manchester Guardian Weekly*, May 21, 1959, p. 10.

66. Philip Larkin, *Selected Letters, 1940–1985*, ed. Anthony Thwaite (NY: Farrar, Straus and Giroux, 1993), p. 382.

67. Bishop and Lowell, *Words in the Air*, p. 745.

68. Meyers, Interview with Ivana Lowell.

69. Solomon Volkov, *Conversations with Joseph Brodsky*, trans. Marian Schwartz (NY: Free Press, 1998), pp. 134–135.

70. Joseph Brodsky, "Elegy: For Robert Lowell," *A Part of Speech* (NY: Farrar, Straus and Giroux, 1980), pp. 135–137.

71. Spivack, *Lowell and His Circle*, p. 126.

72. Frank Bidart, "An Interview," *In the Western Night: Collected Poems, 1965–1990* (NY: Farrar, Straus and Giroux, 1990), p. 234.

73. Priscilla Martin, "Caroline Blackwood," *British Novelists since 1960. Part 1: A–G*, in *Dictionary of Literary Biography*, Volume 14 (Detroit: Gale, 1983), p. 99.

74. Caroline Blackwood, *The Stepdaughter* (London: Duckworth, 1976), pp. 19, 45.

75. Blackwood, *Stepdaughter,* pp. 87, 75, 82.

76. Kenneth Clark, *Looking at Pictures* (London: John Murray, 1960), p. 101.

77. Lowell, *Poems,* p. 838.

78. Meyers, Interview with Ivana Lowell.

79. Meyers, Interview with Robert Pinsky, September 5, 2013.

80. Mariani, *Lost Puritan,* p. 448.

81. Hamilton, Interview with Jonathan Raban, British Library.

82. Hamilton, Interview with Caroline Blackwood, British Library.

83. Meredith, "Remembering Robert Lowell," p. 32.

84. Caroline Blackwood, *In the Pink* (London: Bloomsbury, 1987), p. 157.

85. Hamilton, *Lowell,* p. 472.

86. Hamilton, Interview with Jonathan Raban, British Library.

87. Meyers, Interview with Grey Gowrie.

88. Hamilton, Interview with Christina Brazelton, British Library.

89. Lowell, *Letters,* pp. 668, 671.

90. Meyers, Interview with Ivana Lowell.

91. Meyers, Interview with Caroline Blackwood.

92. Hamilton, Interview with Caroline Blackwood, British Library.

I met Blackwood in London in March 1986, when she was fifty-five and looked ten years older. She had dull gray hair, a haggard blotchy face, gravelly smoker's voice and tottering walk, and wore a huge man's white shirt hanging outside her skirt, black tights and pointed pixie-shoes. Drinking steadily as we talked, she seemed like a ravaged ghost of her old self. Not at all the grande dame, she seemed pathetic and wounded, yet charming and eager to please. With a touch of irony, she said she'd seen me on television—as if I, not she, were the celebrity. She rashly offered to show me her valuable Lucian Freud paintings (in storage while her house was being redecorated) in the lobby of a Marble Arch hotel, but then changed her mind and canceled our next appointment. I was relieved to know she would not be staggering down Oxford Street with a few million pounds' worth of art. While we spoke Sheridan sulked silently in the corner.

93. Lowell, *Letters,* p. 465.

94. Meyers, *Interviews and Memoirs,* p. 286.

95. Mariani, *Lost Puritan,* p. 456.

96. Gordon, "Elizabeth Hardwick," p. 94.

97. Darryl Pinckney, Introduction to Elizabeth Hardwick, *New York Stories* (NY: New York Review Books, 2010), p. xx.

98. Seamus Heaney, "Pit Stop Near Castletown," *Agni,* 57 (April 2003), 4.

99. Gowrie, "Robert Lowell," pp. 34–35.

100. Meyers, Interview with Esther Brooks.

101. John Donne, *Poems,* ed. Herbert Grierson (London: Oxford University Press, 1957), p. 45.

102. Meyers, Interview with Frank Bidart.

This list includes Louis Untermeyer, Diego Rivera and Freda Kahlo, Erich Maria Remarque, Rex Warner, William Saroyan, Alfred Ayer, Irwin Shaw, Carson McCullers, Alexander Solzhenitsyn, Elizabeth Taylor and Richard Burton, Natalie Wood and Robert Wagner.

103. For *Girl in Bed,* see Sarah Howgate, *Lucian Freud Portraits* (New Haven: Yale University Press, 2012), p. 76.

104. Lowell, *Letters,* pp. 663, 665.

105. Meyers, Interview with Gail Mazur.

106. Lowell, *Poems,* p. 716.

After his stroke Samuel Johnson, who suffered from lifelong depression and fear of insanity, expressed the same wish as Lowell: "I was alarmed and prayed God, that however he might afflict my body he would spare my understanding. This prayer, that I might try the integrity of my faculties, I made in Latin verse. The lines were not very good, but I knew them not to be very good. I made them easily, and concluded myself to be unimpaired in my faculties" (Jeffrey Meyers, *Samuel Johnson: The Struggle,* NY: Basic Books, 2008, p. 422).

107. Heymann, *American Aristocracy,* p. 501.

108. Gowrie, "Robert Lowell," p. 35.

109. Laskin, *Partisans,* p. 280.

110. Hamilton, Interview with Christina Brazelton, British Library.

111. Letter from Seamus Heaney to Jeffrey Meyers, August 11, 2013 (sadly, one of the last he ever wrote).

112. Heaney, "Pit Stop Near Castletown," p. 4.

Appendix Three. Robert Lowell vs. Lyndon Johnson

1. Eric Goldman, *The Tragedy of Lyndon Johnson* (NY: Knopf, 1969), p. 423.

2. Goldman, *Lyndon Johnson,* p. 427.

3. Letter from Eric Goldman to George Reedy, Lyndon Johnson Library, Austin, Texas.

4. Goldman, *Lyndon Johnson,* p. 429.

5. Lowell, *Letters,* p. 459.

6. Telegram from twenty writers to Lyndon Johnson, Johnson Library.

7. Saul Bellow, *Letters,* ed. Benjamin Taylor (NY: Viking, 2010), p. xxvii.

8. Goldman, *Lyndon Johnson,* p. 447.

9. Letter from Jack Valenti to Lyndon Johnson, Johnson Library.

10. Lady Bird Johnson, *A White House Diary* (NY: Holt, Rinehart & Winston, 1970), p. 287.

11. Letter from Barbaralee Diamonstein to Eric Goldman, Johnson Library.

12. Hamilton, *Lowell,* pp. 323, 326.

13. Lowell, *Poems,* p. 385.

14. Robert Brustein, *Making Scenes* (NY: Random House, 1981), p. 31.

15. Robert Lowell, *Prometheus Bound* (NY: Farrar, Straus and Giroux, 1969), pp. v–vi.

BIBLIOGRAPHY

Als, Hilton, "A Singular Woman," *New Yorker,* 74 (July 13, 1998), 66–74 (on Hardwick).

Arendt, Hannah, and Mary McCarthy. *Between Friends: Correspondence, 1949– 1975.* Ed. Carol Brightman. NY: Harcourt Brace, 1995.

Axelrod, Steven. *Robert Lowell: Life and Art.* Princeton: Princeton University Press, 1978.

Barker, Rafaella. "Once, Twice, Three Times a Muse," *Harpers and Queen,* September 1993, pp. 156–159, 206 (on Blackwood).

Bishop, Elizabeth and Robert Lowell. *Words in the Air: The Complete Correspondence.* Ed. Thomas Travisano and Saskia Hamilton. NY: Farrar, Straus and Giroux, 2008.

Blackwood, Caroline. "Burns Unit." *For All That I Found There.* London: Duckworth, 1973. Pp. 108–113.

———. *The Stepdaughter.* London: Duckworth, 1976.

Boyers, Robert. "The Visit." *Excitable Women, Damaged Men.* NY: Turtle Point Press, 2005. Pp. 48–71.

Brightman, Carol. *Writing Dangerously: Mary McCarthy and Her World.* NY: Potter, 1992.

Davison, Peter. *The Fading Smile: Poets in Boston, 1955–1960.* NY: Knopf, 1994.

Doreski, William. *The Years of Our Friendship: Robert Lowell and Allen Tate.* Jackson: University Press of Mississippi, 1990.

Gordon, Mary. "The Tiger and the Pelican: Mentors Elizabeth Hardwick and Janice Thaddeus." *Mentors, Muses & Monsters: 30 Writers on People Who Changed Their Lives.* Ed. Elizabeth Benedict. NY: Free Press, 2009. Pp. 88–97. See also pp. 9–16.

Gowrie, Grey. "Robert Lowell: A Memoir." *News from the Royal Society of Literature.* London: RSL, 2003. Pp. 34–40.

Gray, Janet. "Elizabeth Hardwick." *American Writers, Supplement III.* Ed. Walton Litz and Lea Baechler. NY: Scribner's, 1991. Part I: 193–215.

Hamilton, Ian. *Robert Lowell: A Biography.* NY: Random House, 1982.

———. "A Biographer's Misgivings." *Walking Possession.* London: Bloomsbury, 1994. Pp. 5–21.

Hardwick, Elizabeth, "The Art of Fiction," *Paris Review,* 96 (Summer 1985), 20-51.

———. "Going Home in America: Lexington, Kentucky," *Harper's,* 239 (July 1969), 78–82.

———. *Melville.* NY: Viking, 2000.

———. *Seduction and Betrayal.* NY: Vintage, 1975.

———. *Sleepless Nights.* NY: Vintage, 1980.

———. *A View of My Own.* 1962; NY: Ecco, 1982.

Heaney, Seamus, "Robert Lowell: A Memorial Address," *Agenda,* 18 (Autumn 1980), 23–28.

Hecht, Anthony. *Robert Lowell.* Washington: Library of Congress, 1983.

Heymann, C. David. *American Aristocracy: The Lives and Times of James Russell, Amy and Robert Lowell.* NY: Dodd, Mead, 1980.

Jarrell, Randall. *Letters.* Ed. Mary Jarrell. Boston: Houghton Mifflin, 1985.

Kenyon Review, "Celebration of Robert Lowell," 22 (Winter 2000), 199–281.

Laskin, David. *Partisans: Marriage, Politics and Betrayal Among the New York Intellectuals.* NY: Simon and Schuster, 2000.

Lehmann-Haupt, Christopher, "Elizabeth Hardwick, Writer, Dies at 91," *New York Times,* December 4, 2007.

Locke, Richard, "Conversation on a Book," *New York Times,* April 2, 1979 (on Hardwick).

Logan, William, "Lowell in the Shadows," *New Criterion,* 13 (December 1994), 61–67.

———. "Lowell's Skunk, Heaney's Skunk," *Salmagundi,* 177 (Winter 2013), 84–110.

Lowell, Ivana. *Why Not Say What Happened?* NY: Knopf, 2010.

Lowell, Robert. *Collected Poems.* Ed. Frank Bidart and David Gewanter. NY: Farrar, Straus and Giroux, 2003.

———. *Collected Prose.* Ed. Robert Giroux. NY: Farrar, Straus and Giroux, 1987.

———. *Letters.* Ed. Saskia Hamilton. NY: Farrar, Straus and Giroux, 2005.

Mariani, Paul. *Lost Puritan: A Life of Robert Lowell.* NY: Norton, 1994.

Martin, Priscilla. "Caroline Blackwood." *British Novelists since 1960. Part 1: A–G,* in *Dictionary of Literary Biography.* Volume 14. Detroit: Gale, 1983. Pp. 98–102.

McAlexander, Hubert. *Peter Taylor: A Writer's Life.* Baton Rouge: Louisiana State University Press, 2001.

Meredith, William. "Remembering Robert Lowell." *Poems Are Hard to Read.* Ann Arbor: University of Michigan Press, 1991. Pp. 32–36, 223–225.

Meyers, Jeffrey. "Glimpses of Lowell: Scenes from a Life," *Salmagundi,* 176 (Fall 2012), 143–161.

———. "Lowell's Politics: Ambivalence and Commitment," *Kenyon Review,* 34 (Summer 2012), 179–201.

———. *Manic Power: Robert Lowell and His Circle.* London: Macmillan, 1987.

———. "Review of Ian Hamilton's *Robert Lowell: A Biography,*" *Virginia Quarterly Review,* 59 (Summer 1983), 516–522.

———. "Review of Robert Lowell's *Letters,*" *Yale Review,* 93 (October 2005), 146–157.

———. "Robert Lowell and the Classics," *Kenyon Review,* 33 (Fall 2011), 173–200.

———. "Robert Lowell as Critic," *Journal of Modern Literature,* 14 (Summer 1987), 127–146.

———. "The Tragic Destiny of Basil Blackwood," *Standpoint,* 61 (April 2014), 46–49.

———, ed. *Robert Lowell: Interviews and Memoirs.* Ann Arbor: University of Michigan Press, 1988.

Miehe, Patrick. *The Robert Lowell Papers at the Houghton Library, Harvard University: A Guide to the Collections.* NY: Greenwood, 1990.

Millier, Brett. *Elizabeth Bishop: Life and the Memory of It.* Berkeley: University of California Press, 1993.

Plath, Sylvia. *Unabridged Journals.* Ed. Karen Kukil. NY: Anchor, 2000.

Ricks, Christopher, "For Robert Lowell," *Harvard Advocate,* Special Issue on Robert Lowell, 113 (November 1979), 17–18.

Roache, Joel. *Richard Eberhart: The Progress of an American Poet.* NY: Oxford University Press, 1971.

Roberts, David. *Jean Stafford: A Biography.* Boston: Little, Brown, 1988.

Salmagundi, "Fourteen Poets Remember Robert Lowell," 141–142 (Spring 2004), 108–262.

Schoenberger, Nancy. *Dangerous Muse: The Life of Caroline Blackwood.* NY: Doubleday, 2001.

Sexton, Anne. *A Self-Portrait in Letters.* Ed. Linda Gray Sexton and Lois Ames. Boston: Houghton Mifflin, 1977.

Simpson, Eileen. *Poets in Their Youth.* NY: Random House, 1982.

Snodgrass, W. D., "A Liberal Education: Mentors, Fomentors and Tormentors," *Southern Review,* 28 (Summer 1992), 445–468.

Spivack, Kathleen. *With Robert Lowell and His Circle.* Boston: Northeastern University Press, 2012.

Stafford, Jean. "A Country Love Story" and "The Interior Castle." *Collected Stories.* NY: Farrar, Straus and Giroux, 1969. Pp. 133–145, 179–193.

———, "An Influx of Poets," *New Yorker,* 54 (November 6, 1978), 43–60.

Stuart, Sarah Payne. *My First Cousin Once Removed: Money, Madness and the Family of Robert Lowell.* NY: HarperCollins, 1998.

Tillinghast, Richard. *Robert Lowell's Life and Work: Damaged Grandeur.* Ann Arbor: University of Michigan Press, 1995.

Underwood, Thomas. *Allen Tate: Orphan of the South.* Princeton: Princeton University Press, 2000.

Voices & Visions: Robert Lowell. Documentary film, 60 minutes. Produced for PBS by New York Center for Visual History, 1998.

Walcott, Derek. "Robert Lowell." *The Company They Kept: Writers on Unforgettable Friendships.* Ed. Robert Silvers and Barbara Epstein. NY: New York Review Books, 2006. Pp. 115–132.

Williamson, Alan. *Pity the Monsters: The Political Vision of Robert Lowell.* New Haven: Yale University Press, 1974.

Witek, Terri. *Robert Lowell and "Life Studies."* Columbia: University of Missouri
    Press, 1993.
Young, Thomas Daniel. *Gentleman in a Dustcoat: A Biography of John Crowe
    Ransom.* Baton Rouge: Louisiana State University Press, 1976.

INDEX

Compiled by Valerie Meyers